HIJACKED JUSTICE

HIJACKED JUSTICE

Dealing with the Past
in the Balkans

Jelena Subotić

CORNELL UNIVERSITY PRESS   **ITHACA AND LONDON**

First published 2009 by Cornell University Press
First printing, Cornell Paperbacks, 2016

Library of Congress Cataloging-in-Publication Data

Subotić, Jelena.
   Hijacked justice : dealing with the past in the Balkans / Jelena Subotić.
      p. cm.
   Includes bibliographical references and index.
   ISBN 978-0-8014-4802-7 (cloth : alk. paper)
   ISBN 978-1-5017-0576-2 (pbk. : alk. paper)
   1. War crimes—Former Yugoslav republics.   2. Transitional justice—Former Yugoslav republics.   3. Truth commissions—Former Yugoslav republics.
4. Postwar reconstruction—Former Yugoslav republics.   5. Yugoslav War, 1991–1995—Atrocities.   I. Title.

   KKZ4545.S83   2009
   341.6'909497—dc22

                                        2009013037

Cornell University Press strives to use environmentally responsible suppliers and materials to the fullest extent possible in the publishing of its books. Such materials include vegetable-based, low-VOC inks and acid-free papers that are recycled, totally chlorine-free, or partly composed of nonwood fibers. For further information, visit our website at www.cornellpress.cornell.edu.

For Doug and Leo

Contents

Preface and Acknowledgments

I don't remember where I was in July 1995, when I first heard of the genocide in Srebrenica. I have been trying to remember ever since I read Emir Suljagić's harrowing account of surviving Srebrenica, in which he asks all of his former friends to remember where they were while his family was being slaughtered and he ran for his life. But I don't remember, and this fills me with a profound sense of shame. I should be able to remember. I lived in Belgrade, just a few hundred miles from Srebrenica. I considered myself very political, liberal, and as harsh a critic of Slobodan Milošević and his policies as anyone I knew. I worked for an international nongovernmental organization and for a progressive Belgrade radio station. I had access to news reports and to foreign media. Still, I don't remember.

I do remember many other things. I remember watching Milošević's televised takeover of the Socialist Party in 1987 and the sense of dread I felt, even as a teenager, at his aggressive rhetoric, his messianic tone, his language. I remember watching his now famous address in Kosovo in 1989, where he announced to the world and to Serbs everywhere that "no one will beat the Serbs anymore." I remember my high school teachers sending us to one of Milošević's political rallies in Belgrade because this was where "history was happening." I remember the first tanks rolling toward Croatia. I remember driving in Belgrade behind lines and lines of tanks and Yugoslav army soldiers waving at me, blowing me kisses. I remember Vukovar. I remember almost every single one of my male friends trying to dodge the draft, hiding from the military police, sleeping in a different house every night. One of my friends successfully faked a serious psychiatric disorder and was discharged. Another never slept consecutive nights in the same bed for two years. A third was caught in the middle of the night, taken to the army barracks, and put on a truck to Vukovar. By a pure stroke of luck, the truck broke down, and he never made it to Croatia.

I remember watching the demonstrations in Sarajevo in April 1992. Like many others, I thought the war would never spread there—it would be unimaginable. And then it did. I remember the siege of Sarajevo and the stories my mother would occasionally receive in letters from her close friend, a Bosniac trapped in a dilapidated apartment complex on the Serb-controlled side of town. The stories were horrific. She had to change her name to a more Serbian-sounding one in order to survive. She made food out of grass. She gave away all her possessions to Serbian soldiers, hoping they would spare her life. She got cancer. Her friends died trying to get food. The stories only got worse. We heard about cemeteries overflowing with bodies so victims had to be buried in parks, about Sarajevo surrounded by Serbs on mountaintops, about people starving. When I visited Sarajevo as an adult for the first time in 2006 to do research for this book, I couldn't shake that feeling of vulnerability, of being trapped in a bowl, surrounded by snipers who could follow your every move and who killed for fun, for amusement, to show off.

And they killed in my name. They killed in the name of a mythologized Serbia, a country that Milošević and his supporters wanted to make so large as to include every Serb on the planet. "Wherever there is a Serbian bone, that is where Serbia is," they would say. They killed to protect us, "the Serbs," from imagined enemies. But mostly, they killed in order to kill. They killed in order to kill Yugoslavia, a vast, prosperous, diverse country they could no longer control—and without control there was no point in preserving it. And they killed in order to eliminate as many non-Serbs as possible from the territory they wanted. The war was not about controlling the territory through killing. The war was *about* the killing. This terrible thing was done in my name.

How does a society deal with the legacy of such evil, such violence? These crimes are so massive that they are unfathomable to any decent person. How do we go about punishing the perpetrators, acknowledging the victims, and, most important, making sure the crimes never happen again? And how do we understand the kind of society that allows such atrocities to happen? What kind of people are we? What is wrong with us?

When I started fieldwork in Serbia for this book, one of the first things I did was join a local gym. I suppose I wanted to preserve the trappings of my now fully Americanized life and keep a sense of order and place, for doing fieldwork in my hometown, surrounded by family and old friends, was wreaking havoc on my brain. The TV set at the gym was tuned to a local station that was broadcasting live the Hague trial of Slobodan Milošević. I was thrilled; here, I thought, even people working out in a Belgrade gym were interested in the trial and wanted to know more about what had happened in the war. The TV was set to mute, though, and I asked the gym attendant to turn it up. Oh no, he said, we don't listen to that crap—we are waiting for the station to switch over to MTV. That, I thought, was dealing with the past in Serbia.

The genocide at Srebrenica and hundreds of other massacres marked the 1990s in the Balkans. With each passing year, memories fade, witnesses are lost, priorities of investigative reporters change, budgets of human rights groups shrink, and the countries of the former Yugoslavia march on, some faster than others, toward the ultimate prize—membership in the European Union (EU). Once they become "European," they hope this ugly past will all go away. Serbia, Croatia, and Bosnia will finally become "normal," former communist countries now adapting to European markets and liberal democracy, just like Hungary or Slovakia or Bulgaria. And while other East European countries need to fix their economies, change pension systems and citizenship requirements, or carry out police reforms, the countries of the former Yugoslavia are asked to do all that, plus cooperate with international institutions of justice. They are asked to arrest and transfer war crimes suspects to The Hague. The faster they do so, the faster they will join the European Union. "Transitional justice" has now become an international requirement; it is a necessary condition for European accession. It has become like any other EU requirement, something normal that countries need to do in order to move on.

But what happened in the former Yugoslavia was not normal, and normalizing the past to meet bureaucratic requirements for EU accession makes me profoundly uneasy. Out of my fear that something important will be lost if we fail to remember, if we deal with the legacy of war crimes and genocide as if it were on a par with pension reform, came the urge to write this book.

At its most basic, this book is about why it is important that we remember and why remembering, accounting, exploring, and acknowledging the past should be a matter of state policy. This book therefore represents a long working through of the events, debates, hopes, and disappointments I lived and observed in the former Yugoslavia throughout the 1990s and in the war's long aftermath. I wanted to know how these horrific atrocities could have happened in plain sight and with such public knowledge. How could so many otherwise decent people have been quietly supportive and tacitly approving of mass detentions, even extermination of their neighbors, friends, and relatives—people who were their fellow citizens, who spoke the same language and rooted for the same football teams? But even more disturbing, why does nobody want to talk about it? How is it possible that more than a decade after the atrocities happened, public interest in uncovering the crimes is low, and the promise of ideological transformation that was supposed to follow "Europeanization" of the Western Balkans has brought only new layers of denial, not the public reckoning with the past that I wanted?

I argue in this book for a maximalist interpretation of transitional justice. I am very critical of the impact of international war-crimes tribunals, not because I believe they should not exist but because I believe they are not enough. I am critical of the truth commissions that were set up in the region, not because I think they are ineffective but because they have been easily used by political elites to perpetuate the nationalist mythology that allowed the crimes to happen in the first place. I am skeptical of the effectiveness of institutions of transitional justice, not because I believe they are dangerous for political stability but because they let states and societies off the hook. Dealing with the past is obviously important for the victims so they can get some sort of acknowledgment for what they suffered. But it is just as important for the perpetrators and their societies. Addressing the crimes of the past—through individual prosecutions but also through social awareness campaigns, media stories, and perhaps most critically, leaders' admissions and calls to action—is the only way a society can again learn what is right and what is wrong. A society can truly become normal again only when crimes of such breathtaking brutality and magnitude, carried out in the name of a state and a nation, become broadly understood as profoundly, humanly, and morally unacceptable. This is as true for Serbia and Croatia as for the United States. When we deal with the past not as a comprehensive social enterprise but as a mechanistic international requirement, we give political elites who do not think what happened was wrong an opportunity to close accounts on the past instead of opening them. I hope my book cracks the past wide open.

This book would have been impossible without the tremendous help of many friends, colleagues, and experts who showed interest in the project from its infancy. Jeremy Shiffman at Syracuse University first encouraged me to pursue a doctoral degree and has supported my work and career ever since. He deserves my greatest thanks. Once in Madison, I had the great fortune to work with outstanding scholars and mentors at the University of Wisconsin. They welcomed my project, provided precious advice and guidance, and offered unlimited support and encouragement. Michael Barnett, Leigh Payne, David Leheny, Jon Pevehouse, and Joe Soss were there all the way—from the early stages of the project to the final publishing days—and I thank them with tremendous humility. Michael Barnett provides a model of scholarship to which I can only aspire. He took an early interest in this project and helped me find nuances, recraft it, and make it so much stronger over the years we worked together. I cannot thank him enough. Leigh Payne was the kindest of mentors, and her deep understanding of memory politics made this project so much broader than I initially intended. Dave Leheny was not only a great colleague but such a wonderful friend in Madison that he deserves thanks twice, if only for the hundreds of movies we saw together.

I was also incredibly fortunate to receive generous financial support for this project from a variety of sources. The American Council of Learned Societies supported the writing stage, the United States Institute of Peace fellowship allowed me to do extensive fieldwork, and the University of Wisconsin European Union, Vilas, and Scott Kloeck-Jenson travel grants helped greatly in pre-fieldwork and follow-up visits.

Many colleagues in Madison read this project at different stages of development. Orfeo Fioretos, Tamir Moustafa, Scott Straus, and Jason Wittenberg provided valuable comments and suggestions. My fellow graduate students, especially Patrick Cottrell, Travis Nelson, and Ayse Zarakol, provided great help and support as we all slogged in what sometimes seemed like a snail's pace toward the finish line.

My colleagues at Georgia State University have provided great support to me and my work since I joined the faculty in 2007. I especially appreciate the guidance of William Downs and John Duffield, as well as the friendship of the entire faculty. I also benefited greatly from research assistance by Georgia State graduate students Shannon Jones, Vanja Petričević, and Xinsong Wang. I am grateful to Roger Haydon at Cornell University Press for showing an early interest in the book and guiding me through the publication process with expertise and professionalism that are truly exceptional. I also thank the anonymous reviewers of the book manuscript for a very careful read and thoughtful suggestions.

The fieldwork for this book would never have been possible without the generous time and effort of many human rights activists, government officials, scholars, journalists, and international bureaucrats who agreed to be interviewed. There are simply too many of them to name here, but they all deserve my deepest thanks.

In Belgrade, special thanks go to Sonja Biserko, Vojin Dimitrijević, Bogdan Ivanišević, Ivan Jovanović, Biljana Kovačević Vučo, and Marijana Toma, who all went above and beyond interviewee duty to offer great insights, further contacts, and a lot of their time in helping me along. And then there are my friends: Duška Anastasijević, Suzana Blesić, Ana Miljanić, and Dubravka Stojanović spent endless hours listening to my ideas. Their comments and suggestions were invaluable, and I respect their input greatly, especially as they all confront issues of human rights, justice, and democracy in their own respective work. I cannot thank them enough. My dear friends Gordan Paunović and Susanne Simon also made my months in Belgrade more fun and enjoyable. The intellectual footprints of Srđan Rajković, my best friend of twenty years, are also all over this book. His tragic early death is something I will never quite recover from. I miss him more than words can possibly describe.

In Zagreb, special thanks go to Ivo Banac, Ivica Đikić, Vesna Kesić, Marina Škrabalo, Martina Tenko, and Vesna Teršelič. Gabrijela Gavran was also of tremendous help as she gave me access to the fabulous War Crimes Digital Documentation database housed in Zagreb's law school.

In Sarajevo, journalist Slavko Šantić deserves so much more than just a note of acknowledgment. He took on this project with as much interest and dedication as if it were his own and helped set up almost all of my interviews, provided numerous documents and materials, and patiently answered all my questions about the bewildering place that is Bosnia today. I quite literally could not have done fieldwork in Bosnia without his help, which he provided every day, without any compensation or questions asked. Nevena Ršumović helped me so much with the logistics of my stay in Sarajevo, even before we met. She also introduced me to the invaluable online research tool, the IDoc digital archive of the Bosnian press, a phenomenal project indispensable to anyone doing research on Bosnia. Meliha Husedžinović and Dunja Blažević took care of me, fed and entertained me, and offered many more different perspectives on Bosnian politics and culture. Jelena Šantić showed me Sarajevo nightlife, introduced me to her friends and professors, and was a lot of fun. I also greatly appreciate Dino Abazović, Jakob Finci, Emir Suljagić and Mirsad Tokača, who all dedicated much time for extensive interviews for this project.

The last few years of working on this book also brought me tremendous personal joy. We welcomed a little person named Leo Sebastian Rose, who made himself such an essential part of our life that we cannot imagine what it was like before him. He deserves his share of thanks for this project—he dealt with Mom's anxieties and mysterious trips with the computer to a local Starbucks with smiles, giggles, and not too much complaining. I think he even decided to sleep a little more as it was getting closer to the deadline. Leo is absolutely the most wonderful son ever, and I hope I will make him proud.

Finally, I owe much to my family. My parents, Gojko and Irina Subotić, welcomed me back home after years of self-imposed exile and took care of every single thing to make my stay in Belgrade as easy and comfortable as possible. My sister Ivana's annual question, "Are you done yet?" became a running joke with us, and it felt so great to finally tell her, "Yes, I am!" My cousin Irina Ljubić provided great (and unpaid!) research assistance and priceless companionship in Belgrade. Both Irina and her husband, Aleksandar Stojanovski, deserve my deepest love and gratitude. My in-laws, Doug and Karol Ross, were tremendously generous throughout this process. They opened their home in South Florida to us as a writing and working refuge, and most of this book was written there.

And how do I begin to thank Doug? He has endured years of graduate school and junior faculty anxieties, doubts, and worries. He has put up with my more or less constant stress, with long fieldwork, a seven-hour time difference, and really bad telephone and Internet connections. Doug helped in so many ways that nothing I say will quite capture his love, support, and patience. This work could have never happened without him.

Abbreviations

AU	African Union
BH	Bosnia-Herzegovina
CAVR	Commission for Reception, Truth and Reconciliation
CHCHR	Croatian Helsinki Committee for Human Rights
CNDD–FDD	Defense of Democracy–Forces for the Defense of Democracy
CTF	Commission of Truth and Friendship
DOS	Demokratska opozicija Srbije (Democratic Opposition of Serbia)
DRC	Democratic Republic of Congo
DS	Demokratska stranka (Democratic Party)
DSS	Demokratska stranka Srbije (Democratic Party of Serbia)
ECCC	Extraordinary Chambers in the Courts of Cambodia
EU	European Union
FDD	Forces for the Defense of Democracy
FNL	National Liberation Forces
HCHRS	Helsinki Committee for Human Rights in Serbia
HDZ	Hrvatska demokratska zajednica (Croatian Democratic Union)
HRW	Human Rights Watch
HSLS	Hrvatska socijalno liberalna stranka (Croatian Social Liberal Party)
HSP	Hrvatska stranka prava (Croatian Rights Party)
ICC	International Criminal Court
ICG	International Crisis Group
ICJ	International Court of Justice

ICTJ	International Center for Transitional Justice
ICTR	International Criminal Tribunal for Rwanda
ICTY	International Criminal Tribunal for the Former Yugoslavia
INGO	international nongovernmental organization
IWPR	Institute for War and Peace Reporting
JNA	Jugoslovenska narodna armija (Yugoslav National Army)
LDP	Liberalno demokratska partija (Liberal Democratic Party)
LRA	Lord's Resistance Army
NATO	North Atlantic Treaty Organization
NGO	nongovernmental organization
OHR	Office of the High Representative
OSCE	Organization for Security and Cooperation in Europe
RDC	Research and Documentation Center
RS	Republika Srpska (Serb Republic)
SAA	stabilization and association agreement
SCIU	Serious Crimes Investigation Unit
SDA	Stranka demokratske akcije (Party of Democratic Action)
SDP	Socijaldemokratska partija Hrvatske (Social Democratic Party of Croatia)
SDS	Srpska demokratska stranka (Serbian Democratic Party)
SFOR	Stabilization Force
SPO	Srpski pokret obnove (Serbian Renewal Movement)
SPS	Socijalistička partija Srbije (Socialist Party of Serbia)
SRS	Srpska radikalna stranka (Serbian Radical Party)
TRC	truth and reconciliation commission
UN	United Nations
UNAMID	UN-African Union Mission in Darfur
UNDP	United Nations Development Program
UNMIS	UN Mission in Sudan
UNTAET	United Nations Transitional Administration in Timor-Leste
USIP	United States Institute of Peace
WCC	War Crimes Chamber

HIJACKED JUSTICE

Introduction

THE IMPORTANCE OF DEALING WITH THE PAST

He was good with children, the news stories said. He helped "cure" an autistic child through bioenergy. He gave excellent massages. He practiced an ancient Christian Orthodox method of "silencing," a form of meditation. He had an attractive middle-aged mistress. He had a long white beard and long white hair. He was mysterious and spiritual and had a soothing manner about him. He was a poet. He wrote for *Healthy Life* magazine. His name was Dragan Dabić, and he was a holistic healer. Only he wasn't. He was Radovan Karadžić, the Bosnian Serb wartime leader accused by the International Criminal Tribunal for the Former Yugoslavia (ICTY) of genocide, crimes against humanity, and war crimes against non-Serb populations of Bosnia and Herzegovina during the 1992–95 war.

Radovan Karadžić was arrested on a Belgrade commuter bus in July 2008 after thirteen years in hiding. His arrest was sudden and surprising and came only a few weeks after the new, reformist government had come to power in Serbia. And while the Serbian press devoted hundreds of stories to his bizarre disguise and to his mistress, friends, neighbors, and favorite Belgrade bars, the Serbian government looked at Karadžić and saw the country's ticket to the European Union (EU). Suddenly the doors to Europe could open for a country shunned for years because of its reluctance to apprehend war-crimes suspects.

The Serbian government wasted no time in placing Karadžić's arrest in the context of Serbia's European aspirations. The arrest was a sign that the Serbian government had a "very ambitious European agenda," Serbia's foreign minister proudly announced, adding, "We want to be an EU member."[1] "[Serbs] see their manifest destiny in Europe," was an often-heard refrain in the Serbian press following the arrest.[2] "Karadžić's arrest is a great step towards European integration," Serbia's defense minister said.[3]

But the Serbian government used Karadžić's arrest to make an even larger political point. If Serbia respected international law by cooperating with the ICTY, the international community should respect it as well, by siding with Serbia's claim that Kosovo should remain part of Serbia, based on international rules of sovereignty and territorial integrity.[4] Serbia's prime minister Mirko Cvetković made this link very clear: "Serbia respects international law in every respect, whether the issue is cooperation with The Hague or acting against Kosovo's unilateral declaration of independence."[5]

The European Union also reaped immediate political benefits from Karadžić's arrest. European officials boasted that the arrest was the result of sustained European pressures on Serbia. "This is a big success for Europe," French foreign minister Bernard Kouchner proclaimed.[6] It was seen as a triumph of the European Union's enlargement strategy and its clever use of "soft power."[7]

What was missing amid all the self-congratulation of politicians from Belgrade to Brussels to Washington was the substantive moral dimension of why Karadžić was accused of genocide in the first place, what his role was in the killing, and what implications for truth, justice, and reconciliation his arrest would have in the region. Although the Serbian media provided wall-to-wall coverage of the most bizarre tabloid details of his years in refuge, a startlingly few news stories spent any time at all on the content of the Hague indictments, or even more generally on the crimes he was accused of masterminding in Bosnia.[8] It is on these crimes that we should focus our attention.

---

1. B92 (Belgrade-based broadcast network), July 22, 2008, http://www.b92.net.

2. Ljiljana Smajlović, editor of the leading Belgrade daily newspaper *Politika*, quoted in Dan Bilefsky, "Karadžić Arrest Is Big Step for a Land Tired of Being Europe's Pariah," *New York Times,* July 23, 2008.

3. B92, July 22, 2008.

4. B92, August 2, 2008. Kosovo, a former province of Serbia, unilaterally declared independence in February 2008. Serbia has vigorously opposed Kosovo's independence, claiming it is in violation of international law.

5. B92, July 26, 2008.

6. Stephen Castle and Steven Erlanger, "With Karadžić's Arrest, Europe Sees Triumph," *New York Times,* July 23, 2008.

7. "Karadžić Caught," *Economist,* July 24, 2008; "Karadžić in The Hague a Victory for EU Values," Radio Free Europe, July 30, 2008; "Karadžić's Arrest Hailed as Victory for EU Enlargement Policy," *Irish Times,* August 5, 2008.

8. Vesna Perić Zimonjić, "Serbian Press Lionises the Cunning Fugitive, Not the Criminal," *Independent,* July 25, 2008.

Over the course of five days in July 1995, Karadžić's Bosnian Serb troops and Slobodan Milošević's Serbian paramilitaries committed the single worst atrocity in Europe since World War II. The massacre occurred in the Bosnian city of Srebrenica, a designated United Nations (UN) "save haven." Within thirty hours, twenty-three thousand women and children were deported, while the Serbian soldiers separated out all men aged sixteen to sixty and held them in trucks and warehouses, tortured them, and killed all who attempted to flee. In the mountains around Srebrenica, the massacre went on for weeks. When the reports and evidence of the carnage became public, Srebrenica became a symbol of Bosnian genocide, as the graveyard of more than seven thousand Bosniac boys and men.[9]

The international response to atrocities such as Srebrenica was woefully delayed and inadequate.[10] International apathy included failure to acknowledge the seriousness of atrocities, lackluster interest in intervening to stop the killing, and even standing idly by and watching as thousands were taken to slaughter. And as sluggish as the international will to prevent the atrocities was at the time of the killings, international actors have since expended a tremendous amount of energy and effort in developing an increasingly elaborate system of "transitional justice"—systematic addressing of crimes of the past—to deal with the atrocities' political aftermath. The last decade has seen an unprecedented rise in institutions of transitional justice, which now include international and domestic trials for human rights abusers, truth commissions, reparations for victims, and many other projects aimed at helping societies deal with legacies of past violence.

Rapidly expanding scholarship on transitional justice has also developed a complex set of expectations for countries coming out of violent conflict, including a multitude of reasons why transitional justice is a positive, even necessary step a country should take in the aftermath of mass atrocity.

First, it is said to promote social healing and reconciliation. By revealing the truth about past crimes, victims and survivors can begin to heal from the trauma, obtain closure, and then work toward reconciling with their former enemies. Transitional justice, in other words, is therapeutic. It should also lead to peace by

---

9. I use "Bosniac" instead of Bosnian Muslim. A point of some controversy, this change in designation is preferred by Bosniacs themselves and in the recent literature in order to stress ethnicity over religion. When I use "Bosnian Muslim" it reflects the preferred term used by an interviewee. On the controversy over the "Bosniac" (also interchangeably spelled "Bosniak") identity, see Bohdana Dimitrovova, "Bosniak or Muslim? Dilemma of One Nation with Two Names," *Southeast European Politics* 2, no. 2 (2001): 94–108.

10. Samantha Power, *A Problem from Hell: America and the Age of Genocide* (New York: Basic Books, 2002), ch. 9. Also see Thomas Cushman and Stjepan Gabriel Mestrovic, *This Time We Knew: Western Responses to Genocide in Bosnia* (New York: New York University Press, 1996).

promoting justice for victims. Finding out the truth, identifying the perpetrators, and punishing them or forcing them to publicly admit their crimes help achieve justice by ending impunity. The objective accounting of the past helps develop a commonly shared history, which is the basis for reconciliation. In addition, creating a trustworthy account of human rights violations allows a society to learn from its past and prevent a recurrence of such violence in the future. Focusing on justice also helps consolidate the rule of law, the foundation of democracy. Conflicts can then be settled through political deliberation instead of violence. Finally, punishing perpetrators is a sign that society will no longer tolerate such behavior. This deters potential human rights abusers from acting with impunity in the future.[11]

In light of these positive and ambitious expectations, the last decade has seen an unprecedented proliferation of different transitional justice models, as well as the establishment of a veritable international justice industry, with international nongovernmental organizations (NGOs), experts, and entrepreneurs busily lobbying states coming out of a violent period to set up some model of transitional justice to address past wrongs. Recent empirical studies show that more than two-thirds of all transitional states in the past twenty years have instituted or debated instituting some mechanism of transitional justice, most often domestic trials or truth commissions.[12]

Discussing appropriate transitional justice mechanisms has also become routine practice in conflict resolution and peacekeeping negotiations. The relationship between transitional justice and postconflict peacebuilding is especially notable, as it is now promoted by different agencies of the United Nations,[13] international NGOs,[14] and even military strategists[15] as one of the necessary pillars of successful postconflict reconstruction and rebuilding.[16] In addition, expectations

---

11. Adapted from David Mendeloff, "Truth-Seeking, Truth-Telling, and Postconflict Peacebuilding: Curb the Enthusiasm?" *International Studies Review* 6, no. 3 (2004): 355–80.

12. Kathryn Sikkink and Carrie Booth Walling, "The Impact of Human Rights Trials in Latin America," *Journal of Peace Research* 44, no. 4 (2007): 427–45.

13. UN Security Council press release, SC/7880, September 24, 2003.

14. International Institute for Democracy and Electoral Assistance, *Reconciliation after Violent Conflict: A Handbook* (Stockholm: IDEA, 2003); Human Rights Watch, "International Justice," http://hrw.org/justice/about.htm.

15. Michele Flournoy and Michael Pan, "Dealing with Demons: Justice and Reconciliation," *Washington Quarterly* 25, no. 4 (2002): 111–23; John J. Hamre and Gordon R. Sullivan, "Toward Postconflict Reconstruction," *Washington Quarterly* 25, no. 4 (2002): 85–96; Edward Newman, "'Transitional Justice': The Impact of Transnational Norms and the UN," *International Peacekeeping* 9, no. 2 (2002): 31–50.

16. Former UN Secretary General Kofi Annan was explicit in this regard: "We have learned that the rule of law delayed is lasting peace denied, and that justice is a handmaiden of true peace....There cannot be real peace without justice." UN Security Council, SC/7880.

for some kind of a transitional justice arrangement have become incorporated into various kinds of multilateral as well as bilateral agreements with transitional states in search of foreign aid, reconstruction, or club membership. Transitional justice is increasingly becoming part of regional integration requirements, as European Union or North Atlantic Treaty Organization (NATO) candidate states are being required to implement some form of institutional reckoning with the past as a condition for joining.

These trends represent a major change in the way states and international society deal with issues of past crimes. Transitional justice, in other words, is quickly becoming an international norm, a standard of proper state behavior, violation of which will be internationally sanctioned. Yet the way this new international norm has played itself out in the real politics of countries that have adopted it has departed greatly from international expectations.

In the case of justice for Srebrenica, hundreds of direct perpetrators of the atrocity still live free in Bosnia or Serbia, without fear of prosecution.[17] The man who started the Yugoslav wars, Slobodan Milošević, died in his prison cell in The Hague before his trial was over. Most significantly, in Serbia, the country that produced most of the perpetrators of the Yugoslav war atrocities and that became the test case for international justice, the new democratic government managed to put the entire enterprise of justice back into the service of nationalist ideology. International trials at The Hague were domestically rejected as illegitimate victor's justice, and the government provided those indicted with generous legal budgets, helped coordinate their criminal defense, and offered long-term guaranteed financial assistance to their families. The government even strongly encouraged war-crimes suspects to surrender to The Hague, presenting their surrender as the final act of patriotism for the common good of the nation and the state.

Even more surprisingly, the international community has largely accepted this outcome—it has conditioned Serbia's financial well-being as well as its candidacy for the EU on the continuing stream of war-crimes suspects arriving in The Hague. How and under what conditions they get there, whether the Serbian people know what heinous crimes these suspects are accused of committing, and what the domestic political consequences of this "streamlined justice" are no longer concern the international community. As a result, this strategy has allowed Serbia to go through the motions of complying with international norms and standards while in fact rejecting the profound social transformation these norms require.

---

17. International Crisis Group, "War Criminals in Bosnia's Republika Srpska: Who Are the People in Your Neighborhood?" Europe Report no. 103, Sarajevo, November 2, 2000.

This is a puzzling political phenomenon and a disappointing outcome of an elaborate set of international transitional justice policies. The question we need to urgently address is why did this happen? How did domestic political elites manage to use international institutions designed to resolve conflict to such different ends? And, most important, since what happened in Serbia happened in many other states that adopted mechanisms of transitional justice, we have a paradox that is emblematic of a larger problem facing transitional justice norms and institutions.

This paradox can be summed up as follows. Transitional justice institutions have become such a popular way of addressing past abuses that more and more states are adopting some mechanism of transitional justice. At the same time, states use these mechanisms to achieve goals quite different from those envisaged by international justice institutions and activists. States now use transitional justice to get rid of domestic political opponents, obtain international material benefits, or gain membership in prestigious international clubs, such as the European Union. The use of international norms and institutions for local political ends then leads to policy outcomes far removed from international transitional justice expectations. This domestic misuse of transitional justice norms, a phenomenon I call "hijacked justice," is tremendously problematic and significant in that it greatly reduces the effectiveness of international justice projects, jeopardizes their legitimacy, and does not bring about the profound social transformation that countries coming out of violent conflict require.

Domestic use of international norms is important politically because it points to the limits these norms and the actors who promote them face. When domestic actors are able to use international rules and institutions for ulterior political purposes, the rules become less potent and more open to manipulation in the future. This is why, if we believe that there should be international standards about the rule of law and justice in reckoning with massive human rights abuses, we need to pay more attention to domestic political conditions and the consequences of international policy interventions. This will help us understand why some clearly noble international goals, such as those of bringing justice to victims of horrific mass crimes, remain unfulfilled and deeply entangled in domestic political fights. This understanding will in turn help us make better choices about how to reach the goals of justice in the future.

The Argument

My book sets out to achieve this objective by analyzing the domestic strategic use of international models of transitional justice. It challenges optimistic accounts that predict increasing social support for these models as international actors make lasting coalitions with domestic allies and pressure domestic governments to change their policies. Instead, this book examines how domestic translation and appropriation of international norms and institutional models always faces significant and varied domestic challenges, which often produce unexpected and contradictory policy effects. It shows that complying with international norms becomes a strategic, even subversive, choice for those states that do not have much interest in following them. This book therefore opens up the concept of normative and institutional compliance to explore not only *whether* states comply with international norms and institutions but also *how* and *why* they comply.

The theoretical approach presented in this book departs from the existing models of normative compliance in a number of significant ways. Existing explanations of why states adopt international norms often rely on domestic-norm "true believers"—antiregime activists—to bring about normative shifts. In these "boomerang"[18] and "spiral"[19] models of normative change, states comply with international norms and institutions as a result of a sustained effort of domestic-norm believers. These activists then mobilize international actors to exert pressure, socialize, or persuade the norm-offending state to change its policies. Over time, through iteration or habit, international norms become internalized as part of routine state practice.

In many states, however, norm true believers are absent or lack the authority to influence social change, while states still display institutional markers of compliance. This contradiction makes boomerang and spiral explanations inoperable in many empirical cases. This is why I identify three other major coalitions that act as agents of normative and institutional compliance: norm resisters, instrumental adopters, and international norm promoters who act as domestic political stakeholders. Diffusion of international norms and institutional models always produces domestic conflict among different groups who choose to accept, reject, or ignore international normative and institutional pressures. Which domestic coalition comes out on top during the political infighting that follows all international normative advances will shape a state's strategy of normative compliance and its political outcomes.

While international pressure is a given, it is not a constant. It varies in intensity, internal coherence, sustainability, and reliability. I identify three major types

---

18. Margaret E. Keck and Kathryn Sikkink, *Activists beyond Borders: Advocacy Networks in International Politics* (Ithaca: Cornell University Press, 1998).

19. Thomas Risse and Kathryn Sikkink, "The Socialization of International Human Rights Norms into Domestic Practices: Introduction," in *The Power of Human Rights: International Norms and Domestic Change*, ed. Thomas Risse, Steve C. Ropp, and Kathryn Sikkink (New York: Cambridge University Press, 1999).

of international pressure that influence how states approach compliance with international norms and institutions. *Coercive* pressure directly ties compliance with international demands to material rewards such as foreign aid and investment or membership in international organizations. *Symbolic* pressure induces compliance through appeals to a state's desire to be perceived as a legitimate international actor. *Bureaucratic* pressure works under conditions of political uncertainty, when states choose to comply with international requests because they believe international actors can solve their domestic problems.

By highlighting different types of international pressure and domestic responses to them, this book demonstrates the limitations of existing approaches to normative compliance, which miss outcome possibilities different from norm acceptance and internalization. Instead, I focus on how domestic actors understand, interpret, and use international norms for their own political purposes and what consequences this domestic appropriation has for the strength and vitality of the norm itself. Using the empirical example of international norms of transitional justice, this book is an invitation for norms scholarship to move beyond the unintended consequences of good norms that produce bad outcomes and instead explain how domestic use of international norms and institutions can be predicted and incorporated into our understanding of norm diffusion and compliance.

A Note on Research Design and Methods

The challenge of transitional justice literature has long been overwhelming reliance on single case studies without comparisons across cases. International relations norms scholarship has faced a different problem. Until recently largely theoretical in nature, it broadened its scope to include empirical studies, but rarely were norms systematically studied from the vantage point of domestic norm recipients. This book attempts to correct for both methodological and conceptual shortcomings. It starts with the assumption that rich description of nuanced domestic processes and their interaction with international normative and institutional interventions requires comparison of a number of in-depth studies.

Why the Balkans?

This book engages in qualitative methodology and centers on the three case studies of Serbia, Croatia, and Bosnia. The book employs the case-study technique because it is particularly well suited for determining scope conditions as well as causal mechanisms.[20] Understanding the variable effects of international transitional justice interventions requires selecting cases with strong but varied international pressures and significant differences in their domestic effects. The case-selection method used in this project was to choose one region (former Yugoslavia) to conduct in-depth analysis of three cases (Serbia, Croatia, Bosnia) where internationalized transitional justice projects—international and domestic trials and truth-seeking efforts—have been domestically used to local political ends. The advantage of this approach is that this case selection holds the setting and the type of conflict constant and looks at variation in different transitional regimes responding to different kinds of international pressures (coercive in Serbia, symbolic in Croatia, and bureaucratic in Bosnia), spearheaded by different domestic political coalitions (norm resisters in Serbia, instrumental adopters in Croatia, and international norm promoters in Bosnia), leading to very different transitional justice outcomes.

International promotion of transitional justice has been directed at all three countries, but the interaction of international pressures, level of international control of transitional justice mechanisms, and domestic political conditions has produced very different results. All three countries studied here have aspirations for joining the EU to maximize their security and wealth. International scrutiny of all three countries has been intense. In other words, the penalties for not engaging international rules and standards have been very high. However, different domestic power constellations have empowered norm resisters, instrumental norm adopters, and true believers in different ways in the three countries, leading to very different policy outcomes. The choice of the three cases from the former Yugoslavia is also useful as a global test case of the feasibility of high-profile transitional justice projects—lessons learned from ICTY jurisprudence will be applied in other trials before the International Criminal Court as well as in future domestic and hybrid trials.

Research Methods

The book employs a combination of historical process tracing, comparative case study technique, elite interviewing, archival research, discursive methods, and institutional analysis. I use process tracing to examine whether the intervening variables between a hypothesized cause and observed effect shift as predicted. In other words, I use process tracing to examine causal mechanisms at work.[21]

---

20. Alexander L. George and Andrew Bennett, *Case Studies and Theory Development* (Cambridge, Mass.: MIT Press, 2005).

21. Ibid.

In applying this method, I triangulate across multiple data pools, including in-person interviews, public opinion surveys, newspaper and other media reports, primary archival sources, institutional documentation, government and NGO reports, and secondary literature. I also use process tracing to ascertain spatial and temporal linkages among the cases themselves. What happened in Serbia influenced how the international justice industry dealt with Croatia and Bosnia, and observing internal debates about transitional justice "in the neighborhood" guided how governments responded to domestic and international pressures.

International norms influence patterns of behavior in accordance with their prescribed rules and expectations. They can also be directly or indirectly articulated in public discourse. This is why the empirical chapters of the book track elite public behavior in the three countries—Serbia, Croatia, and Bosnia—and match up this behavior as it relates to international transitional justice prescriptions. The chapters follow the public discourse surrounding debates about whether transitional justice models should be adopted, rejected, or something in between. The very existence of rigorous debates about transitional justice indicates the presence of a normative framework that makes public debate meaningful. Presumably, if no norm were present, competing elites would not bitterly fight about it. The process of norm compliance is measured by examining policies, institutions, and political discourse, and triangulating changes in these three elements over time.

The interviews conducted for this study were extensive. They included over seventy formal meetings with international and domestic transitional justice entrepreneurs, domestic policymakers and government officials, NGO activists, journalists and justice experts in Serbia, Croatia, and Bosnia, and many more informal conversations and e-mail and telephone exchanges over the course of two years (2004–6).

The Layout of the Book

This book has two main goals. The first is to contribute to theory building on the domestic use of international norms by exploring different domestic strategies of normative and institutional compliance, using the empirical background of transitional justice. The second, interconnected goal is to analyze how these strategic motives to comply influence international policy outcomes in states that use international norms and institutions. The book's principal theoretical contribution is to add these two dimensions to our understanding of how norms and models diffuse through the international system and to what policy effect. In a way, this book is a response to the constructivist challenge of ten years ago to expand our analysis to focus on "ways in which international norms worked their effects *inside* the many states of the system, and...the ways in which the norms were eventually affected by those individual state experiences."[22]

Chapter 1 introduces the theoretical framework for a domestic politics approach to compliance with international norms of transitional justice. This chapter rethinks the process of international normative compliance by examining why both accepting and outright rejecting international norms are costly to domestic political actors, who have to resort to alternative political strategies. I present three different strategies of compliance, each a response to a specific type of international normative pressure. I then identify specific domestic political conditions that influence how domestic actors choose to comply with international norms under conditions of international pressure. The chapter concludes with a discussion of how different domestic strategies of normative and institutional compliance matter for both domestic adopters and international promoters of norms.

While the domestic political context and international environment frame the boundaries of political action, domestic actors still act in unexpected ways, producing a variety of different political outcomes. The purpose of the three empirical chapters is to trace different strategies of compliance with international transitional justice models and explain their outcomes in multiple domestic political settings. Chapters 2, 3, and 4 provide in-depth analyses of transitional justice in three former Yugoslav states—Serbia, Croatia, and Bosnia.

Chapter 2 explains the experience of transitional justice in Serbia as a consequence of international coercion. Transitional justice efforts in Serbia have been numerous and complex but also erratic and incomplete, leaving in their aftermath significant domestic political disturbances, perhaps none more profound than the 2003 assassination of Serbian reformist prime minister Zoran Đinđić by an organized crime group that called itself "anti-Hague patriots." This chapter first describes the goals and expectations of the international community in introducing transitional justice to Serbia after the overthrow of the Milošević regime. Then it looks at the types of international transitional justice mechanisms Serbia implemented—international trials, a truth commission, and domestic trials— and their domestic political effects. I then analyze specific domestic political conditions in Serbia that guided the state's response to international coercion. The chapter concludes by evaluating the consequences of the domestic misuse of transitional justice in Serbia and of domestic political maneuvers by powerful norm resisters that circumvented the meaning of transitional justice by complying with its institutional requirements.

---

22. Martha Finnemore, *National Interests in International Society* (Ithaca: Cornell University Press, 1996), 137, emphasis added.

Chapter 3 examines transitional justice processes in Croatia, a country with a unique distinction of being both the victim and the perpetrator of Yugoslav war atrocities. Croatia is the only country in the region that has fulfilled its obligations to the ICTY and is now firmly on the path to EU membership. But this path has been a difficult one for Croatia. Contemporary domestic debates about the nature of the war, Croatia's complicity in war atrocities, and what to do with suspected war criminals indicate that while institutional obligations have been met—all suspects have been transferred to The Hague—profound divisions about the Croatian past still remain deeply embedded in the national consciousness. This chapter analyzes in depth the characteristics of the Croatian democratic transition, especially the strategy of integrating Croatia into the EU. This strategy has guided Croatian elites to instrumentally comply with international transitional justice institutions, primarily to obtain international legitimacy for Croatia as a European state while keeping domestic norm resisters marginalized and too weak to successfully mobilize against adoption of transitional justice.

Chapter 4 turns the analysis to Bosnia. Unlike Serbia and Croatia, whose sovereign governments could be pressured into compliance with threats of external sanctions or appeals to legitimacy, the main problem facing Bosnian transitional justice efforts is that the Bosnian state effectively does not exist. It is still a largely internationally run protectorate, divided into two ethnic entities, with an incredibly weak and ineffective national government, uncertain about both its territorial scope and its political authority. In this domestic context of political uncertainty, international justice promoters, norm true believers, have exerted pressure on Bosnia from within by working through the de facto government in charge, the international Office of the High Representative. The chapter concludes by putting the Bosnian transitional justice strategy in the larger context of creating a mature and independent state from an international protectorate with uncertain status. Transitional justice in Bosnia has been used to strengthen state institutions but also to weaken and delegitimize the noncooperative Bosnian Serb entity, Republika Srpska, in order to make calls for a unitary and centralized Bosnian state more acceptable and internationally legitimate.

The conclusion summarizes the book's findings and applies lessons learned from these empirical cases to a final discussion on the impact of domestic political use of international norms and institutions for international policy outcomes. I extend the discussion of hijacked justice to political contexts beyond the former Yugoslavia and offer a number of linkages, similarities, and generalizations that can be explored in future research. I conclude by considering whether international organizations learn from these experiences and what may be possible models of institutional adaptation in the field of transitional justice.

Implications for Scholarship and Public Policy

Why is hijacked justice significant? If states are complying with the requirements of transitional justice institutions, if they are arresting and transferring suspects to international courts, if they are setting up domestic tribunals or truth commissions, then why does a specific path to compliance matter?

This book argues that different strategies of compliance matter because they influence the outcomes of transitional justice efforts. They shape the effects of transitional justice both domestically, in terms of political and justice processes they set in motion, and internationally, in terms of lessons learned for future justice projects held in different political contexts. Although international organizations may initiate international justice projects for all the noble reasons, their effects may be quite different when they are strategically adopted by local political actors in the context of domestic political contention and mobilization.

Domestic political use of international norms of transitional justice also fundamentally impacts those norms and institutions themselves, as well as the future justice interventions they generate. If states comply with international justice for reasons of local political strategy and not from adherence to the norm's expectations, the norm itself becomes challenged; it loses cohesion, it means different things to different audiences, and the institutional models that international justice produces will begin to lose their transnational reputation. If states can achieve the same results in terms of international prestige or international rewards by going through the motions of transitional justice compliance, while in fact using the norm instrumentally to get at other payoffs, the international norm has not achieved its goals. States will rhetorically accept international standards while not putting them into state practice. This is why many states find it much easier to create a truth commission or cooperate with international tribunals than to embark on reflective reevaluation of past state crimes, elite complicity in them, and nationalist mythology that led to abuses in the first place. Hijacked justice, therefore, has profound political consequences on the ground. As many countries eventually discover, legacies of past violence are too embedded in the political identities of postconflict states to be glossed over by creating a ministry or research commission or by signing a law on extraditions.

The book's conclusions are unsettling and might be unwelcome news to many proponents of transitional justice norms and institutions who have been intrepid in their advocacy, lobbying, support, and management of transitional justice projects around the world. The purpose of the book, however, is not to devalue the power and necessity of these projects. Instead, the book's findings call for a better institutional design that can account for the inevitable domestic contestation transitional justice sets in motion. While the book is critical of international coercive policies of conditionality and issue linkage, it does not argue that the international community should remove itself from postconflict states. It promotes more international involvement, not less. Instead of measuring state compliance with transitional justice norms only by administrative tools such as numbers of arrests and transfers of war-crimes suspects, this book calls for a more substantive, sustained, and comprehensive international involvement in postconflict states. Instead of rewarding states for paying lip service to transitional justice, we should promote and support more sweeping domestic normative changes, such as education reform, media professionalization, and strengthening the political culture of human rights. Only when postconflict societies choose to talk about the horrors that happened, the state and societal complicity in the atrocities, and begin to change the way the past is taught will we be able to say that justice has been done.

1

THE POLITICS OF HIJACKED JUSTICE

Over the past twenty years, a global norm has emerged prescribing the appropriate way for states to deal with crimes of the past. This international norm presents a set of expectations for transitional governments to fulfill when facing a state's criminal history. Crudely, it can be reduced to the statement that gross human rights abuses, such as war crimes, crimes against humanity, and genocide, should be adjudicated in a court of law or another type of justice institution and not left to either vengeful justice or forgiveness. While these crimes were previously dealt with by executions or summary trials set up by victors after conflict, or simply remained unpunished, they are now considered just like other crimes that demand a proper trial and due process.[1] In other words, crimes of such magnitude for which no appropriate punishment was ever thought possible[2] have in the past few decades begun to be seen as triable and belonging in a court of law or other highly structured institutional setting, such as a truth commission.[3]

---

1. See Naomi Roht-Arriaza and Javier Mariezcurrena, eds., *Transitional Justice in the Twenty-First Century: Beyond Truth vs. Justice* (Cambridge: Cambridge University Press, 2006).

2. See the famous statement by Hannah Arendt about the Nuremberg trials: "For these crimes, no punishment is severe enough. It may well be essential to hang Göring, but it is totally inadequate. That is, this guilt, in contrast to all criminal guilt, oversteps and shatters any and all legal systems. That is the reason why the Nazis in Nuremberg are so smug." In Hannah Arendt, Karl Jaspers, Lotte Köhler, and Hans Saner, *Hannah Arendt/Karl Jaspers correspondence, 1926–1969* (New York: Harcourt Brace Jovanovich, 1992), 54.

3. Steven R. Ratner and Jason S. Abrams, *Accountability for Human Rights Atrocities in International Law: Beyond the Nuremberg Legacy* (Oxford: Oxford University Press, 2001); Chandra Sriram,

But how do we know that this international expectation is on its way to becoming institutionalized as an international norm? Unlike international justice, which we can trace back at least to the Nuremberg trials, the idea of transitional justice truly attracted international attention only as recently as the 1980s.[4] The Greek trials of military leadership in the mid-1970s were the beginning of this trend, which gained much more steam with the internationally publicized Argentinean junta trials in 1985. A decade later, the phenomenal international attention paid to the South African truth and reconciliation commission (TRC) permanently institutionalized that transitional justice model as an alternative or complementary mechanism to trials as a way to deal with a country's violent past. Detailed studies of truth commissions have also noted an explosion of this particular transitional justice mechanism. One of the leading experts on truth commissions, Priscilla Hayner, even declared that *"virtually every state* that has recently emerged from authoritarian rule or civil war," has expressed some interest in creating a truth commission.[5]

The perceived success of these new institutions provided them with international legitimacy as workable and appropriate models for dealing with serious human rights abuses, even though they remained greatly controversial in their local communities.[6] Domestic trials followed in Chile, Guatemala, Panama, Honduras, Peru, Paraguay, Ethiopia, and Rwanda, and truth commissions were established in Burundi, Chad, East Timor, Guatemala, Haiti, South Africa, and Sri Lanka—to name just a few prominent examples.

More broadly, the global trend toward legalization and "judicialization" of politics, in which transitional justice is embedded, is also showing signs of spreading and institutionalization.[7] Transitional justice was further established, legalized,

---

"Revolutions in Accountability: New Approaches to Past Abuse," *American University International Law Review* 19 (2003): 304–429.

4. Gary Jonathan Bass traces the development of international justice to the Napoleonic trials of 1815, the Leipzig trials after World War I, and the Nuremberg and Tokyo trials after World War II. *Stay the Hand of Vengeance: The Politics of War Crimes Tribunals* (Princeton: Princeton University Press, 2000).

5. Priscilla B. Hayner, *Unspeakable Truths: Confronting State Terror and Atrocity* (New York: Routledge, 2001), 23 (emphasis added).

6. On Argentina, see Luis Roniger and Mario Sznajder, *The Legacy of Human-Rights Violations in the Southern Cone: Argentina, Chile, and Uruguay* (Oxford: Oxford University Press, 1999). On South Africa, see James Gibson and Amanda Gouws, "Truth and Reconciliation in South Africa: Attributions of Blame and the Struggle over Apartheid," *American Political Science Review* 93, no. 3 (1999): 501–18; Charles Villa-Vicencio and Wilhelm Verwoerd, *Looking Back, Reaching Forward: Reflections on the Truth and Reconciliation Commission of South Africa* (Cape Town: University of Cape Town Press, 2000); Lyn S. Graybill, *Truth and Reconciliation in South Africa: Miracle or Model?* (Boulder: Lynne Rienner, 2002).

7. Kenneth W. Abbott, Robert O. Keohane, Andrew Moravcsik, Anne-Marie Slaughter, and Duncan Snidal, "The Concept of Legalization," *International Organization* 54, no. 3 (2000): 401–19; Rachel

and codified with the establishment of ad hoc tribunals for the former Yugo-slavia and Rwanda in 1993–94 and then with the creation of the permanent International Criminal Court (ICC) in 1998. The most recent pillar of emerging international justice structure is the notion of universal jurisdiction, according to which national courts can investigate and prosecute alleged perpetrators on their territory, regardless of where the crime was committed or the nationality of the accused or the victim.[8] International justice advocates have pointed to the recent successful prosecution of human rights abuses committed in other coun-tries by courts in Spain, France, Belgium, the United Kingdom, and the Nether-lands as an indication that universal jurisdiction is now a practical and political reality, on the path to becoming fully assimilated into the domestic criminal law systems of some countries, mostly in Western Europe.[9]

Models of Transitional Justice

As mentioned earlier, the most common mechanisms of transitional justice are domestic trials, international trials, truth commissions, and more recently tri-als in front of foreign courts (based on universal jurisdiction) and hybrid trials (mixed domestic-international). There are, however, other options available to countries, such as reparations to victims,[10] lustration,[11] museums or other sites

---

Sieder and Line Schjolden, eds., *The Judicialization of Politics in Latin America* (New York: Palgrave Macmillan, 2005).

8. Universal jurisdiction gained international prominence when a Spanish judge opened an inves-tigation against former Chilean leader Augusto Pinochet that led to his arrest in the United Kingdom in 1998 and subsequent extradition proceedings. The Pinochet case inspired new prosecutions of crimes by militaries in Latin America and elsewhere, creating a so-called Pinochet effect. See Naomi Roht-Arriaza, *The Pinochet Effect: Transnational Justice in the Age of Human Rights* (Philadelphia: University of Pennsylvania Press, 2005).

9. Human Rights Watch, "Universal Jurisdiction in Europe: The State of the Art," vol. 18, no. 5(D), New York, June 27, 2006. Some analysts, however, have noticed a recent retrenchment of the uni-versal jurisdiction principle, such as Belgium's repeal of its universal jurisdiction statute. See Ellen L. Lutz, "Universal Jurisdiction and the Surge in Domestic Prosecutions for Human Rights and Humanitarian Law Crimes" (paper presented at the SSRC International Law and International Relations Project: Workshop on International Criminal Accountability, Washington, DC, Novem-ber 6–7, 2003).

10. Ellen L. Lutz, "After the Elections: Compensating Victims of Human Rights Abuses," in *New Directions in Human Rights,* ed. Ellen L. Lutz, Hurst Hannum, and Kathryn Burke (Philadelphia: University of Pennsylvania Press, 1989).

11. Lustration, which means "illumination" or "purification," is the vetting of public officials based on their participation in the human rights abuses of the previous regime. This has been an impor-tant transitional justice mechanism in Eastern Europe. See Herman Schwartz, "Lustration in Eastern Europe," *Parker School of East European Law* 1, no. 2 (1994): 141–71.

commemorating the victims,[12] state apologies,[13] community initiatives,[14] unofficial mechanisms,[15] or amnesties. This book focuses on the most prominent and politically most controversial transitional justice institutions—trials (domestic, international, and hybrid) and truth commissions. These institutions represent test cases for the analysis of transitional justice norm diffusion, as they involve much deeper domestic political debate and conflict than more limited and "softer" models such as lustration or sites of memory. Amnesties are increasingly seen as less legitimate, although they are still quite often practiced by transitional states,[16] while lustration and reparations usually go as part of the package with one of the more institutionalized mechanisms, such as trials or truth commissions.

The question still remains, however, why should the very different models analyzed here be considered under the unifying umbrella of transitional justice? The quick answer is that they all deal with essentially the same problem—what, if anything, transitional states should do to publicly deal with crimes of the past. The transitional justice literature until recently made clear distinctions between "truth-seeking" institutions, such as truth commissions, and "justice-seeking" models, such as courts and tribunals—and these indeed are institutions quite different in design, objective, and process.[17] However, they all arise out of the

---

12. Elizabeth Jelin, Judy Rein, and Marcial Godoy-Anativia, *State Repression and the Labors of Memory* (Minneapolis: University of Minnesota Press, 2003).

13. Jennifer Lind, *Sorry States: Apologies in International Politics* (Ithaca: Cornell University Press, 2008).

14. For example, *gacaca* hearings in Rwanda are community justice initiatives. These village-based courts conduct outdoor hearings in thousands of local jurisdictions. They place emphasis on truth telling over retributive justice, and are designed to promote reconciliation between former victims and perpetrators. See Erin Daly, "Between Punitive and Reconstructive Justice: The Gacaca Courts in Rwanda," *New York University Journal of International Law and Politics* 34, no. 2 (2002); Alana Erin Tiemessen, "After Arusha: Gacaca Justice in Post-Genocide Rwanda," *Africa Studies Quarterly* 8, no. 1 (2004): 57–76.

15. For example, unofficial reports not sanctioned by the state. For Brazil, see Catholic Church Archdiocese of Sao Paulo and Joan Dassin, *Torture in Brazil: A Report* (New York: Vintage Books, 1986). For Namibia, see Siegfried Groth, *Namibia, the Wall of Silence: The Dark Days of the Liberation Struggle* (Wuppertal, Ger.: P. Hammer, 1995).

16. See position statements on the illegitimacy of amnesties by Human Rights Watch, http://hrw. org/justice/about.htm, and Amnesty International, http://web.archive.org/web/20040604002622/ http://web.amnesty.org/pages/jus-index-eng. For an opposing view that promotes amnesties as stability-building measures after the conflict, see Jack L. Goldsmith and Stephen Krasner, "The Limits of Idealism," *Daedalus* 132, no. 1 (2003): 47–64; Jack L. Snyder and Leslie Vinjamuri, "Trials and Errors: Principle and Pragmatism in Strategies of International Justice," *International Security* 28, no. 3 (2003): 5–44. On the relationship between amnesties and international justice, see Louise Mallinder, "Can Amnesties and International Justice be Reconciled?" *International Journal of Transitional Justice* 2, no. 1 (2007): 208–30.

17. Indicative of this division in the literature is the debate between José Zalaquett and Juan Méndez. José Zalaquett, "Balancing Ethical Imperatives and Political Constraints: The Dilemma of New Democracies Confronting Past Human Rights Violations," *Hastings Law Journal* 43, no. 6

same normative position—that crimes of the past cannot be dealt with either through victor's justice or through impunity, that there needs to be an open and transparent process of transitional justice—and this is why I discuss these different models as institutional outgrowths of the transitional justice norm.

Furthermore, neat separation of these different institutional arrangements into "domestic" and "international" is misleading. The most clearly international mechanism—an international trial—still interacts with domestic political needs and strategies. Another international model—universal jurisdiction—opens up space for later domestic prosecutions.[18] Domestic mechanisms, such as local truth commissions, are now increasingly guided, staffed, or advised by international justice experts. What this indicates is that the international/domestic relationship in the field of transitional justice has changed. More prominent early models (Greece, Argentina, South Africa) may have genuinely arisen out of domestic social demand, but their international popularity, legitimacy, and perceived success have made them into models to be imitated abroad, even in countries with a much more limited domestic interest in dealing with the past.[19]

For all these reasons, this book employs a multidimensional approach to domestic compliance with transitional justice norms and institutions. It does not deal only with state cooperation with international tribunals, such as the ICTY.[20] Instead, it looks at domestic compliance with transitional justice more broadly, through evaluation of domestic trials and truth-finding efforts, such as truth commissions or institutes of memory. This is an important expansion of the universe of cases of domestic compliance with transitional justice norms, and it proves an important point. States are now subject to pressures—although different kinds of pressures—to respond to transitional justice norms even in the

---

(1992): 1426–32; Juan Méndez, "In Defense of Transitional Justice," in *Transitional Justice and the Rule of Law in New Democracies*, ed. A. James McAdams (Notre Dame: University of Notre Dame Press, 1997). Also Robert I. Rotberg and Dennis F. Thompson, *Truth v. Justice: The Morality of Truth Commissions* (Princeton: Princeton University Press, 2000). New work on transitional justice, however, claims that the truth-versus-justice dichotomy has largely been overcome. See Roht-Arriaza and Mariezcurrena, *Transitional Justice in the Twenty-First Century.*

18. Ellen L. Lutz and Kathryn Sikkink, "The Justice Cascade: The Evolution and Impact of Foreign Human Rights Trials in Latin America," *Chicago Journal of International Law* 2, no. 1 (2001): 1–34.

19. These early models have only recently been flagged as major transitional justice successes. At the time, however, the domestic trial of generals in Argentina was condemned as a major political destabilizer, so much so that its perceived failure led to the increasing popularity of the alternative truth commission model. Recently the pendulum has swung again, and international transitional justice activists are now promoting domestic trials in Argentina with a renewed enthusiasm. See Human Rights Watch, "Argentina: 'Disappearances' Trial Breaks Years of Impunity," June 18, 2006, http://www.hrw.org/en/news/2006/06/18/argentina-disappearances-trial-breaks-years-impunity.

20. For a comprehensive analysis of problems of state cooperation with international tribunals, see Victor Peskin, *International Justice in Rwanda and the Balkans: Virtual Trials and the Struggle for State Cooperation* (Cambridge: Cambridge University Press, 2008).

absence of direct sanctions or rewards. While cooperation with international trials is often secured through use of coercive international tactics, there are other mechanisms at work that motivate domestic elites to start a transitional justice process. As the cases of Serbia, Croatia, and Bosnia will show, when the domestic demand for transitional justice is low or inconsistent, domestic elites will find creative ways to respond to other international pressures—such as symbolic or bureaucratic pressures—by setting up domestic war-crimes tribunals or truth commissions, but they will do so to pursue local political goals that are removed from the purpose and goal of international norms of transitional justice.

The International Justice Industry

The institutionalization of transitional justice is best viewed as embedded in the larger norm of global liberalism, which is evident in the increasing legalization of the international system and reliance on the rule of law as the appropriate model of state practice.[21] The move toward internationalization of accountability for human rights abuses and war crimes is also nested in a wider normative shift in world politics that incorporates human rights norms as an integral part of international relations and foreign policy.[22] For example, Amnesty International, one of the leading international human rights organizations, makes a direct link between legalization and human rights in the field of international justice:

> If the twenty first century is to avoid the brutality that was a hallmark of the twentieth, *a legal system* that ends impunity to the perpetrators of the worst crimes known to humanity—genocide, crimes against humanity, war crimes, torture, extrajudicial executions and disappearances—must be established and implemented worldwide. Such a system is essential to deter people contemplating such crimes, to allow victims to obtain justice and redress and to support reconciliation between the groups or states involved in a conflict.[23]

---

21. Kenneth W. Abbott, Robert O. Keohane, Andrew Moravcsik, Anne-Marie Slaughter, and Duncan Snidal, "The Concept of Legalization," *International Organization* 54, no. 3 (2000): 401–19.

22. Kathryn Sikkink, "Memo for SSRC International Law and International Relations Project: Workshop on International Criminal Accountability" (paper presented at the SSRC International Law and International Relations Project: Workshop on International Criminal Accountability, Washington, DC, November 6–7, 2003).

23. Amnesty International, "Establishing a System of International Justice to End Impunity," http://web.archive.org/web/20040604002622/http://web.amnesty.org/pages/jus-index-eng (emphasis added).

The normative shift at the international level toward legalization as a solution for human rights abuses has led to a massive proliferation of transitional justice initiatives around the world. The institutional designs of transitional justice models are becoming increasingly regulated as professionalized and specialized international organizations supply specific models of policy change for domestic actors to implement.

The growing international supply of specific models for dealing with past crimes also creates its own demand from states. States are now expected, encouraged, or even coerced by other states, by international organizations, and by the growing international justice expert industry—an active group of institutions and individuals with expert authority and policy objectives in the international justice issue area—to conduct transitional justice projects as one of the first steps in postconflict rebuilding.[24]

The role of the international justice industry is vital in this process. International organizations make rules, set standards, and define principles, even "represent humanity" to other states and international actors.[25] They formulate global issues, promote ways in which these issues should be resolved, and lobby states to enact policies consistent with these principles.[26] They are locations of "transnational contextual knowledge."[27] They may have limited implementation power, but they appeal to a sense of justice and fairness and use moral condemnation and shaming when their appeals go unresolved. Their authority therefore is informal, but it is no less real.

The professionalized international justice industry now includes many new international organizations, such as international justice NGOs, pressure groups, courts (notably international criminal tribunals for the former Yugoslavia and Rwanda and the ICC), and truth commissions, as well as other states and individuals, acting as international justice entrepreneurs.[28] Different segments of the international justice industry promote transitional justice for different reasons.

---

24. My understanding of the international justice industry corresponds to what sociological institutionalists call an "organizational field," defined as "those organizations that, in the aggregate, constitute a recognized area of institutional life: key suppliers, resource and product consumers, regulatory agencies, and other organizations that produce similar services or products." Paul DiMaggio and Walter W. Powell, "The Iron Cage Revisited: Institutional Isomorphism and Collective Rationality in Organizational Fields," *American Sociological Review* 48, no. 2 (1983): 147–60, 148.

25. John Boli and George M. Thomas, *Constructing World Culture: International Nongovernmental Organizations since 1875* (Stanford: Stanford University Press, 1999), 14.

26. Susan Burgerman, *Moral Victories: How Activists Provoke Multilateral Action* (Ithaca: Cornell University Press, 2001).

27. Boli and Thomas, *Constructing World Culture*, 34.

28. On the importance of professionalization for international organizational diffusion, see John W. Meyer, John Boli, George M. Thomas, and Francisco O. Ramirez, "World Society and the Nation State," *American Journal of Sociology* 103, no. 1 (1997): 144–81. For a more specific discussion of

Many international justice organizations are true believers in the cause of transitional justice, as many of their staff members have been personally affected and their opinions shaped by working on earlier transitional justice institutions, such as the South African truth and reconciliation commission.[29] Other international justice organizations, such as the ICTY, the ICTR (International Criminal Tribunal for Rwanda), and ICC courts are engaged in norm promotion for bureaucratic reasons. They need to justify their continuing operations, and they need a show of success to further advance their institutional legitimacy. Individual states or quasi-states, such as the EU, use transitional justice as leverage to force adopter states into changing their behavior in internationally appropriate and desirable ways.

This varied and expansive international justice industry no longer only generally supports the international justice regime, but is much more directly involved. International justice organizations help set up and design transitional justice institutions, and provide staff and consulting services. They are also direct agents of transitional justice projects: they collect witness testimony and evidence, they serve as expert witnesses and advisers, and they help generate the political pressure necessary for the arrest of suspects. They lobby on states' behalf, raise funds, and link transitional justice adoption with other international benefits.[30] As a consequence of this unprecedented activism, the international justice industry has succeeded in framing the states' choice as one of which model of justice to adopt, not whether any should be adopted at all.[31]

These professional experts have developed and specified international organizational models of transitional justice, producing a self-reinforcing cycle that

---

international norm entrepreneurs, see Martha Finnemore, "International Organizations as Teachers of Norms," *International Organization* 47, no. 4 (1993): 565–97.

29. This is clearly the case with the International Center for Transitional Justice (ICTJ), since many of its experts came from the South African TRC.

30. For an example of international justice organizations advocating suspension of EU negotiation due to Serbia's lack of cooperation with the ICTY, see Human Rights Watch briefing to the EU foreign ministers in March 2006, Human Rights Watch, "Human Rights Watch Concerns on the Western Balkans," March 6, 2006, http://www.hrw.org/en/news/2006/03/06/human-rights-watch-concerns-western-balkans.

31. To give a flavor of the extent of international involvement in domestic justice initiatives, the ICTJ, only one of the many active international justice organizations, is currently involved in designing, consulting, or setting up truth commissions or alternative transitional justice arrangements in Afghanistan, Algeria, Argentina, Burma/Myanmar, Burundi, Cambodia, Canada, Colombia, Democratic Republic of Congo, Guatemala, Indonesia, Iraq, Israel/Palestine, Kenya, Lebanon, Liberia, Mexico, Morocco, Nepal, Nicaragua, Nigeria, Northern Ireland, Panama, Paraguay, Peru, Sierra Leone, South Africa, Timor Leste, Turkey, Uganda, the United States, and former Yugoslavia (www.ictj.org).

has further institutionalized their professional authority.[32] The international justice organizations have therefore managed to present themselves as objectively and professionally helping states pursue their exogenous goals. These goals are presumed to be justice for victims, punishment for perpetrators, coming to terms with the past, reconciliation, and deterrence of future atrocities.[33] They are assumed, unquestioned, and understood as "best practices" for transitional states. What states now need in order to achieve these goals are international guidance, expertise, resources, and advocacy to get to where they need to be.

The purpose of this book, however, is to show that what happens in real politics differs significantly from the ideals set out by international justice entrepreneurs. The great proliferation of available models of transitional justice makes adopting these institutions an easy way to show compliance with international rules without making broader domestic normative changes. As a consequence, some of the original goals of transitional justice—reconciliation and stability—become subordinated to ulterior state strategies, as justice becomes hijacked in favor of domestic political mobilization.

Internationalized Transitional Justice: What We Know

Two distinct sets of literatures in international relations (IR) and comparative politics speak to the questions of diffusion and adoption of transitional justice norms. The IR literature on international organizations has largely focused on the establishment of very formalized justice institutions (such as international tribunals) and has paid insufficient attention to what these institutions actually do and to what effect. The comparative literature on transitional justice has in turn mostly kept the internationalization aspect without adequate theoretical explanation, and has instead focused on issues of institutional design and optimal conditions for reaching the idealized transitional justice goals (justice, truth, and reconciliation). This literature has mostly centered on truth commissions and much less on international organizations such as the UN criminal courts. This compartmentalization of the problem is unfortunate, as it reveals that both bodies of work have observed the phenomenon somewhat in isolation.

---

32. Meyer et al., "World Society."

33. For a clear enumeration of international justice goals, see the international justice position statement by Human Rights Watch, http://hrw.org/justice/about.htm, and Amnesty International, http://web.archive.org/web/20040604002622/http://web.amnesty.org/pages/jus-index-eng.

The international organizations literature considers international justice another type of "regime," with which states do or do not comply.[34] The transitional justice literature, on the other hand, has been mostly descriptive and prescriptive and even quite teleological in nature.[35] As a consequence, very little has so far been said about either the role of international factors in transitional justice initiatives or the domestic effects of international justice projects.

Transitional Justice as a Social Need

The past decade has seen an unprecedented surge in transitional justice literature, which reflects the great proliferation of transitional justice projects around the world. However, most of this scholarship has been markedly atheoretical and has instead focused on two major pragmatic and normative debates. The first question is whether societies coming out of violent authoritarian pasts should set up any transitional justice initiatives at all or should instead focus on the future, leaving the past to rest. The second debate is about institutional design, where the choice for transitional democracies is limited to sequencing—what should come first, trials or truth commissions (justice or truth/healing).

Most transitional justice literature sees reconciliation as the ultimate goal of transitional justice projects, regardless of the institutional form chosen.[36] Reconciliation can come in many ways. It can include the creation of a reliable record of past events, offer a platform for victims to tell their stories and get some (emotional or material) compensation, propose legal or political remedies to avoid future atrocities, and ascertain guilt and determine accountability of perpetrators.[37]

Others argue, however, that opening the wounds of the past never heals the conflict but instead creates new political and social divisions.[38] Instead of seeking truth and punishing the perpetrators, it is better "not to prosecute, not to punish, not to forgive, and not to forget."[39] This strand in the transitional justice

---

34. Judith Goldstein, Miles Kahler, Robert O. Keohane, and Anne-Marie Slaughter, "Introduction: Legalization and World Politics," *International Organization* 54, no. 3 (2000): 385–99; Christopher Rudolph, "Constructing an Atrocities Regime: The Politics of War Crimes Tribunals," *International Organization* 55, no. 3 (2001): 655–91.

35. Neil J. Kritz, *Transitional Justice: How Emerging Democracies Reckon with Former Regimes* (Washington, DC: United States Institute of Peace Press, 1995).

36. Martha Minow, *Between Vengeance and Forgiveness: Facing History after Genocide and Mass Violence* (Boston: Beacon Press, 1998).

37. Margaret Popkin and Naomi Roht-Arriaza, "Truth as Justice: Investigatory Commissions in Latin America," *Law and Social Inquiry* 20, no. 1 (1995): 79–116.

38. Laurel E. Fletcher and Harvey M. Weinstein, "Violence and Social Repair: Rethinking the Contribution of Justice to Reconciliation," *Human Rights Quarterly* 24 (2002): 573–639.

39. Samuel P. Huntington, *The Third Wave: Democratization in the Late Twentieth Century* (Norman: University of Oklahoma Press, 1991).

literature warns against the politically destabilizing potential of truth-seeking efforts in fragile transitional democracies, as brutal dictators may refuse to hand over power peacefully if they fear prosecution by the new regime.[40] Snyder and Vinjamuri make a similar argument in their very critical appraisal of international justice initiatives.[41] They come out strongly against international trials and approve of truth commissions only if they grant amnesties.

Other scholars and transitional justice activists stress the beneficial consequences of societal catharsis that follow truth-seeking efforts and the prosecution of perpetrators.[42] In this view, proportionate to the punishment of the perpetrators is the acknowledgment of victims' suffering, which can come about only by the public reconstruction of the violent past, by establishing who did what to whom, why, and under whose orders.[43] Furthermore, transitional justice projects can have a demonstrative effect in that procedural justice helps reinforce democratic consolidation and imbue society with respect for the rule of law.[44] Some arguments in favor of transitional justice are made on purely moral grounds—it is the right thing to do, and transitional countries have a duty to bring former perpetrators to justice.[45]

As is evident from this brief overview, transitional justice literature leaves many questions open. Its most serious failing is the lack of serious theorizing about the causes and consequences of many of these projects. For example, despite all the discussion about truth and reconciliation, there are very few clear mechanisms at work here.[46] How exactly does truth lead to reconciliation and

---

40. Guillermo A. O'Donnell and Philippe C. Schmitter, *Transitions from Authoritarian Rule* (Baltimore: Johns Hopkins University Press, 1986); Jamar Benomar, "Justice after Transition," *Journal of Democracy* 4, no. 1 (1993): 3–14.

41. Snyder and Vinjamuri, "Trials and Errors." Also Stephen Krasner, "After War Time Atrocities Politics Can Do More Than the Courts," *International Herald Tribune*, January 16, 2001.

42. Richard Wilson and Brandon Hamber, "Symbolic Closure through Memory, Reparation and Revenge in Post-Conflict Societies," *Journal of Human Rights* 1, no. 1 (2002): 35–53.

43. Aryeh Neier, "What Should Be Done about the Guilty?" *New York Review of Books*, February 1, 1990, 32–35; Robert I. Rotberg, "Truth Commissions and the Provision of Truth, Justice and Reconciliation," in *Truth v. Justice: The Morality of Truth Commissions*, ed. Robert I. Rotberg and Dennis F. Thompson (Princeton: Princeton University Press, 2000), 3.

44. Juan Méndez, "Accountability for Past Abuses," *Human Rights Quarterly* 19, no. 2 (1997): 255–82; Ruti G. Teitel, *Transitional Justice* (Oxford: Oxford University Press, 2000).

45. Diane Orentlicher, "Settling Accounts: The Duty to Prosecute Human Rights Violations of a Prior Regime," *Yale Law Review* 100 (1991): 2539–615; M. C. Bassiouni, "Justice and Peace: The Importance of Choosing Accountability over Realpolitik," *Case Western Reserve Journal of International Law* 35 (2003): 191–204.

46. James L. Gibson, "Does Truth Lead to Reconciliation? Testing the Causal Assumptions of the South African Truth and Reconciliation Process," *American Journal of Political Science* 48, no. 2 (2004): 201–17; David Mendeloff, "Truth-Seeking, Truth-Telling, and Postconflict Peacebuilding: Curb the Enthusiasm?" *International Studies Review* 6, no. 3 (2004): 355–80.

how does reconciliation lead to democratic stability?[47] But more significant for the purposes of my argument, most transitional justice literature assumes that the impetus for setting up transitional justice institutions is domestic in nature, as states will naturally want to deal with their violent pasts as soon as the political transition provides them with that opportunity. If international justice institutions are discussed at all, they are understood to be facilitators of a fundamentally domestic desire for justice arrangements. In contrast, this book claims that the international community (and the international justice industry embedded in it) has developed a set of expectations for state behavior during democratic transitions. Dealing with past crimes has become a fundamental part of the transitional moment, and states adopt these models for reasons that can be profoundly at odds with what the international community has envisaged. This is why we need to understand more fully how domestic societies interpret international normative and organizational models, and we also need to have a systematic explanation for the role of international organizations and norm entrepreneurs in the domestic politics of the states in which they intervene.

Transitional Justice as an International Regime

Within the international organizations literature, two research programs—liberalism and constructivism—have offered insights into why states may adopt certain models of transitional justice. The rationalist liberal framework that stresses domestic politics and social group interests suggests that transitional governments in fledgling democracies may deliberately cooperate with international human rights institutions as a means to (1) lock in and consolidate domestic democratic institutions and (2) strengthen their credibility and stability in respect to nondemocratic political threats.[48] Although this account may not explain why these institutions emerged in the first place, it does offer a good explanation of why transitional governments may cooperate with them. This "self-binding" explanation therefore corresponds to my hypothesis that states use international justice models to get rid of domestic political opponents. However, I identify a broader range of domestic motives for the adoption of international legal models than that offered by liberal IR theory. In addition to domestic power politics hypothesis, this book argues that states adopt international justice models because they are coerced into adoption through material benefits but also

---

47. Mark R. Amstutz, *The Healing of Nations: The Promise and Limits of Political Forgiveness* (Lanham, MD: Rowman & Littlefield, 2005).

48. Andrew Moravcsik, "The Origins of Human Rights Regimes: Democratic Delegation in Postwar Europe," *International Organization* 54, no. 2 (2000): 217–52.

for reasons of legitimacy and symbolic politics or as a consequence of a growing international supply of international justice models that is creating its own demand from states.

Gary Bass offers the most direct application of liberal IR theory to the issue of international legalization of justice.[49] In his work on the politics of international war-crimes tribunals, Bass argues that only domestically liberal states support these tribunals.[50] This is a result of domestic norms spilling over into foreign policy. Liberal states choose trials because they are in the grip of a principled idea—"war crimes legalism."[51] However, these states are hypocritical: they do not risk their own soldiers for the sake of international justice, and they are much more likely to pursue prosecution of war criminals when the victims are their own citizens. Bass's analysis, however, stops with the creation of international tribunals and does not consider the social and political consequences these tribunals have had in the societies over which they have jurisdiction. The emphasis on state liberalism as the best predictor of state adoption or nonadoption of international justice models therefore leaves out an entire set of domestic motivations for cooperation with these international institutions.[52] Instead, even illiberal states—or rather, *specifically* illiberal states—may comply with international justice mechanisms but for quite different reasons than the international community expects them to.[53]

Alternatively, constructivist approaches have been quite insightful in advancing our understanding of why states choose to adopt certain international practices. They may do so because they want to look like modern states, and they learn what that means from proactive international organizations.[54] In addition, the consequence to their reputation of the strategies of naming and shaming pursued by transnational advocacy networks and international NGOs may create incentives for states to change their behavior and conform to new international expectations.[55]

---

49. Bass, *Stay the Hand of Vengeance.*

50. For a liberal perspective in international law that deals with the same issue, see Anne-Marie Slaughter, "International Law in a World of Liberal States," *European Journal of International Law* 6, no. 4 (1995).

51. Bass, *Stay the Hand of Vengeance.*

52. Note that Bass considers only international tribunals, not truth commissions.

53. Emilie Hafner-Burton, Kiyoteru Tsutsui, and John W. Meyer, "International Human Rights Law and the Politics of Legitimation: Repressive States and Human Rights Treaties," *International Sociology* 23, no. 1 (2008): 115–41.

54. Martha Finnemore, *National Interests in International Society* (Ithaca: Cornell University Press, 1996), 137.

55. Margaret E. Keck and Kathryn Sikkink, *Activists beyond Borders: Advocacy Networks in International Politics* (Ithaca: Cornell University Press, 1998).

Constructivist theories have also offered significant insights into issues of international justice. Scholars have identified the phenomenon of "justice cascade," which occurs when the international prestige of a domestic transitional justice arrangement makes the model more attractive domestically and opens up more political space for domestic justice initiatives.[56] Much of the current human rights literature focuses on this effect.[57] Alternatively, diffusion of human rights policies across the international system follows the strengthening of the international human rights regime; as more and more states sign human rights treaties, the regime itself becomes stronger and more states feel an obligation to join.[58]

International justice, however, produces other effects that need to be explained, and most current human rights literature does not offer sufficient guidance.[59] This book generates a series of hypotheses regarding why we should expect to see both increasing compliance with transitional justice models and divergent behaviors of states that adopt them. This recasting of the argument enables us to explore the domestic and international conditions under which states adopt transitional justice projects and the outcomes those factors produce in terms of achieving policy ideals. This move, however, first requires the infusion of a healthy dose of domestic politics into our understanding of international norm diffusion and compliance. This is a challenge this book hopes to meet.

Domestic Politics of Compliance under Pressure

Any work on international norms today must begin with the fundamental premise that they always enter already existing domestic political debates, beliefs, and understandings, which influence the process of norm diffusion in many significant ways.[60] Local political actors work as domestic norm entrepreneurs,

56. Lutz and Sikkink, "The Justice Cascade."

57. Keck and Sikkink, *Activists beyond Borders;* Thomas Risse-Kappen, Steve C. Ropp, and Kathryn Sikkink, *The Power of Human Rights: International Norms and Domestic Change* (New York: Cambridge University Press, 1999); Ellen L. Lutz and Kathryn Sikkink, "International Human Rights Law and Practice in Latin America," *International Organization* 54, no. 3 (2000): 633–59; Daniel C. Thomas, *The Helsinki Effect: International Norms, Human Rights, and the Demise of Communism* (Princeton: Princeton University Press, 2001).

58. Emilie Hafner-Burton and Tsutui Kiyoteru, "Human Rights in a Globalizing World: The Paradox of Empty Promises," *American Journal of Sociology* 110, no. 5 (2005): 1373–411.

59. Sonia Cardenas, "Norm Collision: Explaining the Effects of International Human Rights Pressure on State Behavior," *International Studies Review* 6 (2004): 213–31.

60. A. P. Cortell and James W. Davis, "How Do International Institutions Matter? The Domestic Impact of International Rules and Norms," *International Studies Quarterly* 40, no. 4 (1996): 451–78; Jeffrey W. Legro, "Which Norms Matter? Revisiting the "Failure" of Internationalism," *International*

promoters, and interpreters, making international rules and standards meaning-ful to domestic political audiences.[61] However, domestic actors may be interested in complying with a new global norm not because they want to advance it but because they want to challenge it. Much of norms scholarship has measured nor-mative compliance using indicators such as the change of public discourse, articu-lation or establishment of a policy, or creation of a national institution.[62] Research has shown, however, that many states show signs of normative compliance—they ratify an international treaty or change domestic law—but they do so for window dressing in order to ease international pressure while in fact continuing, and even stepping up, normative violations at home.[63]

The process of norm diffusion, therefore, is inextricably linked to domestic politics. As norms travel through the domestic political space, they get strategi-cally appropriated and utilized by different local actors for a variety of motives. Employing rhetorical tools of argumentation and persuasion, domestic actors use international norms to validate their preexisting self-interested claims and to frame their preferences and actions as consistent with the norm.[64] By doing so, they are able to make use of international norms and institutional models while at the same time rejecting or ignoring their substance. They violate the norm by complying with its institutional demands. In such cases, international norms and the institutional models they generate become part of a domes-tic political struggle as local actors instrumentalize them for narrow political gains.[65] They become detached from the international value and produce a series of discrete, disconnected, and sometimes contradictory strategies by state actors. This domestic use of international norms is therefore not an aberration by some states but an inevitable function of norm diffusion.

Organization 51, no. 1 (1997): 31–63; Jeffrey Checkel, "Norms, Institutions and National Identity in Contemporary Europe," *International Studies Quarterly* 43 (1999): 83–114; Jeffrey Checkel, "Why Comply? Social Learning and European Identity Change," *International Organization* 55, no. 3 (2001): 553–88.

61. Amitav Acharya, "How Ideas Spread: Whose Norms Matter? Norm Localization and Institu-tional Change in Asian Regionalism," *International Organization* 58, no. 2 (2004): 239–75.

62. Andrew P. Cortell and James W. Davis, "Understanding the Domestic Impact of International Norms: A Research Agenda," *International Studies Review* 2, no. 1 (2000): 65–87.

63. Sonia Cardenas, *Conflict and Compliance: State Responses to International Human Rights Pres-sure* (Philadelphia: University of Pennsylvania Press, 2007); Emilie Hafner-Burton and Kiyoteru Tsut-sui, "Justice Lost! The Failure of International Human Rights Law to Matter Where Needed Most," *Journal of Peace Research* 44, no. 7 (2007): 407–25.

64. Thomas Risse, "Let's Argue! Communicative Action in International Relations," *International Organization* 54, no. 1 (2000): 1–39; Frank Schimmelfennig, "Strategic Calculation and International Socialization: Membership Incentives, Party Constellations, and Sustained Compliance in Central and Eastern Europe," *International Organization* 59, no. 4 (2005): 827–60.

65. Hans Peter Schmitz, *Transnational Mobilization and Domestic Regime Change: Africa in Com-parative Perspective* (New York: Palgrave Macmillan, 2006).

However, let me clarify from the outset: the theoretical argument I propose deals with a very specific subset of normative compliance. It explores compliance with international norms under conditions of strong international pressure and limited domestic demand for normative change. In other words, I am not interested in cases of compliance that are primarily driven by normative shifts already taking place in society. When the domestic demand for change is strong, states comply with international norms because these are the norms they already share or because strong domestic constituencies are able to put pressure on governments to change their behavior in response to international demands. I also do not discuss cases where international pressures are low or absent and there are no domestic actors pushing for normative change. In such cases, we can expect that international norms will be soundly rejected or simply ignored.

My argument, then, works within a universe of compliance possibilities that react to sustained but varied international pressures in the domestic political context of strong normative resistance. International pressures to change are great, but the domestic demand for change is weak. The theoretical model I present, therefore, is a domestic politics approach to compliance under pressure and a theory of how this international pressure is resisted and appropriated by local political actors.

International Pressures and Domestic Responses

Coercion

In states where the social demand for normative change is weak and the state unresponsive, international actors will use issue linkage (tying compliance with international demands to rewards such as foreign aid and investment or membership in international organizations) to effectively coerce the state into complying with or adopting an international institutional project.[66] States facing international sticks (withholding of aid, imposition of sanctions) or carrots (exclusive club membership, financial investment) will then comply with international norms and institutions to ease international coercion and obtain material rewards. Coercive pressure produces a simple political bargaining dynamic: if you comply with our requirements, you will get our benefits.

---

66. Heather Grabbe, "How Does Europeanization Affect CEE Governance? Conditionality, Diffusion and Diversity," *Journal of European Public Policy* 8, no. 6 (2001): 1013–31; Judith Kelley, "International Actors on the Domestic Scene: Membership Conditionality and Socialization by International Institutions," *International Organization* 58, no. 3 (2004): 425–57.

Under conditions of international coercion, domestic elites do not have many appealing choices: refusing to comply comes with steep international costs, but compliance can be costly domestically as international demands are perceived as unfair or unacceptable. In such political conditions, domestic elites are best off complying with some international requirements and ignoring others, while repacking compliance as a necessary step that will yield great benefits for everyone at home. Domestic politics will not change, and deeply held social norms will not be transformed. Such coerced compliance then becomes just one in a series of requirements for securing tangible international rewards. It becomes an easy institutional way for states to acquire international benefits, producing outcomes far removed from international policy ideals, as normative social change is effectively traded in for an international reward.

Symbolic Pressure

States are social actors and as such have a desire to form associational ties with other states.[67] They want to belong to international clubs and to be with other like-minded states. They also want to be perceived as legitimate international actors.[68] In states with a strong desire for international membership and recognition, international actors will use symbolic pressure to entice a reluctant state to comply with domestically unpopular norms.[69] Symbolic pressure works something like this: if you comply, you will become one of us.[70]

While membership in international organizations or clubs, such as the EU or NATO, carries obvious economic and political benefits (alliance military protection, full access to regional markets, economic subsidies, and participation or veto-power in regional decision making), there are other pulls for countries to do all they can in order to join.[71] Increasingly, state participation in international organizations and other kinds of multilateral behavior are considered necessary and

---

67. Meyer et al., "World Society."

68. Finnemore, *National Interests*.

69. Finnemore, "International Organizations as Teachers of Norms."

70. For a somewhat similar discussion of the "acculturation" mechanism of social influence, see Ryan Goodman and Derek Jinks, "How to Influence States: Socialization and International Human Rights Law," *Duke Law Journal* 54, no. 4 (2005): 983–98.

71. At the very least, the price of not joining is higher than the price of joining. For this point see Lloyd Gruber, *Ruling the World: Power Politics and the Rise of Supranational Institutions* (Princeton: Princeton University Press, 2000). Also Frank Schimmelfennig and Ulrich Sedelmeier, *The Europeanization of Central and Eastern Europe* (Ithaca: Cornell University Press, 2005); Milada Anna Vachudová, *Europe Undivided: Democracy, Leverage, and Integration after Communism* (Oxford: Oxford University Press, 2005).

appropriate if a state is to be considered a good global citizen.[72] International participation therefore affects state interests and identities. Membership in exclusive clubs such as the EU constitutes what candidate states want to be or what they think they already are—European, liberal, democratic.[73] Joining a prestigious international institution or engaging in other types of multilateral behavior may seem contrary to the immediate national interests of states, but it embodies larger global values that shape strategic choices states make.[74] In other words, states comply with international norms and institutions not because of what they *do* but because of what they *signify*, because of their symbolic and normative properties.[75]

Bureaucratic Pressure

Under conditions of domestic political uncertainty (such as instability, infighting, or weak institutions), international actors will rely on bureaucratic pressures to ensure compliance with international norms and institutions. If they can find no domestic solution to a policy problem and international actors are offering institutional solutions that can be easily adopted, some states will choose to comply with international rules because they believe international actors can solve their domestic issues. Such states are ambiguous about international goals and processes, but they are influenced by the neighborhood effects of international normative and institutional diffusion and are likely to respond strongly to the increasing supply of institutional models available to them by mimicking the behavior of other states. Under bureaucratic pressure, the message international actors send is, comply, and we will fix your problems.

Under conditions of political uncertainty, states will adopt the specific institutional solutions that have obtained the most symbolic legitimacy and have the international authority that alternative models lack.[76] These success models serve

---

72. James March and Johan P. Olsen, *Rediscovering Institutions: The Organizational Basis of Politics* (New York: Free Press, 1989); Martha Finnemore, "Norms, Culture, and World Politics: Insights from Sociology's Institutionalism," *International Organization* 50, no. 2 (1996): 325–47.

73. Finnemore, *National Interests*; Alastair Iain Johnston, "Treating International Institutions as Social Environments," *International Studies Quarterly* 45 (2001): 487–515; Michael N. Barnett and Martha Finnemore, *Rules for the World: International Organizations in Global Politics* (Ithaca: Cornell University Press, 2004).

74. John Gerard Ruggie, "Multilateralism: The Anatomy of an Institution," in *Multilateralism Matters: The History and Praxis of an Institutional Form*, ed. John Gerard Ruggie (New York: Columbia University Press, 1993).

75. DiMaggio and Powell, "The Iron Cage"; Walter W. Powell and Paul DiMaggio, *The New Institutionalism in Organizational Analysis* (Chicago: University of Chicago Press, 1991); John W. Meyer and W. Richard Scott, *Organizational Environments: Ritual and Rationality* (Newbury Park, CA: Sage, 1992).

76. Meyer et al., "World Society."

as a convenient source of the best practices the borrowing states will use.[77] They diffuse across the international system through the activities of a relatively small set of major professionalized international organizations, which present, explain, and sometimes help implement success models to interested states. Institutional models can also diffuse less directly, through neighborhood or regional effects, when states model themselves after their neighbors to be competitive or for fear of lagging behind.

Domestic Political Conditions

International pressures on states do not enter a domestic political vacuum. They always interact with domestic political conditions to guide state strategies of compliance. A number of domestic political factors are particularly salient for this discussion.

Domestic Demand for Normative Change

This domestic demand from below is guided by the nature of normative violation and the broad social consensus developed around public beliefs, understandings, and commitments the international norm is set to change. Some indicators of societal demand from below include social attitudes toward proposed policy change, the political strength of domestic norm promoters, and citizens' demands for accountability at the ballot box, as well as political support for leaders who carried out norm-violating policies.[78] As indicated earlier in the chapter, if the domestic demand for change is high, we can expect the state to adopt international norms and institutions with strong domestic support. Even in states where the demand for change is low, however, there may still be international pressures to comply. It is in such cases that the paradox of hijacked justice will be most pronounced.

Veto Players

Second, we need to determine the location of power in the state and the authority of political spoilers, or "veto players." For states transitioning from a violent

---

77. DiMaggio and Powell, "The Iron Cage."
78. Tricia Olsen, Leigh Payne and Andrew Reiter, "Demand for Justice: Domestic Support for Transitional Justice Mechanisms" (paper presented at the Annual Convention of the International Studies Association, San Francisco, CA, March 26–29, 2008).

period, the question is to what extent members and supporters of the previous regime are still involved in policymaking. Do they have access to the apparatus of repression?

For example, in states transitioning from an authoritarian rule to democracy, unless the transition was brought on by a massive social revolution, the likelihood is that there are still powerful old-regime elements who are embedded, officially or unofficially, in the transitional state's apparatus of force—the military, police, or intelligence agencies. The more "pacted" the transition was (the stronger the compromise made between the old and incoming regimes), the more power old-regime loyalists have in the new transitional state. If the coming international norm is set to fundamentally alter their place in the new state order by requiring a clean slate and their removal from positions of power and control, the transitional elites will fear political reprisal, even a coup, and will be reluctant to destabilize the country and jeopardize their own power by complying with international rules. Compliance here is shallow and rewards-driven; under sustained international pressure, governments will sign laws, they might ratify international treaties, and they will even change domestic legislation and set up new national institutions—but they will not threaten old-regime veto players with political extinction. Instead, they will comply with international demands while keeping the domestic balance of power intact.

Competing Coalitions

Norm compliance is always accompanied by multiple and conflicting points of normative resistance and support in target states. One of the shortcomings of the transnational advocacy network boomerang argument was that it underestimated the strength of elite resistance to international norms and overestimated the power of norm supporters—domestic allies of transnational groups, such as nongovernmental organizations and civil society. While domestic elites in general and government elites in particular may be strongly opposed to policy change, what further complicates international norm compliance are frequent differences and domestic political struggles between elite factions, who use international norms and institutions as domestic wedge issues to score quite localized political points by, for example, instrumentalizing a particular international policy intervention in a coming election campaign.

The major domestic coalitions whose interaction helps determine the mechanism of international norm compliance can be roughly grouped as norm resisters, instrumental norm adopters, and norm-supporting true believers.

Norm resisters are political elites ideologically, politically, or pragmatically opposed to policy change. In countries where elite legitimacy is based on ideologies squarely at odds with norms of the international liberal order, domestic actors are ideologically unable to internalize international norms because norm adoption undermines the basis of their domestic political rule. Nevertheless, these actors will still pursue cosmetic changes to their domestic practices and tactical concessions in order to obtain international benefits and payoffs. They will use international norms and institutions to further consolidate their rule and not to undertake the social transformation these international rules require.

Other domestic political elites may be *instrumental norm adopters*. They use international norms to distinguish themselves from other political groups and to position themselves as internationalist and reformist forces in society. Instrumental norm adopters may face serious political challenges from norm resisters and their constituencies. Still, they agree to implement international institutional changes because they consider them legitimate and necessary if they are to be taken seriously by international actors on whom they depend. International club membership and other status incentives therefore lead domestic instrumental adopters to rebrand themselves as pro-international and dedicated to compliance with international norms. Norm compliance, however, is still driven by external incentives—appeals to legitimacy—and not by norm acceptance and internalization.[79]

Finally, international models are fully accepted by *true believers*—civil-society groups or other political coalitions that are at odds with both norm resisters and instrumental adopters. As we know from boomerang and spiral models of norm diffusion, it is these groups that spearhead norm adoption by making lasting coalitions with international norm promoters who put pressure on domestic governments to initiate policy change.[80] If domestic true believers win the domestic political infighting, we can expect states to fully comply with international norms and institutions.

However, the political environment in which domestic allies of international norm promoters operate is often much more complicated. Civil society in transitional states is just as likely to be bitterly divided over a specific international issue as it is united against a common enemy (the previous authoritarian regime).[81] In addition, close alliances with international actors may become a domestic political liability, giving norm resisters an easy way to delegitimate true believers

79. Jeffrey Checkel considers role playing a half step to internalization. I conceptualize these mechanisms as quite separate. See Checkel, "International Institutions and Socialization in Europe: Introduction and Framework," *International Organization* 59, no. 4 (2005): 801–26.

80. Risse-Kappen, Ropp, and Sikkink, *The Power of Human Rights.*

81. Schmitz, *Transnational Mobilization.*

as unpatriotic and dangerous.[82] This further distracts domestic groups from transmitting international norms by making it much more difficult to build effective broad domestic coalitions in an increasingly hostile political environment.

Under conditions of political uncertainty, however, none of the three groups may have a monopoly over domestic legitimacy and authority, and normative contestation between resisters and adopters may reach a stalemate. It is in these conditions that international norm promoters have the most room to move and implement international institutional projects aimed at domestic normative change. They function as norm transmitters, providing states with appropriate institutional models to choose from, educating them about the benefits of instituting specific domestic projects and the proper ways of going about it. In other words, they provide bureaucratic solutions to state problems.

All groups use posturing, positioning, and rhetorical tools to try to amass stronger coalitions among both international and domestic audiences. For example, norm resisters may appeal to a sense of nationalism, sovereignty, and independence in rejecting international institutional intervention. Instrumental adopters may stress the benefits to society of being on the international community's good side by accepting international models. And true believers—domestic as well as international—may appeal to a sense of morality, or the right thing to do, and try to generate support through claims of righteousness and justice. The more persuasive these different appeals are, the broader the domestic coalitions they are able to build; and the stronger the enforcement mechanisms at their disposal are, the more likely they are to prevail and directly influence the strategy of normative compliance a state will pursue.

Hijacked Justice and Policy Outcomes

If international norms and institutions are accepted as a result of coercion, compliance will be shallow and narrow. International actors may see institutional results of their policy interventions, but international norms that generated policies will not take hold. International policies may also end up providing new space for norm resisters to mobilize, to hijack international norms and institutions for local political goals. Entrenched elites can adapt quickly to preferences of international actors and develop strategies of quasi compliance or even outright deception and countermobilization.[83] Politics in target states will not

---

82. Sarah Elizabeth Mendelson and John K. Glenn, *The Power and Limits of NGOs: A Critical Look at Building Democracy in Eastern Europe and Eurasia* (New York: Columbia University Press, 2002).

83. Schmitz, *Transnational Mobilization*.

change. International projects will therefore at best miss their mark and at worst produce perverse results, as domestic elites use international models for ulterior political purposes. This domestic move will then delegitimize international policy interventions in other political environments.

If a state complies out of concerns for legitimacy, policy change will be instrumental and directly tied to international symbols of reputation and status. As long as international actors maintain significant leverage over domestic politics in the target state, domestic elites will comply. If the international policy presence is sustained, concerns for legitimacy will translate into acceptance of international norms and institutions, as they will become an integral part of what domestic actors understand constitutes appropriate international behavior. However, even though international actors may observe the successes of their policy interventions, international normative and institutional change will be only as deep as domestic elites judge is absolutely necessary to maintain international good standing. While compliance here is deeper than in the case of coercion, it is still a long way from norm adoption and internalization.

Finally, if a state complies to resolve political uncertainty through bureaucratic solutions, international norms and institutions will be accepted for a while or until the uncertainty is resolved. International policies can then be used to settle domestic political disputes. Furthermore, if primary agents of change are international norm promoters, as soon as they leave the stage, lose their domestic political leverage, or move their attention elsewhere, we can expect politics to return to the way it was prior to the international policy intervention. In other words, compliance in response to international bureaucratic pressures will be only as sustainable as the commitment of the international actors promoting the policy change. For all these reasons, international projects may get things done in the short term, but they may end up undermining the larger process of substantive acceptance of international norms and standards.

The purpose of the following chapters is to apply the theoretical argument to the field of transitional justice norms and institutions. Transitional justice models are being implemented with increasing speed in different political environments around the globe, but the outcomes of these policy interventions have been decidedly mixed. The empirical chapters that follow trace the differing policy outcomes to different strategies used by Serbia, Croatia, and Bosnia in response to international pressures to comply with transitional justice norms and institutions.

2

THE PAST IS NOT YET OVER

The experience of transitional justice in Serbia has been one of great disappointment for international justice promoters. Serbia was supposed to be the hard test case for transitional justice. It is the country where most of the alleged perpetrators of the worst human rights abuses in Europe since World War II originated. It is the country in whose name, and in the name of whose people, the Balkan wars were waged. And it is the country that went through a mostly peaceful transition, overthrowing the autocratic regime of Slobodan Milošević at the ballot box and ushering in a new generation of democratic political elites who were expected to put the break with Milošević's legacy at the top of their agendas. Moreover, Serbia matters regionally. It is the largest and most populated country in the Western Balkans; it is a state with regional ambitions whose stability is essential for long-term sustainable peace and cooperation in the neighborhood.

Transitional justice efforts in Serbia have been numerous and complex but also erratic and incomplete, leaving in their aftermath significant domestic political disturbances, perhaps none more profound than the 2003 assassination of Serbian reformist prime minister Zoran Ðinđić by an organized crime group that called itself "anti-Hague patriots."[1]

In analyzing the experience of transitional justice in Serbia, I first lay out the international goals and expectations of introducing transitional justice to Serbia

---

1. In Serbia, "The Hague" is the generally adopted shorthand for the International Criminal Tribunal for the Former Yugoslavia located in The Hague, Netherlands.

and the coercive pressures used to achieve them. I look in detail at the different types of international transitional justice mechanisms Serbia has implemented—international trials, truth commission, and domestic trials—and their domestic political effects. I then analyze specific domestic political conditions—social demand from below, the power of old-regime spoilers, and competing elite strategies—that led to Serbia's coerced compliance with international transitional justice institutions. In closing, I evaluate the consequences of coercive pressure on Serbia for the pursuit of truth and justice.

Serbia Back in the World

Serbia has been legally subjected to the jurisdiction of the ICTY since the tribunal's creation in 1993. In fact, it is precisely because the government of Slobodan Milošević, seen as most responsible for the atrocities of the 1990s, would not undertake any measures to bring perpetrators of war crimes to justice that the international court was established to take on that responsibility. In addition, the 1995 Dayton Peace Accords obligated parties to the peace deal to full cooperation with international justice institutions, including the ICTY.

More broadly, the international justice environment has greatly changed since the 1980s, with many countries instituting some form of transitional justice, such as domestic trials or truth commissions. Numerous specialized international justice organizations have emerged with the sole purpose of helping countries set up institutional mechanisms for dealing with the past. In such a dense international environment, post-Milošević Serbia was under multiple pressures to cooperate with already existing transitional justice institutions or to set up its own.

Serbia's relationship with international institutions of justice, however, has never been easy.[2] When the ICTY was established in 1993, Slobodan Milošević was in absolute control of the state. Under his command, Serbia refused to acknowledge the ICTY as a legitimate international institution and denied any investigative assistance to The Hague, even when ICTY prosecutors were interested in cases of human rights violations against Serb civilians.[3] Serbian authorities obstructed investigators' access to sites of alleged atrocities, preventing the

---

2. For a detailed history of Serbian cooperation with the ICTY, see Victor Peskin, *International Justice in Rwanda and the Balkans* (Cambridge: Cambridge University Press, 2008), chs. 2–3.

3. Gary Jonathan Bass, *Stay the Hand of Vengeance: The Politics of War Crimes Tribunals* (Princeton: Princeton University Press, 2000), 257.

collection of evidence. Some witnesses and even victims withheld testimony from ICTY investigators in fear of reprisal.[4]

It is, of course, hardly surprising that old-regime elites who put the criminal policies in place would resist cooperation with international or domestic transitional justice institutions. Nobody really expected Milošević's Serbia to begin seriously addressing past abuses—the idea behind transitional justice is that it is *transitional governments* who undertake these projects, which is why all of the international expectations were placed on the transitional government that ousted Milošević in 2000. Serbia after Milošević was to be the true test case for the power of international criminal accountability.

Slobodan Milošević was removed from power by a popular revolt on October 5, 2000. In many ways, he brought his demise upon himself by rigging presidential elections on September 24. After the results showed that his challenger, Vojislav Koštunica, had won more votes, Milošević immediately challenged the process and called for a second election round. The Democratic Opposition of Serbia (DOS), on whose behalf Koštunica had run, refused and invited voters to go out to the streets and demand that their votes be properly counted. On October 5, angry citizens stormed Belgrade. The mass of protesters soon overwhelmed the police, who withdrew in disarray. The crowd then took over main state institutions, including the parliament. By the end of the night, the DOS declared the public uprising a success, and Milošević was forced to concede defeat. Vojislav Koštunica was inaugurated president and Zoran Đinđić prime minister.

The DOS, the winning anti-Milošević coalition, was a hodgepodge alliance of eighteen widely differing parties, ranging in ideology from progressive social democratic left to conservative Christian right. Adding to the instability was the campaign calculation of DOS leaders that the only opposition politician with a high enough public opinion rating was Vojislav Koštunica,[5] leader of the conservative Democratic Party of Serbia (DSS). The de facto manager of the opposition and leader of the centrist Democratic Party (DS), Zoran Đinđić was seen by most in the coalition as a much more able leader, but his public opinion negatives were too high—a result of successful Milošević-era personal attacks on his party and his own integrity. A decision was therefore made to take a chance with

---

4. Theodor Meron, "Answering for War Crimes: Lessons from the Balkans," *Foreign Affairs* 76, no. 1 (1997): 2–8.

5. A reliable public opinion survey showed that only Koštunica would beat Milošević in a head-to-head race, by 42 to 28 percent. The same survey showed Đinđić and Milošević in a tie. B92 network, July 27, 2000, http://www.b92.net. Koštunica was announced the official DOS presidential candidate on August 7, 2000.

Koštunica and deal with any policy and personnel differences among the coalition leaders after the election.[6]

The world reacted to Milošević's ousting with great enthusiasm and instant rewards. Only days after the new government took over, the European Union lifted its long-lasting economic sanctions against Serbia and pledged $2 billion in reconstruction aid. The EU also promised an additional $300 million a year in aid over the next seven years and offered a trade agreement that would allow tax-free access to European markets for most Serbian exports. The new tone in European dealings with Serbia was clear. As then French foreign minister Hubert Védrine noted, "The EU has radically revised its policy toward [Serbia]."[7]

Soon afterward, the United States followed suit, approving a $100 million aid package to Serbia. This package, however, came with serious strings attached—it was conditional on Serbia's cooperation with the ICTY, primarily in apprehending and transferring war-crimes suspects, including Slobodan Milošević. In order to keep the money flowing, the Serbian government was required to provide war-crimes documentation, assist in locating suspects and witnesses, and allow access to ICTY investigators.[8] And finally, on November 1, 2000, the union of Serbia and Montenegro, still under the name of Yugoslavia, rejoined the United Nations after an eight-year suspension.

In the immediate aftermath of Milošević's ouster in 2000, the Serbian transitional government had a unique opportunity to make a clean break with the previous regime and introduce a starkly new national discourse, institutions and policies that would signify departure from its violent past. Part of all political transitions is the adoption of new national strategies that include many decisions on how to run the country domestically and where to situate the new democracy internationally. It is at these moments of transition that the changed polities become more directly exposed to international expectations of proper behavior, to international rules and standards that should guide the reformed state as it transitions toward full membership in international society. For countries that are transitioning from a violent period marked by massive human rights abuses toward a more peaceful and rights-respecting era, the issue of transitional justice—how new democracies deal with past abuses—becomes an urgent question. The way in which Serbian political elites chose to deal with the legacy of

---

6. Author's interviews with major DOS leaders, September—October 2005, Belgrade.

7. Suzanne Daley, "European Union Greets Yugoslav Government," *New York Times*, October 10, 2000.

8. Stephen A. Holmes, "$100 Million Voted for Serbia, but with War-Crimes Strings," *New York Times*, October 26, 2000.

Milošević-era crimes, however, turned out to be a stunning setback for international and domestic advocates of transitional justice.

International Goals of Transitional Justice in Serbia

After welcoming Serbia back to the world after years of Milošević's authoritarian rule, specialized international justice organizations demanded that the human rights platform, including transitional justice, be put on the very top of the new government's agenda. International justice experts, however, were not united on the best transitional justice mechanism to offer Serbia. Immediately upon Milošević's ousting in 2000, major international human rights organizations rallied in support of the ICTY and against amnesty for Milošević, without proposing any alternative transitional justice mechanism.[9] International human rights groups also lobbied for an issue-linkage policy for Serbia, arguing that noncooperation with the ICTY should be punished by denial of international loans and credits.[10] When the Serbian government announced its plans to open domestic trials against perpetrators of atrocities in Kosovo, Human Rights Watch (HRW) was skeptical, warning that domestic trials could not substitute for trials at The Hague.[11]

The International Center for Transitional Justice, a highly specialized international nongovernmental organization (INGO) that deals exclusively with issues of transitional justice, advocated other mechanisms for Serbia. The ICTJ did not argue directly against the ICTY, but it more enthusiastically supported a truth and reconciliation commission and actively participated in setting up the Serbian commission in 2001. In a stark departure from other INGO positions, the ICTJ also supported prosecuting Milošević in Belgrade instead of The Hague and rejected the issue-linkage policy.[12] This softer approach, however, was a minority opinion, and after the Serbian truth commission ended in failure, with no evidence collected and no report issued, coupled with the increasing unwillingness

---

9. International League for Human Rights, Physicians for Human Rights, Institute for the Advancement of Human Rights, Amnesty International-USA, Lawyers Committee for Human Rights, Minnesota Advocates for Human Rights, and Human Rights Watch, "Major Rights Groups Oppose Immunity for Milošević," joint press release, October 5, 2000, http://hrw.org/english/docs/2000/10/05/serbia690.htm.

10. Human Rights Watch, "Serbia/E.U.: Human Rights Agenda for the New Yugoslavia," October 12, 2000, http://hrw.org/english/docs/2000/10/12/serbia677.htm.

11. Human Rights Watch, "Yugoslavia: Domestic War Crimes Trials No Substitute for The Hague," April 26, 2001, http://hrw.org/english/docs/2001/04/26/serbia160.htm.

12. Alex Boraine, "Reconciliation in the Balkans?" *New York Times*, April 22, 2001.

of the Serbian leadership to cooperate with the ICTY, the ICTJ reverted to a harder position, shared by the majority of international justice entrepreneurs.[13]

Other international organizations argued for an even more comprehensive approach to transitional justice for Serbia. The Council of Europe, for example, issued very specific guidelines about Serbian cooperation with the ICTY but also demanded that Serbia "inform [its] people about the crimes committed by the regime of Slobodan Milošević, not only against the other peoples of the region but also against the Serbs" if it wanted to join the organization.[14] However, no long-term monitoring of compliance followed these requirements. More important, the Council of Europe has no sanctions mechanisms for guidelines violation. Once Serbia was admitted to the Council of Europe in 2003, the membership carrot was removed, and the power of the council to impose these broad requirements for transitional justice in Serbia was greatly reduced.[15]

The international thinking about the best transitional justice model for Serbia also followed larger shifts in international justice best practices. The international trial model, which shaped both the ICTY and its sister institution ICTR, the tribunal for Rwanda, was created with the idea that removing the proceedings from the area where the crimes had been committed would give the trials more impartiality and legitimacy, and the international makeup of the judges and prosecutors would assure legal competency and expertise. However, this view began to change a few years into the life of the two international tribunals. Instead of displacing the process from communities where the crimes had been committed and the perpetrators still lived, the new international approach was to make transitional justice appear more local and closer to home.[16]

This subtle shift in international justice strategy resulted in part from the increasing international disillusionment with the ICTY and ICTR—the tribunals' astronomical costs, length of trials, failure to apprehend most-wanted suspects, and consistent negative public relations problem in all the countries over which they had jurisdiction.[17] Furthermore, with the change of administration in the United States, international tribunals lost a major state supporter. The Bush administration's general hostility toward international justice resulted not only

13. Mark Freeman, "Serbia and Montenegro: Selected Developments in Transitional Justice," International Center for Transitional Justice, New York, October 2004.

14. Council of Europe, The Federal Republic of Yugoslavia's Application for Membership in the Council of Europe, Opinion No. 239, Brussels, September 24, 2002.

15. Author's interview with the legal adviser of the Council of Europe's Belgrade office, October 11, 2005, Belgrade.

16. Richard Dicker and Elise Keppler, "Beyond The Hague: The Challenges of International Justice," Human Rights Watch, Washington, DC, January 2004.

17. Vojin Dimitrijević, "The 'Public Relations' Problems of International Criminal Courts," manuscript, Belgrade Center for Human Rights, 2005.

in its rejection and obstruction of the International Criminal Court[18] but also in its visibly decreasing support to the ICTY and ICTR and a push for domestic or hybrid international/domestic trials instead.[19] Finally, the attacks of September 11, 2001, further complicated calls for international justice as the global war on terror took precedence over institutions and practices of international law.[20]

The Serbian government used this changing international environment to at first delay its cooperation with the ICTY, responding to the tribunal's diminished international standing as the best transitional justice solution for the former Yugoslavia. But under renewed international coercion, when the European Union directly linked cooperation with the ICTY to Serbia's EU admission chances, Serbia shifted its strategy to include alternative transitional justice mechanisms, hoping to circumvent the ICTY by displaying its commitment to justice, first through a truth commission in 2001 and then through a domestic war crimes tribunal in 2003, established with great financial and expert assistance from the Organization for Security and Cooperation in Europe (OSCE).[21]

The Serbian hope to marginalize the ICTY by pursuing other transitional justice avenues was, however, difficult to sustain. In fact, the importance placed on ICTY's success as a bellwether of the viability of international criminal tribunals in general made cooperation with the ICTY the international community's primary measurement of Serbia's acceptance of international justice standards. Because cooperation with the ICTY was a measurable indicator— the number of suspects arrested and transferred to The Hague and the number of documents and testimonies sent could all be classified, systematized, and easily counted—it soon became the major, if not the *only*, international measurement of how far along Serbia was in adopting the idea of addressing crimes from its recent past.

This international approach was further enforced by the policy of issue linkage, by which almost all international awards Serbia applied for—international aid, financial loans, removal of sanctions, membership in the EU and NATO, as well as many bilateral arrangements with neighboring countries—were linked to cooperation with the ICTY. In fact, while transitional Serbia managed to

---

18. Jamie Meyerfeld, "Who Shall Be Judge? The United States, the International Criminal Court, and the Global Enforcement of Human Rights," *Human Rights Quarterly* 25 (2003): 93–129.

19. See statements in support of domestic trials in Serbia by the U.S. ambassador-at-large for war-crimes issues Pierre-Richard Prosper, Reuters, July 19, 2004, and undersecretary for political affairs Mark Grossman, July 9, 2004, http://belgrade.usembassy.gov/policy/regional/040712a.html. Both diplomats conditioned their support for domestic trials on the arrest of major suspect Ratko Mladić and his transfer to the ICTY.

20. Kenneth Roth, "The Law of War in the War on Terror," *Foreign Affairs* 83, no. 1 (2004), 2–7.

21. Sonja Biserko (director of the Helsinki Committee for Human Rights in Serbia), in interview with author, September 21, 2005, Belgrade.

carry out significant reforms in many areas of concern—the economy, fiscal and monetary policy, trade, customs, taxes, and even beginning steps toward police and army reform—it was its problematic cooperation with the ICTY that delayed the tastiest carrot—membership in the European Union.

The First Order of Transitional Justice: The Milošević Case

Governing Serbia turned out to be much more difficult than overturning Milošević. What became apparent immediately after October 5, 2000, was the extent to which the issue of the past, specifically the Milošević wars and the war crimes committed, would be an unshakable legacy that the new transitional government was ill equipped to deal with. While conflict and tension within the DOS were widely reported during the campaign, the fragility of the coalition became fully clear only after the October 5 revolt. The early disagreements were about turf control, management of resources, and cabinet posts. But the first serious government crisis erupted over the question of what to do with Milošević.

Unlike President Koštunica, who vigorously opposed transferring Milošević to The Hague and was ambiguous about offering Milošević amnesty in response to stepping down peacefully,[22] Prime Minister Đinđić advocated investigating Milošević for abuses of power, but *not* for war crimes, and proceeding with the arrest and a domestic trial.[23] These differences were both ideological and political. Koštunica was a conservative, suspicious of international institutions and the ideas of transitional justice but also greatly concerned about the threat to domestic political stability of any Milošević trial. Đinđić was a moderate international-ist, but he was primarily a technocratic pragmatist. He did not particularly engage with ideas of international justice, but he was worried that keeping Milošević out of jail would invite domestic political trouble.[24] The two entrenched positions immediately created a domestic political standoff. Complicating matters was increasing impatience from the international community and the ICTY itself for the start of real Serbian cooperation.

The United States, for its part, increased the pressure on the new government by conditioning the badly needed financial aid for the country's postwar reconstruction—$100 million in direct U.S. aid and U.S. support for International Monetary

---

22. "Koštunica Meets Milošević," BBC News, January 14, 2001.
23. "Milošević 'To Face Justice,'" BBC News, December 24, 2000.
24. DOS leaders, interviews.

Fund and World Bank loans to Serbia—on Serbia's full cooperation with the ICTY, the major indicator of which would be Milošević's arrest and extradition to The Hague. The U.S. Congress set a hard deadline for the arrest of March 31, 2001. Worried that the president's reluctance to extradite Milošević would undermine donors' pledges of support, Serbian prime minister Đinđić decided to circumvent Koštunica and arrest Milošević on the U.S. deadline date.[25] This also happened to be the day that Koštunica was out of the country on a state visit and was unable to intervene and block the arrest operation.[26] After a two-day standoff at his residence, Milošević was arrested for corruption and abuse of power and placed in a Belgrade prison.[27] He was then suddenly and quite secretly transferred to The Hague on June 28, 2001, in a clandestine operation coordinated by Prime Minister Đinđić.[28]

However, the government chose not to use Milošević's arrest as an opportunity to ignite a public debate about the past by openly discussing the crimes for which he had been indicted by the ICTY. Instead of approaching transitional justice as an issue of morality, Đinđić justified cooperation with the ICTY on the basis of both international prestige ("Milošević was not exchanged for money, but for [international] credibility";[29] Milošević's extradition was Serbia's "entrance ticket to the democratic world"[30]) and the punishment noncompliance would bring ("Refusal to extradite Milošević would lead to the suspension of financial aid, which would bring the country to the brink of economic collapse, complicate the repayment of foreign debt, and prevent Serbia's membership in international financial institutions"[31]). And of course, good politician that he was, he invoked children: the government's action was taken "not because of us or our parents but because of our children."[32] Đinđić's allies were even more blunt in justifying Milošević's sudden arrest and extrajudicial extradition: "We wanted American money, we wanted EU money."[33] While Đinđić's rhetorical strategy was to couch transitional justice as a purely pragmatic decision, this

---

25. Čedomir Jovanović (Prime Minister Đinđić's closest adviser and former deputy prime minister, later president of the Liberal Democratic Party), interviewed on "Insajder" [Insider] broadcast, B92 TV, April 19, 2005.

26. Steven Erlanger, "Milošević Trial: Test on Many Levels," *New York Times*, June 29, 2001.

27. B92, April 1, 2001.

28. B92, June 29, 2001.

29. Nenad Lj. Stefanović, "Zoran Đinđić, srpski premijer: Nisam najmoćniji čovek u Srbiji [Zoran Đinđić, Serbia's prime minister: I Am Not the Most Powerful Man in Serbia]," *Vreme*, July 26, 2001.

30. *Nedeljni telegraf*, May 9, 2001.

31. B92, June 28, 2001.

32. Jeffrey R. Smith, "Serb Leaders Hand Over Milošević for Trial by War Crimes Tribunal," *Washington Post*, June 29, 2001.

33. Jovanović, interview.

approach had significant consequences for the process of transitional justice in Serbia, as Serbian citizens came to see it as a business transaction and not an issue of justice.[34]

The divisions leading up to and following Milošević's extradition to The Hague soon solidified, and the ruling coalition in Serbia began to lose its cohesion. On August 17, 2001, Koštunica's DSS party resigned from the Serbian government. The first transitional government in post-Milošević Serbia had not survived one year in office.

Cooperation with the ICTY: Bait and Switch

As mentioned earlier, the international community made Serbia's cooperation with the ICTY the main, if not the only, marker of its compliance with the international justice regime. How and under what domestic circumstances ICTY suspects showed up in The Hague was not important as long as there was a continuing stream of the most-wanted on the flights to the Netherlands.

After Milošević was transferred to The Hague in 2001, Serbian elites hoped this unprecedented move (Milošević was the first ever head of state to be prosecuted for war crimes at an international court) would mollify the ICTY and that lower-level suspects would now be forgotten. However, the ICTY, and then the United States and the EU, interpreted Milošević's arrest as a sign that transfers of suspects were indeed possible in Serbia, and they soon pressed for more, again tying material benefits to institutional cooperation.

In the Milošević case, the Serbian government reacted to the immediate threat of international sanctions and withholding of aid with a hastened, uncoordinated, and domestically very controversial arrest and transfer to The Hague. This dynamic was repeated many times after that—the government would promise never to arrest Serbian "heroes" and would pledge to provide them with all the support they needed, and then days before an international deadline that usually

---

34. Bogdan Ivanišević, "Softly-Softly Approach on War Crimes Doesn't Help Democracy in Serbia," Human Rights Watch, August 11, 2004. Most citizens support cooperation for "utilitarian reasons," either to avoid international sanctions or because it is a requirement for international integration. These results have remained remarkably steady over time, ranging from 70 percent to 80 percent of the Serbian population. See annual public opinion surveys on this topic conducted by the Strategic Marketing Research for Belgrade Center for Human Rights and Organization for Security and Cooperation in Europe. OSCE, "Public Opinion in Serbia: Views on Domestic War Crimes Judicial Authorities and the Hague Tribunal, December 2006," http://www.osce.org/docu ments/srb/2007/03/23518_en.pdf.

involved financial or membership sanctions, the heroes would reluctantly but regularly be shipped off to The Hague. A clear example of this strategy was the arrest and transfer to The Hague of Veselin Šljivančanin, indicted by the ICTY for war crimes in Vukovar, Croatia. Šljivančanin was arrested on June 13, 2003 (and transferred in July 2003), just two days before the deadline for the next U.S. Congress certification of financial assistance to Serbia.[35]

This strategy was further tested after the surprising ICTY indictments in 2003 of four generals accused of crimes against humanity during Serbia's war in Kosovo in 1999. These indictments presented a serious problem for the government because some of the generals were still in active duty in the Serbian army and police corps.[36] The indictments caused a public uproar, with the Serbian police minister vowing not to extradite the suspects, calling the indicted general Lukić a "hero" and the minister's "right hand,"[37] and promising that he would do everything in his power to prevent the generals from going to The Hague, "except as tourists."[38] The government issued a public statement accusing ICTY chief prosecutor Carla Del Ponte of having "humiliated the Serbian government and the entire state."[39] A few months later, the government somewhat changed its position and opened the possibility for a domestic trial of the four generals. Government officials later claimed, however, that this was never a realistic expectation but had been circulated only to placate domestic public opinion.[40] For almost a year, the generals remained untouched by the authorities, living in Serbia under government protection while under the shadow of the ICTY indictment.

Ignoring the ICTY proved untenable, however. In early 2005, Serbia faced increasing international isolation over its refusal to arrest suspects. The U.S. State Department announced it was unable to certify Serbian compliance with conditions established by the Congress for foreign assistance. The U.S. ambassador in Belgrade announced that substantial portions of U.S. aid were to be cut, and technical advisers were to be withdrawn. Shortly thereafter, the EU foreign

---

35. International Crisis Group (ICG), "Serbian Reform Stalls Again," Europe Report no. 145, Belgrade, July 17, 2003.

36. Sreten Lukić was the sitting head of the public security department; Vlastimir Đorđević was Lukić's predecessor. Nebojša Pavković was a former army chief of staff; Vladimir Lazarević was a former army general.

37. B92, October 20, 2003.

38. B92, December 2, 2003.

39. "Pavkovića, Lukića, Lazarevića i Đorđevića traži Haški tribunal" [The Hague wants Pavković, Lukić, Lazarević and Đorđević], Balkan, October 8, 2003.

40. Author's interview with Koštunica's senior foreign policy adviser, who requested anonymity, September 27, 2005, Belgrade.

policy chief canceled a planned trip to Belgrade in protest over continuing Serbian noncooperation with the ICTY.[41]

The Serbian government deeply felt and worried about these threats. Serbia was fully dependent on international aid and loans if it was to make any attempt at recovery after Milošević's disastrous economic policies of the 1990s. Playing hardball with international donors was equal to economic suicide. By extension, the government did not want to risk voters' rage if all international monies suddenly disappeared. Although Serbian voters had responded positively to the nationalist hard-line rhetoric, when it came to their pensions and salaries, they would not take a complete international freeze lightly.

In response to this grim political outlook, the Koštunica government instituted a new strategy of "voluntary surrenders," when indeed a dozen ICTY suspects were arrested and transferred to The Hague in just a few months.[42] In a model borrowed from Croatia, the deal was that the state would guarantee the suspects that if they surrendered voluntarily, they would be allowed to return from The Hague to Serbia and face charges while on bail. They were also provided financial assistance for their families, granted under the generous Law on the Rights of Indictees in the Custody of the International Criminal Tribunal and Members of their Families.

This about-face in dealing with international justice institutions, however, had to be persuasively sold to the public. The public relations strategy was multifaceted. In January prominent Serbian Orthodox Church clerics had issued statements warning that the country was suffering because of a few individuals, whose patriotic duty it was to surrender so Serbia could move on. The government also threatened that if the suspects failed to surrender voluntarily, they would be arrested and forcibly transferred to The Hague, forgoing financial support for their families. The government also launched a media offensive, appearing on special television shows and urging suspects to surrender.

In the spring of 2005, after much public bluster, the government arrested and transferred three of the four generals to The Hague, while one remained at large.[43] The way they were transferred was extraordinary. After months of denying the substance of the indictment and legitimacy of the ICTY, one of the four accused generals, Nebojša Pavković, announced that he would surrender. The decision was announced two days before the European Union was to confirm

---

41. International Crisis Group, "Serbia: Spinning Its Wheels," Europe Briefing no. 39, Belgrade, May 23, 2005.

42. Helsinki Committee for Human Rights in Serbia (HCHRS), *Human Security in an Unfinished State: Serbia 2005* (Belgrade: HCHRS, 2006).

43. The fourth indicted general, Vlastimir Đorđević, was arrested in 2007.

a favorable feasibility study for Serbia's EU accession. Pavković's voluntary surrender was a huge media event, and the Koštunica government gave a statement "highly praising [Pavković's] decision, considering it in the best interest of the country, and as his moral, responsible and patriotic attitude toward the country and the people." The government also promised to provide all necessary assistance to his family.[44]

Another member of the group of four generals, Vladimir Lazarević, had an even more VIP send-off. After deciding to surrender, Lazarević was met by the patriarch of the Serbian Orthodox Church and Prime Minister Koštunica, who both praised Lazarević's heroic decision. Koštunica went so far as to say that "the general acted in line with a long-standing tradition of the Serbian army, namely, that our officers fight for the interests of the people and country until the bitter end."[45] As in the case of Pavković, Lazarević's surrender was cast as an act of supreme patriotism, as a "difficult decision in the interest of the homeland."[46] Lazarević was flown to The Hague in a government jet, accompanied by the justice minister.[47]

In Lukić's case, the voluntary part of the surrender was more suspect. After a government spokesman said that Lukić's arrest was "a form of voluntary surrender," it turned out that he had been forcefully arrested while being treated in a hospital for a heart condition.[48] The government, however, reiterated that the surrenders worked as acts of soldiers' devotion to their country at a time of need.[49]

The sudden change of heart and the streamlined process of voluntary surrenders were the results of the larger political calculations of the Serbian government, which was concerned that unless Serbia stepped up its cooperation with the ICTY, it would not be allowed a seat at the table regarding much more important issues—the status of Kosovo and Montenegro. The EU feasibility study also played a crucial role in hastening transfers to the ICTY, but so did the U.S. carrots of granting Serbia most favored nation trade status, which was important for Serbia's struggling textile industry.[50]

The Serbian government's changed strategy was a huge success. The EU approved a positive feasibility study on April 12 and the go-ahead to negotiate a

44. B92, April 22, 2005.
45. "Lazarević ide u Hag" [Lazarević to The Hague], *Glas*, January 29, 2005.
46. B92, February 2, 2005.
47. International Crisis Group, "Serbia: Spinning its Wheels."
48. B92, April 4, 2005.
49. As compensation for their voluntary surrenders, the government provided each indictee 200 euros a month, and their family members would be entitled to three plane tickets to Amsterdam bimonthly and 250 euros per person to cover travel expenses. Tanja Markotić, "U toj igri više ne učestvujem" [I Don't Play That Game Anymore], *Novosti*, November 3, 2005.
50. Koštunica's senior foreign policy adviser, interview.

stabilization and association agreement (SAA) on April 25, 2005, the necessary baby steps toward negotiations for EU membership.[51] The improved cooperation with the ICTY also gave Serbia a much-needed international financial boost in investment. It also allowed the Serbian government to breathe a little easier, as it hoped the ICTY would now leave Serbia alone for a while and forget that the two major suspects, Radovan Karadžić and Ratko Mladić, were still very much fugitives from justice.[52] In effect, the EU reward stalled significant future co-operation with the ICTY instead of boosting it.[53]

At the same time, however, this strategy was clearly aimed at the domestic political audience. The Serbian people were told only that these suspects were leaving for The Hague because it was a requirement of the international community or an act of patriotic duty. They were told repeatedly by their government that these transfers were opening up doors for Serbia to join the EU, an issue that the government of Vojislav Koštunica made a centerpiece of the coming election campaign.[54] They were not once informed about the substance of the indictments—the crimes for which these individuals had been indicted, how they came about, who the victims were, the scope of abuse, or any other details. Instead, masked in the guise of voluntary surrenders, dealing with the past was repackaged as acts of patriotism for which the state was grateful. Thus the stepped-up pressure from the ICTY and other international actors did not translate into any substantial changes in Serbia's understanding of its own past or in any attempt to address past abuses in a systematic way.

In contrast to the policy of voluntary surrenders, there are numerous examples of Serbian transitional justice policies differing sharply from the increased enthusiasm to cooperate with the ICTY. For example, the government made no effort to reform its judiciary or police to the degree that any domestic investigations and prosecutions for war crimes could take place. A comprehensive report by the OSCE found that Serbian courts were woefully unprepared technically, logistically, and professionally to deal with war-crimes prosecution.[55] In addition,

---

51. B92, October 10, 2005.

52. Karadžić was the wartime leader of Bosnian Serbs. Mladić was their military commander. Both men are wanted for gross human rights abuses in Bosnia, including the genocide in Srebrenica. Karadžić was subsequently arrested in 2008.

53. Gareth Evans and James Lyon, "No Mladić, No Talks," *International Herald Tribune*, May 21, 2007.

54. Illustrative of this government's line is the statement by Rasim Ljajić, president of the National Council for Cooperation with the ICTY, that "the voluntary transfer [of general Lazarević] is a great step toward the EU, because it has facilitated the positive EU Feasibility Study." B92, January 29, 2005.

55. Organization for Security and Cooperation in Europe, *War Crimes before Domestic Courts* (Belgrade: OSCE, 2003).

Serbian lawmakers persistently refused to amend Serbian laws to accept command responsibility, a critical element of jurisprudence concerning war crimes and human rights abuses.[56]

In early 2005, at the height of the voluntary surrenders, a few nongovernmental organizations discovered evidence of new mass graves in Serbia filled with the bodies of Kosovo Albanian civilians killed in 1999. Instead of opening investigations, the Serbian Ministry of the Interior, the Ministry of Justice, and the security services all covered up the findings and began a campaign of silencing and intimidating witnesses by forcing them to sign statements on "spiritual peace," admitting in writing that they did not "feel psychological pressure to disclose what had happened…in May 1999."[57] Local police also threatened to file criminal charges for "disclosure of state secrets" against any police officers willing to talk.[58]

The paradox of increasing international cooperation and complete nonaction at home made transitional justice advocates in Serbia complain that the more the Serbian government stepped up its "expedited shipping" of ICTY indictees, the less public debate there was about war crimes. As a leading human rights activist noted, "With each 'voluntary transfer,' Serbia is further away from transitional justice."[59] The Serbian government approach was not the only part of this equation—international actors were also responsible, as they repeatedly showed interest only in a complete package arriving in The Hague, not in the political collateral damage such an approach would create domestically. Transitional justice, in other words, became a trading currency between local elites and international community, effectively removing the substantive issue of addressing past wrongs from the public debate. The Serbian government used international justice and ICTY as a foil to send signals to the domestic audience that nothing significant would change, that the grand narrative of Serbia's victimization and the need for its vindication would continue, and that in fact by trading these suspects one by one, Serbia would achieve great international awards—the most coveted prize being negotiations for EU accession. In other words, this strategy allowed Serbia to go through the motions of complying with international institutional demands while in fact rejecting the profound social transformation that international norms require.

---

56. After much international pressure, mostly from the OSCE, the legislation was eventually changed to include command responsibility, but only for future crimes, not for any prosecution of crimes already committed.

57. Helsinki Committee for Human Rights in Serbia, *Human Rights and Collective Identity: Serbia 2004* (Belgrade: HCHRS, 2005).

58. Humanitarian Law Center, newsletter, February 3, 2006.

59. Biljana Kovačević Vučo (director of the Lawyers Committee for Human Rights), in interview with author, September 29, 2005, Belgrade.

The Serbian TRC: An Institution Designed to Fail

In March 2001, almost out of nowhere and without any public debate or consultation, president Koštunica, a staunch opponent of international justice, established by decree the Serbian truth and reconciliation commission, the only body of its kind in the former Yugoslavia.[60] There is evidence that Koštunica formed the commission in a misguided effort to circumvent the ICTY and appease the international community, which had been putting pressure on the government to address the Milošević-era legacy. This perception that Koštunica was only deflecting international criticism is further reinforced by the fact that the commission was announced the day before the United States was to certify continuing financial aid to Serbia, conditional on its cooperation with international justice institutions.[61] A few months before he declared the establishment of the truth commission, Koštunica had referred to well-known transitional justice mechanisms in other countries, saying,

> I believe there is a need for all countries in the region to return the judicial process home. For example, I have a lot of respect for what the Truth and Reconciliation Commission has done in South Africa. Also, the Chilean example is very good. I believe that leaders responsible for crimes should be held accountable for them in front of their own people.[62]

Because Koštunica's intentions were transparent, the ICTY in fact strongly opposed the forming of the Serbian TRC, arguing precisely that a domestic truth commission would take away international attention and funds from ICTY and that transitional justice projects would become diluted and unfocused.[63]

While Koštunica's motive may have been to delegitimize the ICTY by offering a domestic alternative, international justice entrepreneurs jumped at the opportunity to help set up a truth commission in Serbia. The international involvement in this project began with the International Center for Transitional Justice and the visit of its president, Alex Boraine, to Belgrade soon after Milošević's ousting in October 2000. Boraine had been interested in promoting transitional justice in Serbia even during Milošević's rule, but he was not welcome and was even

---

60. "Odluka o osnivanju Komisije za istinu i pomirenje" [Decision on the Establishment of the Truth and Reconciliation Commission], *Službeni list SRJ* [Official Gazette of the SRJ], no. 15/2001, March 29, 2001.

61. Freeman, "Serbia and Montenegro."

62. B92, December 19, 2000. Alex Boraine, ICTJ director, agreed with this general view and expressed a preference for a domestic truth commission model over the international tribunal. B92, February 12, 2000.

63. Velimir Ćurgus Kazimir (director of the Ebart Media Documentation Center), in interview with author, September 22, 2005, Belgrade.

denied entry visas by the Milošević regime. After October 2000, Boraine renewed his interest and coordinated his visit with local NGOs, who had long lobbied for a Serbian TRC.[64] While in Belgrade, Boraine met with many human rights activists, including some who opposed setting up a TRC while the Koštunica administration, with its record of hostility toward international justice, was in power.[65] The ICTJ's preference was to try and work with the TRC for a few months and see whether the center's experts could positively influence the commission's plans and operations. Since Koštunica was going to establish the TRC anyway, the ICTJ wanted to be in a position to push Koštunica to improve the credibility and diversity of the commission's composition so that the TRC could potentially overcome its inherent legitimacy gap and go on to do some serious work.[66]

The main issue of contention with some domestic skeptics was that the ICTJ insisted the TRC should be an official body endorsed by the president, giving it popular legitimacy. Serbian human rights activists argued, in contrast, that as long as Koštunica was president, this would jeopardize the composition and serious commitment of the truth commission to address crimes from the past. The ICTJ position prevailed, however, and Koštunica ended up with a mandate to appoint TRC members.[67] His first appointments immediately raised red flags—he appointed mostly nationalist conservative academics with a long paper trail of a strongly pro-Serbian interpretation of the past wars and a markedly anti-internationalist bent. There were only two ethnic minority representatives and no members of religious communities other than the Serbian Orthodox Church. There were no representatives from any major human rights group that had worked on transitional justice issues. In addition to poor composition, the main criticism of the commission was its mandate "to uncover evidence on the social, interethnic and political conflicts which led to the war and to shed light on the causal links among these events."[68] In other words, the commission wanted to create a comprehensive historical narrative of how the former Yugoslavia had broken up and who was to blame rather than doing the practical

---

64. Alex Boraine, *A Country Unmasked: South Africa's Truth and Reconciliation Commission* (Cape-town: Oxford University Press, 2001).

65. Ćurgus Kazimir, interview.

66. Mark Freeman (expert on the former Yugoslavia at the International Center for Transitional Justice), in interview with author, September 29, 2005.

67. It is important to note that ICTJ today minimizes its role in setting up the TRC, while domestic human rights activists argue that the project was spearheaded by the ICTJ and was later used by Koštunica. This discrepancy likely reflects the fact that neither side wants to take credit for an institution that failed so publicly.

68. "Odluka o osnivanju Komisije."

work of truth commissions—to conduct hearings with witnesses and survivors of human rights abuses.[69]

The additional conceptual problem was that the Serbian TRC was to be of regional scope; it was to collect evidence of crimes *by all sides* in all Yugoslav wars but conducted by only Serbian researchers. In contrast, Serbian human rights activists and the ICTJ supported a more focused approach dealing with Serbian crimes against other groups and supporting initiatives in Croatia and Bosnia that would deal with Croatian and Bosnian crimes against other ethnicities. The only two regionally and internationally respected scholars immediately resigned in protest over the composition, mandate, and scope of the TRC, causing a serious blow to the commission's legitimacy. In addition to personnel problems, the Koštunica administration provided the TRC with practically no resources, the members met only a few times, and the commission never produced any report. In 2003, the TRC died quietly, a casualty of the bureaucratic reshuffling of the federal government.[70]

The failed Serbian TRC experiment is another example of how the purpose of an internationally designed transitional justice project can be turned on its head—an institution that was supposed to lead to social reconciliation was designed in a way that had the potential to further inflame preexisting ethnic prejudices and exacerbate social divisions. As a leading Serbian human rights activist put it, "the Serbian truth commission perpetrated a fraud on the international justice community."[71]

The Serbian TRC experience indicates that when applied domestically to a society whose elites are unwilling or unable to deal with the substance of international normative demands, international models are used by elites to promote their preexisting agendas. Since Serbia's transitional strategy was one of restoring its lost reputation and improving its international image, it made sense for the elites to use prestigious international models to advance this goal. The truth

---

69. The TRC president, Sveta Stojanović, said that in his view the goal of the TRC was to look at "interconnectedness of Yugoslav wars, and Serbian crimes in relation to crimes of other groups against the Serbs." Author's interview, October 18, 2005, Belgrade.

70. See Nenad Dimitrijević, "Coming to Terms with the Evil Past: Does Serbia Need a Truth and Reconciliation Commission?" (paper presented at "Judging Transitional Justice: An Interdisciplinary Workshop on New Democracies' Coming to Terms with their Past," University of California, Irvine, October 30–31, 2004). Other commission members blamed Serbian NGOs for the commission's demise, arguing that the NGOs had already prejudged Serbia guilty for the crimes of the Yugoslav wars and since that was not the position of the commission, the NGOs "actively lobbied international donors against the commission." Author's interview with a commission member, September 4, 2004.

71. Sonja Biserko, in interview with author, September 1, 2004, Belgrade.

commission was put to perfect use in line with this strategy—it was mandated to show how other groups and international factors were responsible for the Yugoslav breakup and how Serbs were being unfairly portrayed as Balkan bogeymen.

The consequences of the Serbian TRC failure were manifold. First, it was a huge embarrassment for the ICTJ, which had lent its name, its brand, and its authority to what amounted to a fraudulent institution.[72] More important, the utter failure of the Serbian TRC to conduct any hearings, pursue any independent research, collect evidence, or issue any kind of report tainted this transitional justice institutional model in the eyes of the Serbian public as ineffectual, bureaucratic, overly political, and flat-out useless. In fact, so widespread was the sense of the commission's failure that groups that would not agree on anything else—nationalist historians and human rights activists—agreed that the idea of a truth commission for Serbia had been forever used up and discarded. The ICTJ has since supported a regional commission project, which would involve participants from Serbia, Croatia, and Bosnia and would work on identifying all victims of the wars. However, because the brand "truth commission" has been so utterly devalued, the new proposed commission would be named the Regional Commission for Establishing the Facts about War Crimes in the Former Yugoslavia. The commission would collect evidence, process data collected by human rights groups and the ICTY, and act as a forum in which victims could voice their experiences.[73] The regional commission project has not made much progress on establishing an actual institution but has focused instead on regional conferences, workshops, and training seminars. The commission faces significant challenges as it moves, as none of the governments in the region have endorsed the project, and the societies themselves are deeply divided on what kind of a truth institution is most appropriate.[74] Without official support, it is unlikely that the commission will have a broad social and political impact.

Domestic War-Crimes Trials

Serbia conducted only a few domestic war-crimes trials throughout the 1990s and in the first few years after the democratic transition. Higher courts have overturned some of the rare convictions after what human rights activists alleged

---

72. In its report on transitional justice in Serbia, ICTJ calls Serbian TRC an example of how *not* to set up a truth commission. Freeman, "Serbia and Montenegro."

73. Želimir Bojović, "Formirati regionalnu komisiju za činjenice o ratnim zločinima" [Create a Regional Commission for Facts about War Crimes], Radio Free Europe, June 17, 2008.

74. Conor Gaffney and Aida Alić, "First Regional Truth Commission Runs into Doubts," *Balkan Insight,* August 5, 2008.

was clear political pressure.[75] It was really only after the 2003 assassination of Prime Minister Đinđić that the political will to start a serious domestic war-crimes court project kicked into high gear. Displaying a newly found sense of urgency after the assassination shock, the post-Đinđić government quickly set up two twin institutions—the Organized Crime Chamber and the War Crimes Chamber (WCC), as well as a special court to investigate the Đinđić assassination. The WCC was established in July 2003 as the location of all future war-crimes trials in Serbia. The WCC also has a specialized prosecutor for war crimes, a special detention unit, and a special war-crimes investigation service within the Ministry of Internal Affairs.[76]

According to Serbian government officials, two concerns motivated the government to set up the WCC. First, it was the issue of dealing with war crimes: "We really thought that this was a shame, something we have to bring to the surface." Second, "addressing this problem" was important to the government's goal of advancing Serbia's European integration.[77]

The WCC was received with great enthusiasm and encouragement by international organizations and member states. The OSCE was directly involved in setting up and supporting the institution; it helped draft the Law on War Crimes and contributed to witness protection legislation and the development of a witness protection program. The International Center for Transitional Justice was also involved; its experts advised the new prosecutor and shared lessons learned from domestic trials in other transitional countries.[78] This international support for domestic trials also came on the heels of the United States' growing hostility to international tribunals, which manifested itself most clearly in its animosity toward the International Criminal Court but also in an increased sense of urgency to wrap up the remaining ICTY proceedings,[79] focus on arrest and transfer of major

75. Helsinki Committee for Human Rights in Serbia, *Human Rights and Collective Identity,* 149.

76. *Zakon o organizaciji i nadležnosti državnih organa u postupku za ratne zločine* [Law on Organization and Jurisdiction of Government Authorities in Prosecuting Perpetrators of War Crimes], *Službeni glasnik Republike Srbije* [Official Gazette of the Republic of Serbia], no. 67/2003, July 1, 2003, arts. 11 and 12.

77. Dušan Protić (former deputy justice minister), quoted in Diane F. Orentlicher, "Shrinking the Space for Denial: The Impact of the ICTY in Serbia," Open Society Institute, New York, May 2008, 64.

78. International Center for Transitional Justice, "The Former Yugoslavia: ICTJ Activity," March 2006, http://www.ictj.org/en/where/region4/510.html.

79. For example, the U.S. embassy in Belgrade has consistently downplayed the importance of ICTY cooperation, while the State Department has even lobbied Congress and tried to dissuade international justice organizations from supporting continued issue-linkage policy for Serbia. See International Crisis Group, "Serbia's U-Turn," Europe Report no. 154, Belgrade, March 26, 2004. With the appointment of a new, more ICTY-friendly U.S. ambassador in 2004, the U.S. pressure on Serbia somewhat increased.

suspects, and then turn over other, lower-rank suspects for trials in front of Serbian domestic courts.[80] In fact, it is in part as a result of the increasing U.S. reluctance to foot the ICTY bill that The Hague agreed to an exit strategy, by which the high-ranking suspects would be tried in front of the ICTY and the lower-ranking cases would be transferred back to domestic courts in the region.

The international support and enthusiasm for the Serbian WCC was mostly directed at the office of the prosecutor, which was praised for a professional and dedicated staff fully committed to international ideas and standards of transitional justice. As the prosecutor's spokesman explained,

> If a country wants to be a member of a liberal democratic club with liberal democratic norms, then a critical aspect of this process is a break with the politics of war crimes and ethnic political crimes. Societies need to deal with the past not to appease the international community but because of themselves.[81]

This understanding of transitional justice norms is virtually unheard of among Serbian national institutions and has been isolated to a few human rights groups. Despite the best of efforts, however, the WCC was off to a very slow start, with only six cases completed by the spring of 2008, almost five years after the institution was founded.[82] The main obstacles facing the WCC remained intimidation of judges and prosecutors and a poor witness protection program, as well as limited investigative ability and access to evidence, especially lack of cooperation from Serbian police.[83] For example, the war-crimes investigation service within the Serbian police has taken a very restrictive approach in assisting the war-crimes prosecutor. It provides documents to the prosecutor only in response to specific requests rather than at the service's own initiative, greatly undermining the prosecutor's investigative abilities. Some of these initial problems were partly

---

80. See statements by Prosper and Grossman. The Bush administration, however, did not speak with one voice. Ambassador John Danforth, U.S. representative to the United Nations, argued that Serbia's continued lack of cooperation with the ICTY made domestic trials seem less, not more, realistic. UN Security Council press release, SC/8252, New York, November 23, 2004.

81. Bruno Vekarić (spokesman for the Office of the Prosecutor, War Crimes Panel of the Belgrade District Court), in interview with author, December 6, 2005, Belgrade.

82. Two high-profile cases completed are the trial for the massacre of civilians and POWs in Vukovar, Croatia, in 1991 and the trial of members of the paramilitary group Scorpions for the Srebrenica massacre in 1995. Another important case, ongoing as of October 2008, is the trial of police officers accused of killing Albanian civilians in Kosovo in 1999 and then organizing the transport and burial of their remains in a Belgrade suburb. As of October 2008, six cases were completed but had not yet reached the sentencing stage; fourteen were in the trial stage, ten in the investigation stage, and twenty-three in the pretrial stage.

83. Bogdan Ivanišević, "Against the Current: War Crimes Prosecutions in Serbia," International Center for Transitional Justice, New York, February 11, 2008.

alleviated by the amendments to the Law on the Organization and Jurisdiction of State Organs in Proceedings Against Perpetrators of War Crimes, passed in December 2004.[84] Since then, the ICTY has agreed to transfer its first case to the Belgrade court.

After the change in government in 2003 and replacement of the reformist coalition by the Koštunica-led nationalist bloc, political pressures increased on the WCC prosecutor. The difficulties ranged from slashed budgets (by as much as 30 percent in 2005) to lack of cooperation with the executive branch and hostile comments by cabinet and parliament members, who wanted the WCC to take on all war-crimes cases, making further demands from the ICTY obsolete and allowing the government to directly control justice proceedings at home.[85] The prosecutor described his position:

> It hasn't been easy, given the attitude of the public. I felt like the captain of a ship being tossed about far out at sea by the wind, lightning, and huge waves from all sides, and I knew I had to bring that ship to a calm harbor—to trials and judgments.[86]

These difficult and politically hostile conditions weakened "the resolve and effectiveness" of the prosecutor's office and can help explain why there have been so few trials.[87] In addition, Serbian politicians were reluctant to publicly support domestic war-crimes trials because "in political life in Serbia, the topic [of war crimes] is understood to be a theme which can lose you votes."[88] Finally, the prosecution was dealt a serious setback when the Serbian Supreme Court overturned the verdicts in the most high-profile case the WCC had tried, that of the massacre in Ovčara, outside Vukovar, Croatia, in which two hundred Croats were taken from a hospital and executed at a nearby farm.[89] The supreme court also considerably lowered the sentences of the defendants in the *Scorpions* case, discussed in the next section, a very important prosecution and the only one that dealt directly with the Srebrenica genocide.[90] These decisions by the supreme

---

84. *Zakon o organizaciji i nadležnosti državnih organa u postupku za ratne zločine* [Law on the Organization and Jurisdiction of State Organs in Proceedings against Perpetrators of War Crimes], *Službeni glasnik Republike Srbije*, no. 135/04, December 21, 2004.

85. Helsinki Committee for Human Rights in Serbia, *Human Security*, 76.

86. Aleksandra Petrović, "Suočavanje sa zločinom" [Facing the Crime], *Politika*, October 7, 2005.

87. Ivanišević, "Against the Current," vi.

88. Milan Antonijević (executive director of the Lawyers Committee for Human Rights), quoted in Caroline Tosh and Aleksandar Roknić, "Politicians Stymie Belgrade War Crimes Trials," Institute for War and Peace Reporting (IWPR), April 28, 2008, http://www.iwpr.net.

89. Ibid.

90. The Scorpions paramilitary unit was created at the very beginning of the war in Croatia in 1991. It operated under the command of the Serbian police or the former Yugoslav national army.

court significantly undermined the WCC prosecutor and led Serbian human rights groups to accuse the court of "seriously impeding war crimes trials in Serbia and delivery of justice for the defendants as well as their victims."[91]

However, problems with domestic war-crimes prosecutions ran much deeper. Human rights activists immediately pointed out that in all cases only direct perpetrators had been indicted, and even then only members of paramilitary groups or territorial defense, while the indictments did not specify any link between these groups and Serbian official policy, the army, or police forces.[92] In other words, the WCC had treated the perpetrators as if they were a few bad apples, disconnected from the larger chain of command and from a major national project.[93] In the words of leading human rights activists, this strategy amounted to "whitewashing the state."[94] An additional problem has been prosecutors' reluctance to deal with crimes committed by Serb forces against Kosovo Albanians—the result of renewed anti-Albanian public sentiment that engulfed Serbia in the aftermath of Kosovo's declaration of independence in February 2008.[95] Finally, the WCC prosecutors have been reluctant to in any way tie the Serbian state to the Balkan wars, a political perspective reflected in WCC indictments. For example, the indictment in the *Zvornik* case accuses Bosnian Serb militiamen of deporting, torturing, and killing the Bosniac population in the Zvornik municipality in 1992. The indictment, however, states, "In May 1992, in the then Republic of Bosnia and Herzegovina, a civil war began between the members of the Serb, Croat, and Muslim ethnicities. It was a noninternational armed conflict."[96] This interpretation of the Bosnian conflict, however, stands in direct contradiction to ICTY jurisprudence, which has unequivocally stated that the Bosnian war was an

---

Scorpions carried out numerous war crimes in Croatia, Bosnia, and Kosovo. Helsinki Committee for Human Rights in Serbia, "Slučaj Škorpioni" [The Scorpions Case], September 14, 2008.

91. Humanitarian Law Center, "Serbian Supreme Court Obstructs War Crimes Trials," press release, September 19, 2008.

92. The official reason given for this strategy was that Serbian law does not allow for command responsibility. However, legal experts agree that since command responsibility has become common law within international humanitarian law, it supersedes Serbian domestic objections to its application. See Human Rights Watch, "Justice at Risk: War Crimes Trials in Croatia, Bosnia and Herzegovina, and Serbia and Montenegro," vol. 16, no. 7(D), New York, October 13, 2004.

93. Humanitarian Law Center, "Transitional Justice Bulletin: War Crimes Trials in Serbia," January 11, 2007. For example, of the sixty Serbs indicted in nine cases for crimes against Croats, Bosniacs, and Albanians, two were police officers, one was an army officer, and all the remaining defendants were local police officers or paramilitary troops and army reservists. Most often, however, they were simply rank-and-file members of the police or paramilitary forces. Ivanišević, "Against the Current," 8.

94. Biserko, interview, September 21, 2005.

95. Tosh and Roknić, "Politicians Stymie Belgrade War Crimes Trials."

96. Office of the War Crimes Prosecutor, *Indictment against Branko Grujić et al.*, no. *KTRZ 17/04*, August 12, 2005.

international conflict with significant involvement of the Serbian state security, police, and military apparatus.[97]

This strategy of focusing on war crimes as individual, isolated incidents and not state crimes is also in line with a larger Serbian strategy of isolating and defending the state from charges of genocide and aggression and requests for payment of compensatory war damage to Croatia and Bosnia and Herzegovina in two cases against Serbia adjudicated in front of the International Court of Justice (ICJ).[98] Indeed, the ICJ February 2007 ruling that did not find Serbia directly responsible for the genocide in Bosnia (but responsible for not preventing the atrocities) was broadly interpreted in Serbia as finally absolving the state of charges of genocide. This has created a political atmosphere in which it is difficult for the WCC prosecutor to charge any Serbian war-crimes suspect with genocide.[99]

Others in civil society, however, have been kinder to the WCC, arguing that while indictments have been limited, what is important is for a national institution to acknowledge that crimes have indeed been committed and to prosecute those responsible, paving the path for new indictments of more higher-ranking officials.[100] Furthermore, the WCC was praised for its regional cooperation with Croatian and Bosnian counterparts who worked together on investigations and processing of cases.[101]

The question of the WCC's domestic impact, however, remains. According to opinion surveys, the WCC has had only a marginal impact on Serbian society and its commitment to transitional justice.[102] The WCC does not allow free broadcasting of live hearings from the courtroom, which seriously obstructs its public message.[103] Attempts at media outreach have been unsuccessful, as the

---

97. See, for example, *ICTY Appeals Chamber, Prosecutor v. Duško Tadic, Case No. IT-94-A, Judgment*, July 15, 1999.

98. Helsinki Committee for Human Rights in Serbia, *Human Security.*

99. Ivanišević, "Against the Current," 11.

100. Dejan Anastasijević (investigative reporter for the weekly *Vreme* and an expert on Serbian paramilitary and organized crime), in interview with author, October 18, 2005, Belgrade; and Žarko Korać (president of the Social Democratic Union and former Serbian deputy prime minister), in interview with author, October 13, 2005, Belgrade.

101. Tosh and Roknić, "Politicians Stymie Belgrade War Crimes Trials."

102. In an opinion poll conducted three years after the WCC was established, only 27 percent of the citizens surveyed knew a domestic war crimes tribunal existed (although only 5 percent correctly identified the WCC by name), while 56 percent could not name any national institution that dealt with war crimes. A majority (59 percent) could not name a single case. Significantly, however, the public picked up on the government strategy to use domestic trials to counter the ICTY. While only 9 percent of those surveyed held a favorable opinion of the judiciary, 56 percent believed that Serbian courts could handle war-crimes cases, making the ICTY obsolete. OSCE, "Public Opinion in Serbia."

103. Humanitarian Law Center, "HLC on War Crimes Trials in Serbia," July 26, 2006.

Serbian media have shown little interest in regularly reporting on the trial proceedings.[104]

That an institution like the WCC even exists in Serbia is an encouraging sign for proponents of transitional justice. However, the way that elites have managed to manipulate its process, by pushing for indictments that exonerate the state and radically individualize and isolate the crimes, is yet another example of how international models of transitional justice can be used to pursue radically different domestic political agendas.

Missed Opportunity: The Srebrenica Tape

In June 2005, Serbia woke up to bombshell news. The prosecution in the case against Slobodan Milošević in The Hague had shown a video clip with the clearly visible executions of six Bosniac men in Srebrenica in July 1995. What made this video so shocking was that it showed the men, some very young (later identified by relatives as sixteen-year-olds), being tortured, humiliated, verbally abused, made to dig their own graves, and then shot in the back while the Serbian assassins (with clearly marked Serbian paramilitary "Scorpions" insignia on their uniforms) joked, yelled abuses at the victims, and worried that the camera recording the executions would run out of battery power.[105] Even more striking were the first few minutes of the video, which showed a Serbian Orthodox priest blessing the paramilitaries with the following send-off: "Brothers, we are facing a revival of Turkish belligerence, they want Serbian sacred places; please help your faithful army to prevail over our enemies."[106]

The brutality of the scene, the clear identification of the perpetrators and the victims, the role of the church, and the sheer horror of the event shook Serbian society. Even reliable nationalist pundits and church spokesmen could not be counted on to dismiss the video outright. It was played and replayed on most TV

---

104. For example, a WCC spokesperson tried to conduct regular biweekly press briefings but had to abandon the practice because so few journalists showed up. Ivanišević, "Against the Current," 36.

105. As if the Srebrenica massacre was not brutal enough, evidence uncovered at the trial showed that the perpetrators often verbally abused the victims in horrific ways. For example, before the execution of a young Bosniac boy, Aleksandar Medić, one of the perpetrators, asked the boy, "Have you ever had sex?" When the boy answered no, Medić told him, "Well then, you never will!" Medić was sentenced to five years in prison, the minimum sentence prescribed. The supreme court later overturned his conviction. Humanitarian Law Center, "Scorpions Verdict Politically Motivated," press release, April 11, 2007.

106. E. R., "Imam petoricu u paketu" [I Have Five in the Package], *Večernje novosti*, June 3, 2005.

stations.[107] There were public condemnations on talk shows, and even human rights activists were given full airtime to describe the crime, identify perpetrators, and illuminate the events that had led to the tape's surfacing at The Hague.[108] And finally, the police used the tape to identify Serbian perpetrators, and in the following few weeks eight of them—but none of the higher-ups who ordered the killing—were arrested and charged with war crimes in front of the Serbian War Crimes Chamber. The quick reaction by Serbia received a lot of international praise, including that from its most vocal critic on issues of justice, ICTY prosecutor Carla Del Ponte.[109]

But this period of acknowledgment and addressing of crimes lasted no more than a few days, enough for the regime and hard-line nationalists to consolidate. In just a matter of days, public officials changed their message, stressing instead that these were the individual crimes of obviously deranged individuals who had already been or would soon be arrested, and this should be the end of the story. For example, Serbian minister of the interior Dragan Jočić said, "[The killers] were infantile, they wanted to show off."[110]

There were concerted efforts from all levels of government to separate Serbia's role from events in Bosnia, as well as from paramilitary formations that were active there. The third aspect of the strategy was to diminish the importance of the Srebrenica genocide by pointing out that crimes had been committed on all sides and to shift the discussion to crimes committed by Bosniac forces against Serb civilians in the neighboring village of Bratunac. Illustrative of this strategy is the statement by the leader of the Serbian Radical Party:

> A one-sided approach to Srebrenica is unacceptable for my party. It hurts me to see how most people in Serbia are speaking about crimes committed by Serbs, and no one speaks about crimes committed by Muslims. If any Serb in Republika Srpska committed any crime, what kind of sin is that for Serbia?[111]

---

107. A media survey showed that while Serbian print media had published 816 articles on Srebrenica in the two years prior to the airing of the video, as many as 676 stories about the genocide were published in the month of June 2005 alone, immediately after the video was shown. Ebert Consulting, "Mediji o Srebrenici, januar 2003–jun 2005" [Media on Srebrenica, January 2003–June 2005], Belgrade, 2005.

108. Nataša Kandić, director of the Humanitarian Law Center, was instrumental in finding the tape and handing it over to the ICTY prosecutor. Apparently, for years this tape could be rented under the counter at a local video club in the Serbian city of Šid. B92, June 5, 2005.

109. B92, June 2, 2005.

110. Velimir Ćurgus Kazimir, "Jevreji, trgovke belim robljem i škorpioni" [Jews, Human Trafficking, and Scorpions], *Helsinška povelja*, vols. 83–84, May–June 2005.

111. D. Vukelić, "Stranke: Ne deklaraciji o zločinima" [Parties: No to the Declaration on Crimes], *Blic*, June 4, 2005.

Another popular view was that this overhyping of Srebrenica was an international ploy to further destroy Serbia's reputation, making it vulnerable in the coming negotiations on the future of Bosnia, Kosovo, and Montenegro. A representative of the ruling DSS party said, "Some factors in the international community are bent on hurting Serbs, and their goal is to make the Serb public feel the collective guilt, and consequently more easily swallow the intended punishment."[112] Finally, the Serbian defense minister worried that "broadcasting of that recording…once again tainted the international image of Serbia," but he added, "The entire case indicates only the responsibility of individuals and not of the people and the state."[113]

Within weeks, the video was no longer in the news or in the public debate. In the words of the editor–in chief of the major Serbian daily newspaper, "This is only natural because people cannot tolerate bad things being said about their countrymen.…I personally am relieved that I no longer have to be exposed to the video."[114] This sentiment that it was easier not to address the past in a systematic way was also evident in public opinion polls conducted shortly after the Srebrenica video was broadcast. Only 32 percent of the citizens thought the video was authentic, and of those who actually saw it, the number was only 45 percent. The rest either thought it was forged or had no opinion. Another interesting finding was that in a poll conducted prior to the broadcast, 40 percent of the Serbian population acknowledged that a crime had been committed in Srebrenica. After they saw the video, however, there was a visible increase in those who held no opinion or claimed lack of knowledge about the event. This indicates that the population was more ready to acknowledge the crime in the abstract than when faced with the evidence of it.[115] The Serbian citizens were not ready "to publicly acknowledge facts that were privately known."[116]

Srebrenica, however, remained in the news throughout 2005, the tenth anniversary of the massacre. One of the first events to mark this occasion was the May 2005 academic panel at the Belgrade Law School, originally entitled "Tenth Anniversary of the Liberation of Srebrenica," referring to "liberation" from Bosnian Muslims. The title of this panel was too offensive even for the conservative law school, which renamed the event "The Truth about Srebrenica" but refused to change either the panel lineup or the subject matter.[117]

---

112. *Nacional,* June 6, 2005.

113. *Danas,* June 7, 2005.

114. Author's interview, October 14, 2005, Belgrade.

115. Strategic Marketing Research, "Serbian Public Opinion Regarding Airing the Video of the Crime Committed in Srebrenica," June 2005, Belgrade, on file with author.

116. Nenad Dimitrijević, "Serbia after the Criminal Past: What Went Wrong and What Should be Done," *International Journal of Transitional Justice* 2, no. 2 (2008): 5–22, 5.

117. Helsinki Committee for Human Rights in Serbia, *Human Security,* 45–46.

While human rights NGOs and international justice activists pressured Serbia to use this anniversary to open up the question of Srebrenica, the Serbian government strongly resisted this pressure and issued a series of statements aimed at diffusing the Srebrenica issue. The Serbian parliament failed to pass a joint Declaration on Srebrenica, amid fierce debate about whose crimes should be condemned. Two parties, the Democratic Party and the Serbian Renewal Movement (SPO), insisted that the declaration clearly condemn the massacre in Srebrenica and call for an investigation into who ordered and perpetrated the atrocities. The SPO proposal, however, also included a statement that Serb perpetrators of the Srebrenica massacre "did not represent Serbs and Serbia" and were working against "Serbian tradition and culture." In other words, for this political party, it was important to acknowledge and apologize for the crimes in order to clear the Serbs' name and reputation. All other parliamentary parties disagreed. They wanted instead to tone down the document, not mention the specific crime in Srebrenica but issue a general condemnation of war crimes, with special focus on crimes against the Serbs. The human rights community submitted their own declaration document to the parliament for ratification. This document strongly condemned the Srebrenica massacre, called it genocide, and stressed why it was important for the Serbian public to know the truth about the crime. This proposal, however, was supported by only two members of parliament.[118]

Some of the nationalist posturing in the parliament was clearly political in nature. Koštunica's DSS minority government wanted to further secure support from Milošević's Socialists and extremist Radicals, and downplaying the Srebrenica issue was a way of appeasing the two coalition partners. After the failed parliament vote, the ruling party, DSS, issued its own public declaration, which opened with the following message:

> Serbia has a special vital and historical interest in the explanation and judgment of all war crimes committed in the recent history of Yugoslavia in which the Serbian nation was the greatest victim. First in terms of victims, Serbia must be first in the judgment of all crimes.[119]

What is striking in this declaration is the insistence that the Serbs were the greatest victims of the Yugoslav wars—in the face of overwhelming evidence to the contrary.[120] But even more important is the way in which the ruling elite

---

118. B92, June 14, 2005.

119. DSS, "Deklaracija o osudi ratnih zločina na prostoru nekadašnje Jugoslavije" [Declaration on Condemning War Crimes on the Territory of the Former Yugoslavia], June 15, 2005, http://www.dss.org.yu.

120. For example, the most reliable database of all victims of the Bosnian war, compiled by the Sarajevo-based Research Documentation Center, indicates in real numbers that the overwhelming

used the discourse of transitional justice ("explanation and judgment of all war crimes") to further pursue its ideological agenda, which focused on advancing the narrative of Serbia's victimization, suffering, and unfair international condemnation.

This relativization and distancing from crimes, the "opportunistic pacification of the past,"[121] also marked the actual tenth anniversary of the Srebrenica massacre. A day after the massive ceremony to commemorate Srebrenica held on location in Bosnia, the Serbian Orthodox Church organized a parallel ceremony in the neighboring village of Bratunac to mark the atrocities committed there against the Serbs. The Srebrenica ceremony was broadcast only on the liberal television network B92, while the Bratunac event received blanket coverage in the rest of the Serbian media, including a special supplement to *Večernje novosti*, the highest-circulation daily newspaper, which included inflated numbers of Serb victims as well as multiple historical inaccuracies and exaggerations of events in the course of the Bosnian war.[122]

What the elite discourse and public attitudes surrounding the Srebrenica event showed was that even in the case of insurmountable evidence that great numbers of Bosniac civilians had been killed by Serb troops, including paramilitaries from Serbia proper—all caught on tape!—Serbian elites still refused to accept the basic premise of transitional justice—acknowledging the crimes and then punishing the perpetrators. Even more significant was the way in which the elites tried to use the language of transitional justice to reverse its main purpose—and to continue the nationalist ideology that had led to the crimes in the first place.

Domestic Demand from Below

The first major obstacle that international ideas about transitional justice had to overcome was a deeply entrenched public hostility to the goals of transitional justice and consequently very low domestic demand for normative change. The Serbian public largely refused to believe that the Serbs had committed war crimes, and they blamed other nations and ethnic groups for starting the war; they also distrusted the international community and by proxy international justice insti-

---

majority of victims were Bosniacs. See documentation on the Center's Population Losses project, available at http://www.idc.org.ba/project/populationlosses.html.

121. Nenad Dimitrijević, "Srbija kao nedovršena država" [Serbia as an Unfinished State], *Reč* 69, no. 15 (2003): 5–21.

122. Helsinki Committee for Human Rights in Serbia, *Human Security*.

tutions, notably the ICTY, which was the only publicly visible institutional mechanism of transitional justice in Serbia.[123]

There are a number of reasons why the Serbian public was so hostile to ideas of transitional justice. First, Milošević's policies were supported by a significant majority of the Serbian electorate, especially in the first ten years of his rule (1987–96). These elections were neither fully free nor fair, but the system was still open for challengers. And while Milošević surely would not have allowed another winner, he did allow token opponents to run, though they never came even close to winning significant majorities. Opinion polls conducted by respected independent agencies consistently showed Milošević as the most trustworthy and popular politician throughout the war period.[124] It was not until 1996, in the face of large citizen protests over election fraud, that he began to lag in the polls. In other words, Milošević's rule was not simply imposed on unwilling oppressed people; for a long time, his leadership and policies were rooted in a national public consensus.

Societal participation in the criminal past was widespread and multilayered. Some of the participants—political elites, the church, elite intelligentsia, and the military—remained in power after the transition and actively blocked transitional justice projects because of their own responsibility in inciting or conducting them. Other participants were direct perpetrators—troops and paramilitaries who now led civilian lives. Finally, and most intractably, there was the psychological participation of a significant majority of the population who approved of the nationalist policy in its general terms. These people were now unwilling recipients of transitional justice projects that required them to reexamine their own personal responsibility for both action and inaction that had made atrocities possible on such a wide scale.[125]

More generally, the character of the crimes committed directly influenced the Serbian social and political response. The fact that the crimes had been committed against non-Serb populations, against "foreign enemies" in an internationalized war setting, made appeals to address individual and social complicity in them much more difficult to maintain than if the atrocities had been committed by Serbs against other Serbs. This fact was compounded by the character of

---

123. Belgrade Center for Human Rights, *An Analysis of a Public Opinion Survey on the ICTY with Comments and Recommendations* (Belgrade: BCHR, 2005), 372; Srđan Bogosavljević and Svetlana Logar, "Viđenje istine u Srbiji [Perception of Truth in Serbia]," *Reč* 62, no. 8 (2001): 5–34.

124. See regular reports by the Strategic Marketing Research agency, Belgrade, available at http://www.smmri.co.yu. On the continuing popularity of Milošević's Socialist Party, see Marija Obradović, "The Ruling Party," in *The Road to War in Serbia: Trauma and Catharsis*, ed. Nebojša Popov (Budapest: Central European University Press, 2000), 425–48.

125. Korać, interview.

the postwar settlement, which institutionalized ethnic divisions and separated warring groups who now lived in different countries or in highly segregated in-country ethnic entities, without any incentive to cooperate or even interact with one another. This principally ethnic quality of both the crimes committed and the postconflict solution made the search for truth and justice that much more distant and less urgent. Unlike other major transitional justice projects in countries like South Africa or Argentina—where truth, justice, and reconciliation were considered necessary for preserving national unity and building a future together with former political enemies—in Serbia, as well as in other former Yugoslav republics, the major incentive—living together—was absent. In the words of a Serbian journalist, "We don't have victims [in Serbia], only refugees. Serbians don't know what it's like to be victims."[126] This is why it was so difficult for both international and domestic promoters of transitional justice to make facing the past an issue of national priority—the population simply did not care about atrocities committed against groups who lived in other countries and with whom they were unlikely to ever interact again.[127]

Another reason for the low social demand for justice is the profound "ethnification" of Serbian politics in the 1990s through massive nationalist mobilization around "defending Serbian interests." This was the time of great social transformation from communism to nationalism, the time when "the working people became the Serbian people."[128] Ethnic politics became the only lens through which the population saw and interpreted the world and events surrounding them.[129] This is why any discussion of transitional justice more generally and ICTY specifically would always hit the wall of ethnic politics. Society was unequipped to think of crimes committed in the name of politics in any other way other than as an ethnic war of self-defense. Consequently, transitional justice projects that required Serbia to face its crimes, acknowledge abuses, and punish the perpetra-

---

126. Antonela Riha (reporter for B92 network) quoted in Orentlicher, "Shrinking the Space," 91.

127. This low social demand for transitional justice is evident in the results of systematic public opinion surveys. For example, in a 2005 survey, 81 percent of respondents answered that Serbs had suffered the most during the Yugoslav wars, and 74 percent believed that Serbs had committed the fewest crimes of all ethnic groups in the former Yugoslavia. "Public Opinion in Serbia: Views on Domestic War Crimes Judicial Authorities and the Hague Tribunal April 2005," report on file with author. In a similar survey conducted by the same agency in 2006, 64 percent of respondents believed that facing the crimes of the past was important, but 35 percent of those believed this was important to vindicate the Serbs from false accusations of war crimes. OSCE, "Public Opinion in Serbia."

128. I thank Ivan Čolović for this astute observation.

129. Sabrina P. Ramet, "Under the Holy Lime Tree: The Inculcation of Neurotic and Psychotic Syndromes as a Serbian Wartime Strategy, 1986–1995," in *Serbia since 1989: Politics and Society under Milošević and After*, ed. Sabrina P. Ramet and Vjeran Pavlaković (Seattle: University of Washington Press, 2005).

tors flew in the face of the general public's understanding of what the war was about.

To conclude, ever since Milošević came to power in 1987, the Serbian people have been socialized by the elites to believe that their nation is a victim of vast outside conspiracies that want to subjugate or destroy it. The agents of destruction vary in the story and across time, but those most commonly mentioned are Kosovo Albanians, Slovenes, Croats, Muslims, the international community, the United States, and NATO.[130] The narrative for the past twenty years in Serbia has been that of a victimized nation, of people on the run or engaged in self-defense against one of their enemies.[131] It is difficult to overestimate the saturation in the public discourse of this idea. It permeates all aspects of public life, requiring politicians to address and solve it, and it partly explains the public approval of the wars of the 1990s. In such an environment, it is not surprising that attempts at introducing models of transitional justice have hit the wall. There has simply been no discursive space open for this new message. In the words of a Serbian politician, Serbia after Milošević was not ready to face its past, "like a patient is not ready to undergo surgery without anesthetic."[132] Serbian transitional elites entered this space to provide the national anesthetic, to dull the pain of the past by ignoring it.

The Power of Old-Regime Spoilers

Another reason why fully complying with international transitional justice demands would have been too costly for Serbian elites was the robust presence of old-regime spoilers within the military, police, and secret service and the simple fact that the new government did not hold a monopoly over the use of force, the basic element of statehood. In fact, one of the first big cracks in the DOS coalition appeared on the eve of Milošević's ousting, when President-elect Koštunica told his DOS allies he wanted "a deal, not a revolution."[133] The deal included keeping in place Milošević's army and intelligence chiefs, as well as a promise to Milošević that he would not be extradited to The Hague. According to Koštunica's advisers, the decision to keep major old-regime players in the government was made "in order to instrumentalize the old regime so that they would not stage a coup."[134]

130. Bogosavljević and Logar, "Perception of Truth in Serbia."
131. David Bruce MacDonald, *Balkan Holocausts? Serbian and Croatian Victim-Centred Propaganda and the War in Yugoslavia* (Manchester, UK: Manchester University Press, 2002).
132. Author's interview with senior DS official, October 26, 2005, Belgrade.
133. Jovanović, interview.
134. Author's interview with Koštunica's senior foreign policy adviser.

Koštunica's decision to keep Milošević's two close allies, one of whom was indicted by the ICTY for war crimes, was for all intents and purposes a choice to offer amnesty for past abuses, a decision that immediately blocked attempts at a clean break with Milošević's legacy. This compromise then set up a political and institutional structure in which serious justice initiatives would be blocked from the start by old-regime elements that remained in positions of authority and in control of a monopoly of force.

Since human rights abuses committed during the previous regime were *state crimes,* not isolated incidents by a few soldiers but a constitutive part of Milošević's policies, the new government immediately encountered a lot of resistance to investigating perpetrators, as the old state security apparatus almost seamlessly transitioned into the new regime. The insurmountable difficulty in dealing with old-regime spoilers was the extent to which the army, police, paramilitary troops, intelligence services, and organized crime were intertwined. So the question became, who does the arresting and who does the investigating? Who are the agents of justice? The government could not order the arrests of paramilitary leaders if those leaders were themselves integrated, officially or semiofficially, into the police force. In addition, many of the paramilitaries morphed after the war into "regular" organized crime. They had vast networks of coconspirators across the region, easily able to provide shelter. More important, they were motivated to protect themselves at all cost, as shown in the lengths they would take—assassinating a sitting prime minister—to stop further cooperation with The Hague.

Competing Elite Strategies

The public rift over dealing with past abuses revealed sharp differences between two competing elite blocs in transitional Serbia, the conservatives and the reformers. The conservatives gathered around President Koštunica included traditional nationalists but also significant numbers of former Milošević loyalists—mostly from Milošević's Socialist Party (SPS) and the extremist Serbian Radical Party (SRS)—who flocked to Koštunica's DSS. They had significant support among the army, old communist political elites, the Serbian Orthodox Church, establishment intelligentsia, and the largely unreformed and unprofessionalized media.[135] The reformers around Prime Minister Đinđić included most cabinet members and major business and technocratic elites, and they also had wide

---

135. Helsinki Committee for Human Rights in Serbia, *The Press: An Unchanged Matrix* (Belgrade: HCHRS, 2004).

support among most of Serbia's civil-society sector. Although the two camps frequently differed on matters of policy, their biggest point of disagreement was on issues of transitional justice.

The conservatives, norm resisters, displayed general hostility toward the idea of transitional justice; they strongly opposed cooperation with international justice institutions and were enraged by Milošević's extradition, calling it illegal and unconstitutional.[136] Pursuing a vindication strategy, the conservatives used rhetoric and policy efforts to show how the past was in fact not all bad, how international opprobrium was unwarranted, and how with the change in elites the old policies could be better explained and, if not again pursued, then at least vindicated. This strategy was clear already in the first speech President-elect Koštunica gave on the eve of Milošević's ousting: "There are those who did us wrong, who bombed us. We cannot forget the damage or the crimes [against us]; *Serbs will lose their identity if they forget those crimes.*"[137]

Koštunica's first speech was significant because it provided a window into many aspects of the new president's strategy for Serbia in transition. It indicated a clear continuation of the vision of Serbia and Serbian people as victims of crimes committed *against* them and never *by* them. It was the first strong indication, at the level of public narrative, that much that had perpetuated Milošević's hold on his people—the sense of victimization, suffering, and punishment—would continue in transitional Serbia as well. On the level of discourse, not much seemed to have changed.[138]

The conservatives' rage against international justice was especially pronounced in relation to the ICTY. Koštunica's disdain of the ICTY is well documented. He often publicly denigrated the tribunal, once famously referring to it as "the last hole on [his] flute."[139] He also argued that "his stomach rolled" at the thought of the tribunal, but that he had to, in a way, "digest" this institution. "As a man lives with a disease, and in the end manages to overcome it, I think that the ICTY in a way has elements of an illness, and sometimes there is something positive in an

---

136. B92, April 10, 2002.

137. B92, October 6, 2000 (emphasis added).

138. The vindication strategy was also used to guide policy, such as Serbia's official legal strategy in its defense against Croatian and Bosnian charges of genocide and aggression in front of the International Court of Justice. Serbia's legal representative argued that it is in Serbia's interest to process individual war crimes so that "we can go back to the glory days of Serbia's leaders who respected rights of combatants even before there was a Geneva convention." Author's interview with Radoslav Stojanović, Serbia's representative in the ICJ case, October 10, 2005, Belgrade. Interestingly, this same argument was made by the ICTY president, Theodor Meron, who argued that Serbia's cooperation in extraditing ICTY indictees would show how these horrible abuses were "in contrast with the heroic tradition of the Serbian people." B92, November 11, 2005.

139. B92, February 1, 2002.

illness, a man can end up stronger and harder after overcoming it."[140] Comments like this prompted ICTY prosecutor Carla Del Ponte to label Koštunica as the main obstacle to cooperation.[141]

The conservatives' resistance to international justice, and especially the ICTY, was not only ideological; it was also firmly political. The conservatives used the justice issue to present themselves to the voters as a truly patriotic force, which would preserve the Serbian national legacy and not put it up for sale. These messages were clearly aimed beyond Koštunica's DSS party base to the wider swath of Milošević-era SPS and SRS voters. Koštunica's strategy was to expand the DSS electoral base with nationalists and Milošević loyalists who were now looking at the changed political scene in search of a party that would continue Milošević-era nationalist policies.[142] In order to follow this political strategy, the conservatives *had* to resist international notions of transitional justice because this continuing resistance would score them valuable domestic political points and secure their unchallenged place on the right of the political spectrum.

In contrast, Prime Minister Đinđić positioned his own political party as the party of European integration, reform, and internationalism, juxtaposing it to the reactionary and anti-European party of president Koštunica. Đinđić linked cooperation with the ICTY to European integration: "Europe is our house and no price is too high to pay....I am for Europe,"[143] implying that his opponents were not. Đinđić used justice at The Hague as a domestic political wedge issue, a defining difference between the two opposing political groups. In other words, Đinđić's reformers were instrumental adopters of transitional justice; they would invoke the international norm to justify institutional and policy change but also to delegitimize the preferences of their domestic political opponents.

The prime minister's vision for Serbia was of a democratic, "European" state, fully recovered economically and on the way to becoming a regional economic power. For this coalition, the focus was on integrating Serbia into international institutions and ultimately taking it to the European Union. This focus on integration, however, led the reformist coalition into two mutually contradictory strategies of compliance with international transitional justice demands. On the one hand, the reformists chose to instrumentally comply, by cooperating with the

---

140. B92, April 2, 2002.

141. International Crisis Group, "Belgrade's Lagging Reform: Cause for International Concern," Europe Report no. 126, Belgrade, March 7, 2002.

142. Eric Gordy, "Postwar Guilt and Responsibility in Serbia: The Effort to Confront It and the Effort to Avoid It," in Ramet and Pavlaković, *Serbia since 1989.*

143. Sonja Biserko, "Zoran Đinđić i Haški tribunal" [Zoran Đinđić and The Hague Tribunal], in *Zoran Đinđić: Etika odgovornosti* [*Zoran Đinđić: The Ethics of Responsibility*], ed. Latinka Perović (Belgrade: Helsinki Committee for Human Rights in Serbia, 2006), 229.

ICTY and setting up a domestic war-crimes court, in expectation of international approval and awards. They did not, however, interpret compliance to include expectations of more comprehensive, substantive changes to Serbia's politics and its teaching of the past. On the other hand, the focus on international integration prevented the reformists on many occasions from digging deep into past abuses because they feared that reminding the international community of Serbia's recent crimes would somehow undermine the reputation and prestige of "new Serbia."

A clear example of this paradox was the question of how to deal with the mass graves discovered in a Belgrade suburb in 2001 that contained the bodies of more than four hundred Kosovo Albanian civilians killed during Serbian police incursions into Kosovo. By insider accounts, many of the discussions in the cabinet focused on how uncovering the perpetrators among the Serbian police would damage Serbia's international reputation. Officials worried that in this transitional moment, discovering a crime of such magnitude would cool off international support for the new government and would be an international public relations disaster. As one of the participants in the discussions reportedly asked, "How much longer do we have to clean up Milošević's garbage?"[144]

While some of Đinđić's reluctance to tackle transitional justice directly is explained by his lack of appreciation for the urgency of the problem, he also had little room to maneuver in initiating a fundamental change of values and norms in Serbian society. The reformers' core support never went higher than 20–25 percent, which was never enough of a base from which to launch a massive social reeducation effort without suffering immediate political consequences.[145]

In addition to conservative resisters and reformist instrumental adopters, Serbia did have its share of true believers in the ideas of transitional justice. Serbia has a sizable civil society and within it a small but vocal subset of human rights organizations dedicated to acknowledging past abuses, finding justice for victims and perpetrators, and preventing new violence. Human rights organizations and a few independent media began setting up transitional justice projects as early as 2000, even before the Serbian regime change. These early projects were mostly in the form of international academic conferences that, while attended by major international transitional justice experts, were left largely unreported by the mainstream media and occurred in a sort of parallel universe to that of political party strategies, establishment academic institutions, and elite intelligentsia.

---

144. Goran Svilanović (former foreign minister and president of the Civic Alliance of Serbia), in interview with author, September 26, 2005, Belgrade.

145. Author's interview with the director of Strategic Marketing Research agency, October 1, 2005, Belgrade.

Unlike the civil society in many other transitional countries that, along with the media, played a critical role in transitional justice by conducting investigative reports on the crimes committed, publicizing their findings, raising awareness about past abuses, and publicly shaming perpetrators,[146] Serbian civil society was too weak to really matter. Public trust in the civil-society sector in general, and in human rights groups in particular, was incredibly low. Their media reach was limited and their positions often incompletely or unfairly represented. Leaders of human rights groups were victims of both physical and verbal harassment, without any protection from the police.[147] They were also ridiculed and persistently abused in the media, creating an atmosphere in which their statements and public appearances were widely interpreted as anti-Serbian or antipatriotic.[148] They were regularly attacked by members of the Serbian parliament for having a "destructive impact on the consciousness of young people" and for being "anti-Serb," without any rebuke by the parliament speaker.[149] None of this created an atmosphere in which serious questions about the past could be debated.

Politically, civil-society activities could not translate into official policy because there were no political forces—parties, government officials, or leaders—either interested enough in following them or strong enough to push them through a legislative process. The only two political parties that made dealing with Milošević's legacy and crimes of the past centerpieces of their agendas were the Civic Alliance of Serbia and the Social Democratic Union, and later the Liberal Democratic Party (LDP).[150] However, the share of their combined vote was negligible, and they never managed to have more than a token representative elected to the parliament. They potentially had the most power when their leaders were cabinet members in Đinđić's government. Even then, however, the calls for transitional justice were drowned out by what the government perceived

---

146. Perhaps the most famous example of the civil society role in transitional justice was the power and influence of the Argentinean victims group, Mothers of the Plaza de Mayo. In Brazil, in the absence of official investigations of past abuses, the Catholic Church published a report of an "unofficial truth commission" that was widely circulated and became the basis for an unofficial historical transcript of the authoritarian past. See Catholic Church Archdiocese of Sao Paulo, *Torture in Brazil: A Report* (New York: Vintage Books, 1986).

147. Biserko, interview, September 21, 2005; and Vučo, interview. Also Human Rights Watch, "Human Rights Overview: Serbia and Montenegro," January 18, 2006, http://www.hrw.org/legacy/english/docs/2006/01/18/serbia12242.htm.

148. Helsinki Committee for Human Rights in Serbia, *Human Rights and Accountability: Serbia 2003* (Belgrade: HCHRS, 2004); Helsinki Committee for Human Rights in Serbia, *Human Security*.

149. Humanitarian Law Center, "Transitional Justice Report: Serbia, Montenegro and Kosovo, 1999–2005," Belgrade, June 27, 2006, 16.

150. The Liberal Democratic Party (LDP), led by Đinđić's closest disciple, Čedomir Jovanović, was established in 2005. The Civic Alliance was absorbed by the LDP in 2007. The Social Democratic Union works in coalition with the LDP.

were more pressing problems facing the country.[151] The two parties' presence and consistency in matters of transitional justice were of tremendous comfort to the fledgling human rights groups, but this did not help either transform unofficial transitional justice efforts into government policy or give human rights groups enough political clout to become unofficial but broadly accepted chroniclers of the past.

To sum up, the Serbian transitional justice experience points to multiple sites of domestic resistance to the advancement of international transitional justice models. Institutional resisters were many—the president and his political coalition, old-regime spoilers, the media, and the public at large. Locations of institutional acceptance were much fewer and weaker—the political coalition around the prime minister decided to comply with international requirements, but it did so instrumentally, not as true believers. The only point of full normative acceptance could be found in isolated pockets of civil society, but this coalition was weak and politically marginalized and had no enforcement mechanisms at its disposal. The domestic political conflict over competing strategies therefore directly shaped transitional justice outcomes.

"Stop the Hague": The Assassination of Prime Minister Đinđić

Transitional justice and responsibility for past abuses once again became the centerpiece of Serbian politics with the March 12, 2003, assassination of Prime Minister Đinđić by the notorious armed group the Red Berets.[152] Immediately following the assassination, the Serbian government imposed a state of emergency and cast a wide net intent on apprehending major suspects and organized crime figures. The stunning finding was that assassination conspirators called this operation "Stop The Hague," strongly indicating that Đinđić had been murdered to stop further Hague investigations and extraditions.[153] Additional findings in

---

151. Korać, interview, and Svilanović, interview.

152. Officially titled the Special Operations Unit, this group was formed as a paramilitary unit in 1990 to stir up Serbian rebellion in Croatia. Its members were accused of committing some of the most heinous atrocities in the Yugoslav wars. At the end of the war, Milošević officially merged the Red Berets with the regular security forces, and they remained part of the official police forces after Milošević was ousted from power, making them much more difficult to disband and prosecute. Dejan Anastasijević, "Ko su 'Crvene Beretke?'" [Who are the "Red Berets"?], Vreme, October 19, 2000.

153. Testimony of Zvezdan Jovanović, one of the alleged assassins, during the assassination trial proceedings. Glas javnosti, December 26, 2003. For a comprehensive investigative report on the assassination, see Miloš Vasić, Atentat na Zorana Đinđića [The Assassination of Zoran Đinđić] (Belgrade: Politika, 2005).

the assassination inquiry pointed to a strong possibility that Đinđić's killing was an attempted coup—that he was killed by the Red Berets but with logistic support of the state security apparatus.[154] It became clear from later trial testimony that the Red Berets wanted to eliminate Đinđić and his closest associates and overthrow the regime, restoring Milošević-era loyalists to power.[155]

Đinđić's assassination was a pivotal moment in Serbia's transition. His death left a huge power vacuum, which was immediately filled by Koštunica's DSS and by the extreme nationalist SRS. The first post-Đinđić elections indicated a strong normalization and relativization of war crimes and their perpetrators, who made an open comeback into mainstream politics. The 2003 parliamentary elections featured three indicted war criminals—Slobodan Milošević, Vojislav Šešelj and Nebojša Pavković—at the top of their respective parties' (SPS, SRS, and Socialist People's Party) electoral lists, while two generals indicted for war crimes, Vladimir Lazarević and Sreten Lukić, figured on the Liberal Party election list.

Đinđić's assassination stopped Serbian reforms in their tracks. It compromised further cooperation with the ICTY as the only element in the Serbian government inclined to cooperate had been removed, and Koštunica went back to his entrenched position of noncompliance. Furthermore, Koštunica used the fact that the assassination was intended to literally stop The Hague investigations and transfers to make repeated claims that it was The Hague that was somehow responsible for Đinđić's death (by unreasonable pressures placed on the government).[156] The implication was that this tragedy was the final proof that international justice, institutionalized as cooperation with The Hague, was not only unnecessary but outright counterproductive for Serbia and dangerous for its leaders.

The high-profile assassination created a domestic political crisis of major proportions, and the instability that followed significantly weakened the reformist government, which lost reelection in December 2003. Soon after the new administration was inaugurated, it announced that it would no longer recognize indictments based on command responsibility, no further indictees would be transferred to The Hague, and domestic courts would take over ICTY trials.[157]

154. Anastasijević, interview.

155. Trial testimonies uncovered a hit list as part of the same "Stop The Hague" operation, which also targeted Đinđić's advisers Čedomir Jovanović and Vladimir Beba Popović and foreign minister Goran Svilanović.

156. Peter S. Green, "Serbia Cracks Down on Mobsters and War-Crime Suspects," *New York Times*, April 21, 2003.

157. B92, March 6, 2004.

A few weeks later, the government passed a law to fund and legally facilitate the defense of indicted war criminals before the ICTY.[158]

The subsequent round of presidential elections in June 2004 ushered in a new reformist president, who declared his intent to continue Đinđić's legacy and fulfill Serbia's obligations to international justice organizations. The government, however, has remained bitterly divided over transitional justice policies. Conservative hard-liners have continued to control the parliament, and the enduring power struggle over Hague extraditions and renewed international pressures have led to a virtual government paralysis, where the most fundamental decisions about the country's future, such as possible accession to the EU, have all become hostages to the unresolved question of how to deal with the legacies of the past.

Europe's Squeeze

Serbia's strategic quasi compliance with the norms and institutions of transitional justice finally collapsed in 2006. After the surge in transfers in April 2005, cooperation with the ICTY stalled again. The ICTY increased demands for transfers of the two remaining most-wanted indictees—Radovan Karadžić and especially Ratko Mladić, who was widely believed to be hiding in Serbia, protected by the Serbian military. The international squeeze on Serbia to arrest and transfer those two men became increasingly linked to any future negotiations on Serbia's accession to the EU. In many ways, the future of Serbia's international integration was taken hostage by the two men, without whose apprehension Serbia was relegated to the back of the EU accession line, with decreasing financial assistance and a weakening bargaining position on the future of Kosovo.[159]

The Serbian government consistently argued that it had no information on the two men's whereabouts. Karadžić's location became a matter of local mythology, with most speculations suggesting that he was hiding in the rugged unpopulated mountainous terrain between Serbia, Bosnia, and Montenegro, supported by local tribal leaders and members of the Serbian Orthodox Church. The Serbian government's claim that it had no information about Mladić's whereabouts lacked credibility after it was publicly disclosed that Mladić had been living openly in his Belgrade house until 2002 and had since then been spotted in various locations in rural Serbia. The government's position was further complicated by documentation that Mladić had been kept on the Serbian army's payroll

---

158. B92, March 30, 2004.
159. International Crisis Group, "Serbia: Spinning Its Wheels."

until 2002, and that none other than then president Koštunica had signed his retirement papers. The fact that the army was protecting Mladić made his arrest that much more difficult.[160]

The international pressure for Mladić's arrest greatly intensified after Croatia arrested and transferred its most-wanted ICTY suspect, General Ante Gotovina, in December 2005. The ICTY put pressure on Serbia, asking it to step up to Croatia's plate. The Serbian government responded again with a time-buying strategy—it leaked to Serbian media that Mladić had been located and that negotiations for his surrender were under way. The media ran this story for weeks, even though it turned out that it was completely false. During that time, the Serbian government hoped to stall for time and delay the ICTY chief prosecutor's negative report to the UN about Serbia's lack of cooperation. Koštunica even vouched to European officials that he would personally oversee the Mladić case.[161] The highlight of this cat-and-mouse game was the disclosure that the Serbian government had sent ICTY an incomplete file on Mladić, even empty photocopied pages in lieu of his personal dossier, again hoping the ICTY would not notice, or that this tactic would buy Serbia some time.[162] Serbia's recalcitrant position was not helped by Milošević's sudden death in The Hague in March 2006, when the ICTY lost its star defendant. The tribunal now wanted Mladić more than ever.

The European Union finally lost its patience with Serbia, and on May 3, 2006, EU negotiations on Serbia's accession were officially suspended because of the country's failure to deliver Mladić. This unfavorable turn of events put great strain on the Serbian government, leading to the resignation of high-ranking officials. On June 1, 2006, the United States followed suit by suspending financial aid to Serbia as punishment for its continuing lack of cooperation with the ICTY, especially its lack of progress in arresting Ratko Mladić. Serbia finally seemed to have lost all the international goodwill it had earned by getting rid of Milošević in 2000. Serbia's future looked grim. The country not only lost the chance to acquire additional international rewards, but it actually lost the benefits it already had.

In the subsequent few months, however, European policies toward Serbia began to change. In November 2006, NATO came to a surprising decision to admit Serbia to the Partnership for Peace program, even as Serbia continued to ignore ICTY demands, a long-term requirement for NATO admission.[163] And

---

160. Dejan Anastasijević, "Pršti, pršti haška staza" [On the Snowy Path to The Hague], *Vreme*, December 29, 2005.
161. B92, May 1, 2006.
162. Anastasijević, "On the Snowy Path."
163. NATO continued to publicly insist on Serbia's full cooperation with the ICTY. NATO summit declaration, "Riga Summit Declaration," press release, Riga, Latvia, November 29, 2006.

then, in a stunning reversal, the EU announced on February 12, 2007, that SAA negotiations with Serbia would resume, provided the government showed a clear commitment to achieving full cooperation with the ICTY and took concrete and effective action for full cooperation.[164] What "clear commitment" meant was left unspecified, but it was obvious that the government was no longer obliged to arrest Mladić and Karadžić as a condition for SAA talks. In a press conference after the EU Troika meeting with Serbia in early March 2007, Commissioner Rehn cited the following actions Serbia was required to take: a formal commitment to arresting fugitives, placement of "competent and committed people" in the right governmental positions to enable full cooperation with the ICTY, coordination of authorities working on fugitives' arrest, and granting full access to documents and files.[165]

The timing of the EU turnaround was even more surprising since it came on the heels of the February 2007 ruling by the International Court of Justice determining that Serbia's failure to transfer Mladić to the tribunal was a violation of the genocide convention and ordering Serbia to cooperate fully with the ICTY.[166]

The EU officially resumed SAA negotiations with Serbia in June 2007, after the Serbian government cooperated in the arrest of Bosnian Serb general Zdravko Tolimir and Serbian former police general Vlastimir Đorđević. In November 2007, the EU initialized the SAA, the major step toward EU accession. This major reward in the absence of any visible steps toward apprehending the remaining war-crimes suspects angered international human rights organizations, who argued that the EU was effectively rewarding Serbia for harboring suspects accused of genocide and was furthermore considering admitting to the union a state that was in violation of the genocide convention.[167] It also seriously undermined the ICTY prosecutor, Carla Del Ponte, who had consistently issued reports that Serbia was not fully cooperating with the tribunal and that

---

164. European Commission, "Serbia 2007 Progress Report," Brussels, November 6, 2007.

165. General Affairs and External Relations Council, EU-Serbia Troika, Brussels, March 6, 2007.

166. On February 26, 2007, the International Court of Justice ruled that Serbia had breached its obligations under the Convention on the Prevention and Punishment of the Crime of Genocide by failing to prevent the 1995 genocide at Srebrenica or to punish those responsible. It also found that Serbia's continuing failure to transfer Mladić to the ICTY amounted to an ongoing violation of its obligations under the genocide convention. This was the first time the ICJ had ruled that a country was in violation of the convention. International Court of Justice, *Case Concerning the Application of the Convention on the Prevention and Punishment of the Crime of Genocide (Bosnia and Herzegovina v. Serbia and Montenegro)*, Judgment, February 26, 2007.

167. For example, see Human Rights Watch, "Don't Compromise on Mladić: EU Should Insist on Full Cooperation with Yugoslav Tribunal," November 6, 2007, http://hrw.org/english/docs/2007/11/06/serbia17261.htm.

only EU conditionality stood a chance to make Serbia act.[168] Against all appeals by international justice proponents,[169] as well as serious objections by Belgium and the Netherlands, the EU finally signed the SAA with Serbia on April 29, 2008, with the caveat that the implementation of the document would depend on Serbia's cooperation with the ICTY.[170]

The EU's unexpected reversal can only be interpreted as a purely political measure aimed at strengthening pro-European forces within Serbia—namely, the reformist Democratic Party at the expense of the hard-line Democratic Party of Serbia and the Serbian Radical Party—on the eve of parliamentary elections scheduled for May 2008.[171] In fact, Javier Solana, the EU's high representative for foreign and security policy, openly said that the SAA should be offered to Serbia before parliamentary elections to support pro-European forces in the elections and "send a clear message to the Serbian people that we care about them."[172] The EU gamble paid off, and the reformers won a ten-point victory in the May 2008 elections. Their victory, however, was not robust enough to allow them to form a majority government. In a particularly ironic twist, the reformist Democratic Party was forced to invite Milošević's Socialists to join the government.[173]

The change of government, however, quickly led to improvement in cooperation with the ICTY. In a clear sign that norm resisters had been replaced, at least for the time being, with instrumental promoters, the new reformist government surprised international observers and the Hague tribunal itself by arresting Radovan Karadžić in Belgrade in July 2008. Karadžić's arrest, while intensely covered in the Serbian media, revealed that Serbian society is still uncertain about its past and ways to deal with its legacy. An opinion poll conducted immediately after the arrest showed that 54 percent of the Serbian respondents did not approve of Karadžić's transfer to The Hague, while 42 percent approved. A third of those surveyed saw Karadžić as a hero, and only 17 percent as a war criminal, while the overwhelming majority, 86 percent, believed that the ICTY was biased against the Serbs.[174]

---

168. "Del Ponte Urges EU Serbia Caution," BBC News, January 31, 2007.

169. International Crisis Group, "Will the Real Serbia Please Stand Up?" Europe Briefing no. 49, Belgrade, April 23, 2008.

170. B92, April 29, 2008.

171. International Crisis Group, "Serbia's New Government: Turning from Europe," Europe Briefing no. 46, Belgrade, May 31, 2007.

172. Javier Solana, address to the Committee on Foreign Affairs of the European Parliament, April 8, 2008, http://consillium.europa.eu/solana.

173. Dejan Anastasijević, "Serbian Voters Spurn Nationalists," Time, May 12, 2008.

174. The survey was conducted by Strategic Marketing Research for the National Council for Cooperation with the Hague Tribunal. Results were published on B92, July 25, 2008.

Not surprisingly, the international reaction to the arrest was markedly different. International human rights groups quickly hailed the unexpected arrest as a "major blow against impunity" for war crimes,[175] and the EU praised Serbia for "acting in accordance with European values."[176] The EU also indicated that Karadžić's arrest would make it easier for Serbia to fulfill the remaining EU requirements. EU candidate status, however, would still depend on full cooperation with the ICTY, especially the arrest of Ratko Mladić.[177]

Furthermore, it became increasingly clear that the SAA was offered to Serbia not only to strengthen reformists on the eve of elections but also specifically to pressure the Serbian government to recognize Kosovo.[178] The issue of war-crimes justice became much less important as the new crisis—regional instability following Kosovo's declaration of independence—loomed large. The EU ministers gave a clear indication that they were willing to put Serbia on a fast track to Europe, sidestepping the issue of international justice and cooperation with The Hague, in exchange for Serbia's readiness to peacefully give up Kosovo.[179] The earlier trade-off—Europe for The Hague—was now replaced by a new one— Europe for Kosovo. Once again, the issue of justice for crimes against humanity became a political currency of the lowest order, a matter of deal making and compromise setting, removed as far as possible from the ideas and norms of dealing with the past.

Conclusion

Serbia's transitional justice strategy led to a number of outcomes that are normatively and politically detached from the statement and purpose of transitional justice. Serbia managed to get away with domestic politics as usual, limiting or blocking serious consideration of crimes of the past and individual and societal complicity in them, as long as it could plausibly claim it was conforming to international institutional demands by cooperating with the ICTY, setting up a domestic truth commission, and opening domestic war-crimes trials.

The uninspiring story of the Serbian experience indicates the extent to which transitional justice in Serbia was caught up in a domestic power struggle between

---

175. Human Rights Watch, "Bosnia: Karadžić Arrest a Blow against Impunity," July 21, 2008, http://www.hrw.org/english/docs/2008/07/21/bosher19421.htm.

176. B92, July 30, 2008.

177. B92, September 15, 2008.

178. Kosovo unilaterally declared independence on February 17, 2008. Serbia has refused to recognize the new state.

179. "EU Offers Serbia Deal on Kosovo," BBC News, December 14, 2007.

two fractions of the fledgling transitional state. It is a cautionary tale of how transitional justice can become hijacked by domestic political actors who use it as an international and domestic strategy to achieve very specific local goals—turf protection, domestic power, delegitimation of political enemies, and perpetuation of nationalistic historical narratives, as well as obtaining international rewards—objectives all very far removed from international justice policy ideals.

It is also a story about the enthusiasm and naïveté of international norm entrepreneurs, who were so eager to put their models into practice that they failed to see political realities on the ground that made their projects ineffective at best and counterproductive at worst.[180] The particular strategy of coerced quasi compliance, aided by international organizations' mechanistic approach to issues of war crimes, had serious consequences for transitional justice goals in Serbia. This relentless insistence on judging Serbian compliance by counting the numbers of suspects transferred to The Hague hurt the deeper message of transitional justice—that crimes of such magnitude should not happen again. With each year that goes by without a systematic or really *any* examination of past wrongs, crimes are forgotten and public opinion about Serbian innocence and international anti-Serbian bias hardens.[181] This in turn creates an anti-international backlash, with increasing distrust and delegitimation of international institutions in general.

Most significant, Serbia's strategy and international coercive issue-linkage approach both cheapened the very idea of transitional justice, which became commercialized and was viewed by the public exclusively as an issue of trade. A nation's history, truth about its past, and justice for victims could all be negotiated—for an appropriate international price.

---

180. Patrice C. McMahon and David P. Forsythe, "The ICTY's Impact on Serbia: Judicial Romanticism Meets Network Politics," *Human Rights Quarterly* 30, no. 2 (2008): 412–35.

181. Annual public opinion surveys conducted by Serbian polling agencies for the OSCE have shown a trend of *decreasing* numbers of respondents who believe that truth and justice are important for the future of the country and its international relations. Also decreasing is public trust that the truth about the crimes will ever be ascertained. OSCE, "Public Opinion in Serbia."

3

THE TRUTH IS IN CROATIA'S FAVOR

Croatia's commitment to transitional justice has for many years been best described as one step forward, two steps back.[1] The Croatian government has mostly cooperated selectively, reluctantly, and insufficiently with the Hague tribunal. The pressures coming from the ICTY but also from other international organizations and individual states have created deep divisions within the Croatian state, with the "Hague issue" dominating domestic political debates and pitting strong domestic interest constituencies against one another.

This lackluster cooperation ended in 2005 when Croatia transferred the last ICTY indictee to The Hague, effectively fulfilling its obligations to the tribunal. Croatia was generously rewarded for this move with the promise of European Union membership. This journey, however, has been a difficult one for Croatia. Current debates going on in the country about the character of the 1990s war and war crimes committed indicate that while institutional obligations have been met—all suspects have been transferred to The Hague—profound divisions about the Croatian past still remain deeply embedded in the national consciousness.

To begin with, unlike Serbia, Croatia had the misfortune to wage the war on its own territory for an extended period of time. After it declared independence in 1991, the Croatian government was immersed in a war against its sizable Serb minority.[2] Croatia's nationalism began to harden under president Franjo Tuđman,

---

1. For a detailed history of Croatian cooperation with the ICTY, see Victor Peskin, *International Justice in Rwanda and the Balkans* (Cambridge: Cambridge University Press, 2008), chs. 4–5.
2. Available census data from 1991 put the Serb minority in Croatia at 12 percent.

who changed the constitution in 1990 to make Croats the only "constitutive people" of Croatia, de facto relegating Serbs to a minority, an "alien body" in Croatia. With direct prodding from Serbia, Croatian Serbs chose to respond to their
change in status with armed rebellion instead of constitutional negotiation. In
many ways this was not a homegrown effort but an uprising coordinated, financed
and managed from Belgrade.[3] For their part, the Croatian militia was spoiling for
a fight, and in a series of meant-to-provoke incidents by both sides, the large-scale
war began in 1991. It lasted in full force until the spring of 1992, when an even
more brutal conflict erupted in Bosnia, and the Croatian front remained largely
silent, with clearly delineated territories controlled by the Croatian government
and rebel Serbs. Croatia suffered many casualties in the beginning of the war,
as the federal Yugoslav National Army (JNA), as well as volunteer and paramilitary groups from Serbia proper, supported the Serb rebels. The more memorable
atrocities in the war were committed by the Serbs during the three-months-long
brutal siege of Vukovar, while international attention was grabbed by the indis-
criminate Serbian bombardment of the historic city of Dubrovnik, a gorgeous
medieval port on the Adriatic Sea, whose destruction had no strategic value to
the Serbian army other than demoralizing and humiliating Croatia. However, as
the Bosnian war raged on, Croatia became more deeply involved in this conflict
by arming and supporting Bosnian Croats and as part of a widely reported pact
between Milošević and Tuđman to divide Bosnia between Serbia and Croatia.[4]
In the course of the Bosnian war, Croatian troops and paramilitaries and their
Bosnian proxies also carried out atrocities against Bosniacs.

Finally, in 1995, as Serb troops were beginning to lose ground in Bosnia, the
Croatian army regrouped and carried out two complex military operations—
Flash and Storm—which effectively retook control of most of Serb-held territory but in the process also deported, or "ethnically cleansed" the entire Serb
population of Krajina—some two hundred thousand people. In the course of the
operation, the Croatian military and paramilitaries also burned Serbian houses
to the ground and killed almost all the Serbs who refused to or could not leave—
mostly disabled and the elderly.[5] The Croatian message was clear—the state of
Croatia was no longer a welcoming place for Serbs.

---

3. Human Rights Watch, "Weighing the Evidence: Lessons from the Slobodan Milošević Trial,"
vol. 18, no. 10(D), New York, December 14, 2006.

4. For an overview of documents pertaining to the Tuđman–Milošević agreement, see Predrag
Lucić, ed., *Stenogrami o podjeli Bosne* [Notes on the Division of Bosnia] (Split, Croatia: Kultura &
Rasvjeta, 2005).

5. Croatian Helsinki Committee for Human Rights, *Military Operation "Storm" and Its Aftermath*
(Zagreb: CHCHR, 2001). The Croatian Helsinki Committee for Human Rights estimates that the
casualty toll of operation Storm was around seven hundred, while up to twenty-two thousand houses

In this political context, Croatia's war legacy revolved around Croatia's unique position as both the victim and the perpetrator of mass atrocities. Its path to transitional justice was further complicated by the fact that the country was simultaneously undergoing a double transition—from the previous regime and from the war.[6] This paradox and the cycle of ethnic reprisals and revenge killings made the character of the war and the identity of the postwar Croatian state the central focus of attempts to reckon with the past.

In analyzing the transitional justice experience in Croatia, this chapter proceeds as follows. First, it lays the groundwork by outlining international goals and expectations for transitional justice in Croatia following the first fully democratic elections in 2000. Then it looks at the specific mechanisms of transitional justice carried out in Croatia—international and domestic trials and official truth telling—and their domestic political effects. The chapter then analyzes domestic political conditions—domestic demand from below, the power of old-regime spoilers, and competing elite strategies—that led to Croatia's instrumental adoption of international models of transitional justice. The chapter concludes by analyzing the consequences of using transitional justice as a pathway to making Croatia a legitimate European state in light of Croatia's pending accession to the European Union.

After Tuđman: Croatia Back in Europe

Croatia was among the first states to demand that the international community establish a war-crimes tribunal for atrocities committed during the Yugoslav wars.[7] Croatia's enthusiasm for the ICTY was based on the expectation that the tribunal would indict and try only Serbs accused of war crimes against Croatian civilians. In 1995, however, the ICTY indicted the first Croatian national for atrocities committed against Bosniacs in 1993, a move that outraged the Tuđman government, which responded by instituting an almost complete freeze on cooperation with the tribunal and promoting the indicted general. According to the

---

were burned. See *Jutarnji list,* July 21, 2000. These figures are still disputed by the Croatian government and are largely portrayed as overblown in the Croatian media.

6. For a general overview of the main problems of Croatia's democratic transition, see Sabrina P. Ramet and Davorka Matić, eds., *Democratic Transition in Croatia: Value Transformation, Education, Media* (College Station: Texas A&M University Press, 2007).

7. After the ICTY was set up in 1993, Croatia passed a constitutional act in 1996 regulating Croatian cooperation with the ICTY. Also in 1996, Croatia joined the Council of Europe, pledging, among other things, to fully cooperate with the ICTY.

then U.S. ambassador to Croatia, "Tudman's idea of cooperation with the tribunal was to kick his indicted officer upstairs."[8]

Bowing to tremendous pressure from the United States, which threatened to cut Croatia's international financial and military aid, Tudman finally sent the indicted general to The Hague, although he stated publicly that the general had volunteered to go, thereby setting no precedents for further extraditions. In 1998, Tudman sent ten more Croatian nationals to The Hague, again stating that they had surrendered voluntarily. In the last few years of Tudman's presidency, the ICTY led a bitter battle with Croatia over jurisdiction over operations Flash and Storm. Croatia argued that the ICTY had no jurisdiction since these were operations of national defense against Croatian Serb insurgents. The ICTY disagreed, indicting two Croatian paramilitaries for war crimes and finally succeeding in having them arrested and sent to The Hague.

The relationship between Croatia and the ICTY got so bad at the end of Tudman's administration that the Croatian parliament issued a "Resolution on Cooperation with the ICTY," admonishing the tribunal for failing to adequately deal with "war crimes committed against the Croatian people and other non-Serb civilians during Serbian and Montenegrin aggression against Croatia and during the armed rebellion in Croatia."[9] The resolution clearly stated that the Croatian parliament considered the proper role of the ICTY to be "punishing crimes committed during the war and aggression against the Republic of Croatia in 1991 and years of [Serbian] occupation of the Croatian state territory." The resolution also explained the Croatian legislature's interpretation of operations Flash and Storm as "counterterrorist" and carried out on Croatia's own territory, therefore falling outside ICTY jurisdiction.[10]

After years of tense relations with the international community, Croatia's international reputation greatly improved after Tudman's death in 1999 and the general elections of 2000. Weakened by Tudman's death and disarray within its ranks, Tudman's political party, the Croatian Democratic Union (HDZ), suffered major losses at the polls. Stjepan Mesić, a former high-profile communist official and HDZ defector,[11] won the presidency, and the parliament was placed in

---

8. United States ambassador to Croatia Peter Galbraith quoted in Gary Jonathan Bass, *Stay the Hand of Vengeance: The Politics of War Crimes Tribunals* (Princeton: Princeton University Press, 2000), 244.

9. Croatian Parliament, *Rezolucija o suradnji s medunarodnim kaznenim sudom u Haagu* [Resolution on Cooperation with the International Criminal Tribunal in The Hague], *Narodne novine* [Official Gazette], no. 24/1999, March 5, 1999.

10. Ibid.

11. Mesić was the last president of the former Yugoslavia. He left the HDZ in protest of its role in the armed conflict between Bosniacs and Croats in the Bosnian war.

control of the left-leaning six-party coalition led by the Social Democratic Party (SDP) of Prime Minister Ivica Račan and Croatian Social Liberal Party (HSLS) led by Dražen Budiša. This governing coalition showed ideological strain from the beginning. SDP was in effect a communist successor party, with Račan himself a notable communist operative during the previous regime. The HSLS was a party of Croatian nationalists (Budiša himself was a noted nationalist dissident during communism) who distinguished themselves from Tuđman's HDZ mostly by the desire to quickly Europeanize Croatia, without the burden of Tuđman's isolationism. The key to the ruling coalition's cohesion was the successful marriage of the two ideological blocs, with SDP clearly the strongest party in numbers and HSLS supplying the coalition with nationalist credibility that communists-turned-SDP members could never persuasively muster.

Post-Tuđman Croatia was generously rewarded for its change of government and moves to correct its human rights reputation. A few months after the elections, Croatia was admitted to NATO's Partnership for Peace and to the World Trade Organization. The new government also received more than $23 million in EU financial assistance, including $16 million to support refugee return, as well as $30 million in aid from the United States. But most significantly, Croatia received promising signals regarding its chances for joining the EU. In July 2000, the European Commission began steps toward an SAA between the EU and Croatia. Negotiations on the SAA officially started in November 2000, and the agreement itself was signed in October 2001.[12] Croatia was clearly on the fast track back to Europe.

International Goals of Transitional Justice in Croatia

The world's embrace of post-Tuđman Croatia also came with great expectations for the proper way in which Croatia should deal with the violent legacies of its recent past. However, unlike Serbia, for which international justice organizations developed specific protocols and models of transitional justice deemed most appropriate, post-Tuđman Croatia was expected to be a much easier case and less in need of hands-on international guidance. After initial positive outreach by the Croatian government, international justice institutions focused on continuing Croatian cooperation with the ICTY and professionalizing domestic war-crimes

---

12. Amnesty International, "A Shadow on Croatia's Future: Continuing Impunity for War Crimes and Crimes against Humanity," no. EUR 64/005/2004, London, December 13, 2004.

trials within Croatia.[13] In many ways, international justice policies followed a general international attitude toward Croatia, which manifested a "profound relief" at having in power a democratic government and a reliable international partner after years of Tuđman's autocracy.[14] In fact, such was the feeling of promise presented by the new Croatian leadership that the then U.S. secretary of state Madeleine Albright expressed hope that the "Croatian example" would pressure Serbia to "think hard" when it saw "Croatia's rapid move into Europe."[15]

As in Serbia, the international community instituted a policy of issue linkage with Croatia, where each step toward fulfillment of ICTY cooperation requirement would be rewarded with another door opened for Croatia on its path to joining the EU. However, international issue-linkage pressures were much more ad hoc and haphazard than in the case of Serbia. Foreign officials routinely scolded Croatia for lackluster cooperation with the ICTY, but then still approved financial aid to set the country on the path to European integration.[16] EU officials continued to call for Croatia's cooperation but stopped short of issuing an ultimatum in case Croatia reneged on its promises.[17] This toothless issue linkage reflected an understanding among international actors that the international community should be sensitive to domestic political realities in Croatia and be careful not to destabilize the pro-Western Račan government and potentially empower HDZ old-regime spoilers.[18] Some international organizations even worried that Croatia had too much to deal with during its transition to focus on the past. "What is being asked of this country is extraordinary," was the response of an OSCE staffer to Croatia's reluctance to deal with the past.[19] In many ways, therefore, the international belief that Croatia had the foundation of democratic normalcy suited the domestic lack of appetite for serious processes of transitional justice.

13. Amnesty International, "Amnesty International Report 2001: Croatia," London, June 1, 2001; Human Rights Watch, "World Report 2001: Croatia," New York, December 1, 2000; International Crisis Group, "After Milošević: A Practical Agenda for Lasting Balkans Peace," Europe Report no. 108, Brussels, April 1, 2001.

14. International Crisis Group, "Croatia: Facing Up to War Crimes," Europe Briefing no. 24, Brussels, October 16, 2001.

15. Steven Erlanger, "Albright Visits Post-Tudjman Croatia and Hails the New Leadership," New York Times, February 3, 2000.

16. A clear example of inconsistencies in the issue-linkage strategy was a 2002 British call for the indicted Croatian general Ante Gotovina to surrender to The Hague, immediately followed by the announcement of a 5 million British pounds donation for Croatia to carry out economic, legal, and educational reforms. Victor Peskin and Mieczyslaw P. Boduszynski, "International Justice and Domestic Politics: Post-Tudjman Croatia and the International Criminal Tribunal for the Former Yugoslavia," Europe-Asia Studies 55, no. 7 (2003): 1117–42, 1131.

17. "EU Mission Monitors Croatia's Progress," Southeast European Times, October 21, 2002.

18. International Crisis Group, "Croatia"; Peskin and Boduszynski, "International Justice," 1134.

19. OSCE Croatia War Crimes Unit staff member, in interview with author, November 23, 2005, Zagreb.

The pressures on Croatia to begin a process of transitional justice were therefore not as sustained or strong as those on Serbia. This was the result partly of Croatia's insisting on its status as a victim rather than a perpetrator of war atrocities but also of the fact that its involvement in the Bosnian war took a longer time to investigate and prove than in the case of Serbia. As a consequence, international priorities for transitional justice in Croatia were much less focused and in many ways resulted in the neglect of justice processes in Croatia as international attention centered on the more difficult cases of Serbia and Bosnia. This somewhat lax international attitude toward Croatia began to change after it became clear that, away from the international spotlight, Croatia was woefully unprepared to begin the process of facing its violent legacy.

The New Government and International Justice

The new Croatian government initially made significant gestures in the realm of human rights and transitional justice, wanting to differentiate itself from the Tuđman regime and secure international rewards and acclaim. President-elect Mesić publicly invited all Serb refugees to return to Croatia, and the government allocated $55 million to facilitate their return.[20]

But perhaps the most notable change was in the field of cooperation with the ICTY. After years of impasse under Tuđman, the transitional government agreed to provide documentation requested by the ICTY regarding Croatian involvement in alleged war crimes committed by its armed forces during operations Flash and Storm. Furthermore, the government facilitated the transfer of the first Bosnian Croat suspect to The Hague.[21] It allowed ICTY investigators to inspect the site of an alleged Croatian atrocity against Serb civilians.[22] The government also permitted the ICTY to establish a liaison office in Zagreb and approved a declaration that recognized ICTY's jurisdiction over operations Flash and Storm.[23] Things were looking good, and international justice organizations were happy.[24]

---

20. Human Rights Watch, "World Report 2001: Croatia."

21. This was the case of Mladen Naletilić Tuta, a Bosnian Croat accused of atrocities against the Bosniac population in the city of Mostar in 1993.

22. The alleged massacre occurred in the Croatian city of Gospić in 1991.

23. Croatian Parliament, *Deklaracija o suradnji s međunarodnim kaznenim sudom u Den Haagu* [Declaration on Cooperation with the International Criminal Tribunal in The Hague], *Narodne novine*, no. 41/2000, April 14, 2000.

24. Human Rights Watch, "World Report 2001: Croatia."

Internally, however, trouble was brewing. The governing six-party coalition was beginning to show signs of strain, and no issue made this clearer than the way Croatia was dealing with the increasingly aggressive ICTY prosecutions of Croatian nationals as well as Bosnian Croats for atrocities committed against Serbs and Bosniacs. Over the next couple of years, international justice for Croatia was a game of push and pull, a balancing act between the strong elite desire to bring Croatia into the EU fold and the need to appease domestic constituencies, many of which were offended by the very idea of transitional justice for Croatian crimes.

Cooperation with the ICTY: One Step Forward, Two Steps Back

The first jolt to the Croatian feeling of self-satisfaction with its improved international reputation came from The Hague in March 2000 with the conviction and a harsh forty-five-year prison sentence for Bosnian Croat general Tihomir Blaškić. This was the highest sentence issued by the court up to that time.[25] The conviction was especially shocking for the Croatian public because it delineated a direct relationship between the Croatian leadership and its Bosnian proxies, until then largely hidden from public view. Legally, the ICTY ruling was problematic for Croatia because it defined the Bosnian war as an international conflict, with Croatia as an aggressor party. This was precedent-setting and a cause of great concern for the Croatian government. Croatia's relationship with the ICTY deteriorated further in 2000 when ICTY chief prosecutor Carla Del Ponte gave indications that more indictments of Croatian generals were under way and sharply criticized the Croatian government for failure to hand over requested documents and allow interviews of high-profile officials.[26]

The government response was to rebuke the ICTY and redefine the war in Croatia's terms. In October 2000, the Croatian parliament adopted the Declaration on the Homeland War, which asserted that between 1991 and 1995, Croatia had waged "a just and legitimate defense...to defend its internationally

---

25. Blaškić was convicted of personal and command responsibility for the massacre of Bosniacs in the Bosnian village of Ahmići in 1992. In 2004, however, he won on appeal after showing that the Tuđman government had purposefully withheld exonerating evidence from his defense team. He was released in August 2004 and was greeted in Croatia as a wartime hero. Drago Hedl, "Disquiet at 'Hero's Homecoming,'" IWPR, August 27, 2004.

26. International Criminal Tribunal for the Former Yugoslavia, "Address to the UN Security Council by Carla Del Ponte, Prosecutor of the International Criminal Tribunals for the Former Yugoslavia and Rwanda, November 21, 2000," press release, November 24, 2000.

recognized borders against Greater Serbia's aggression" and that this war was one of "liberation," not one of conquest.[27] Later that year, the government issued a thirteen-point list of conditions redefining the terms of Croatia's cooperation with the ICTY.[28]

International Justice and Democratic Consolidation

The issue of the Croatian war legacy and international pressures for justice for the crimes committed put a serious strain on the governing coalition. In February 2001, a local Croatian court acted on ICTY investigations and issued an arrest warrant for Mirko Norac, a famed Croatian general and war hero, now accused of war crimes against Serb civilians in 1991. Croatian right-wing parties and veterans' groups were quick to mobilize and organize street demonstrations throughout Croatia. The biggest protest was held in the city of Split on February 11, 2001, with 150,000 people marching in protest of Norac's pending arrest.[29] Some of the more memorable placards read, "We are all Mirko Norac" and "Hands off our Holy War."[30]

Not only did the protesters express anger over Norac's arrest warrant, but they used his case as a rallying point for a more general grievance against the government's new policy of cooperation with the ICTY, which they saw as unscrupulous giving in to international pressures.[31] The protesters also viewed cooperation with the ICTY as further humiliation of Croatia by Serbs. Mirko Čondić, representative of the main headquarters for the Protection of the Dignity of the Homeland War gave a rousing speech that noted,

> Mesić and Račan seem to want Croatia to kneel down in front of the Serbs and beg for forgiveness. By putting Norac on trial they want to put the whole Croatian army and nation on trial.... For the trial of Norac is

---

27. Drago Hedl, "Croatia: Rewriting History," IWPR, April 16, 2004.

28. International Crisis Group, "Croatia."

29. One of the fiercest anti-ICTY and antigovernment speeches at the Split rally was delivered by HDZ official Ivo Sanader, the current prime minister of Croatia.

30. Opinion polls conducted during the crisis showed that two-thirds of Croatians strongly opposed Norac's extradition to The Hague, while half of those polled believed that Croat generals should not be investigated by either the Croatian or the Hague judiciary. Zdravka Soldić-Arar, "Dvije trećine građana protiv je izručenja Norca u Haag!" [Two Thirds of Citizens against Extradition of Norac to the Hague], *Slobodna Dalmacija*, February 10, 2001.

31. "Croatian Rally Protests U.N. and Demands Early Elections," *New York Times*, February 12, 2001.

the trial of Croatian freedom, and the freedom of Norac is the freedom of the Croatian people. As long as we the creators of the Croatian state are alive there will be no trial against Norac.[32]

The government was at first taken aback by this massive outcry of public support for an indicted war criminal, and it made futile appeals to the public that the demonstrations were hurting Croatia's international reputation and its appeal as a destination for foreign commerce and tourism.[33] It then regrouped and countered the right wing, accusing it of using the veterans to advance its own political goals of destabilizing the government and removing it from power. Prime Minister Račan addressed the parliament and reiterated that the government would not give into the right-wing pressure to end cooperation with the ICTY. The stakes, he argued, were too high; domestically, the crisis threatened to undermine Croatia's democratic legal order and judicial independence, and internationally, it risked further isolating Croatia after the honeymoon it had enjoyed in the aftermath of Tuđman's death.[34] In other words, Račan presented the issue of justice for war crimes as a central part of establishing the rule of law and consolidating democracy in Croatia, necessary for Croatia's European pretensions.[35] President Mesić also had harsh words for the nationalists, whom he accused of manipulating the crisis for their own political gains.[36] Even Dražen Budiša, HSLS leader and cabinet member most opposed to the ICTY, stated that he could not defend Norac given the serious nature of the indictment.[37]

The crisis was finally diffused with a compromise—ICTY prosecutor Carla Del Ponte agreed to defer the Norac case to the Croatian judiciary and, for the time being, to give up on asking for Norac's transfer to The Hague.[38] This unprecedented move helped diffuse the political crisis and relieve some of the pressure on the Croatian government. Croatian papers even declared, "Carla Del Ponte

32. Snježana Šetka, Zoran Šagolj, and Mirjana Ljubić, "Split: 150 tisuća puta 'Svi smo mi Mirko Norac'" [Split: 150 Thousand Times "We Are All Mirko Norac"], *Slobodna Dalmacija*, February 12, 2001.

33. "Croatians Rally to War Crimes Suspect," BBC News, February 11, 2001.

34. B92 network, February 10, 2001, http://www.b92.net.

35. Even at the height of the Norac crisis, opinion polls showed that the overwhelming majority—79 percent—of the Croatian public supported Croatia's EU membership bid. EurActiv, February 20, 2001.

36. "Croatian Protesters Lift Blockade," BBC News, February 12, 2001.

37. "We can't defend this....Only a coward kills women and children." Budiša was quoted in Peter Finn, "In Croatia, Law vs. Patriotism; Thousands Rally for Ex-General Accused of War Crimes," *Washington Post*, February 16, 2001.

38. International Criminal Tribunal for the Former Yugoslavia, "Statement by the Prosecutor concerning the Croatian Judiciary's Investigation of General Mirko Norac," press release, February 21, 2001.

saved Račan."[39] After receiving assurances from The Hague that he would not be transferred there, Norac surrendered to the Croatian authorities and insisted that he had never intended to undermine the nascent democracy in Croatia. In fact, he said, "Fighting for the country, I also fought for its legal institutions."[40]

In many ways, the Račan government came out on top in this first public crisis regarding the issue of justice for past abuses. The strategy the government used focused on accusing the right-wing nationalists of undermining Croatian legal institutions and the rule of law and order that Croatia had fought for in its war of independence. In other words, the government accused the nationalists of undermining the Croatian state that they themselves held so dear.

The Račan government was also helped by the ICTY prosecutor's sensitivity to Croatia's domestic political turmoil and willingness to compromise and defer the controversial case to Croatian courts. It is possible that, at least in part, the reason for ICTY's softer approach was a sense among international actors that exerting too strong a pressure on Croatia at the same time the new Serbian government was enjoying the post-Milošević international honeymoon would be politically inappropriate, especially since the Serbian elites were not showing any significant improvement in the realm of international justice.[41] This delicate dance of mirroring Serbian and Croatian action on issues of transitional justice has remained a constant in the two countries' domestic attitudes and in international approaches to transitional justice in the region.

International Justice Absolving the State

This early leniency by the ICTY was soon to be replaced by a much harsher stance toward Croatia's continuing reluctance to cooperate with The Hague. And again, the impetus for a shift in international policy toward Croatia was influenced by events in Serbia. After Milošević was transferred to The Hague in June 2001, the ICTY prosecutor turned her attention to Croatia and stepped up pressure on the Račan government to improve its lackluster efforts to cooperate with the tribunal. In July 2001, the ICTY prosecutor issued indictments against two high-ranking Croatian generals, Rahmi Ademi and Ante Gotovina. Ademi was charged with committing crimes in the Medžak Pocket area in 1993, and

---

39. Višnja Starešina, "Carla Del Ponte spasila Račana" [Carla Del Ponte Saved Račan], *Večernji list*, February 22, 2001.
40. B92, February 22, 2001.
41. International Crisis Group, "Croatia."

Gotovina with a "joint criminal enterprise" of forced deportation and murder of Croatian Serbs during Operation Storm in 1995.[42]

These indictments sent shock waves through Croatia and caused the Račan government a much greater headache than any previous altercation with the ICTY. The fact that the Gotovina indictment labeled Operation Storm a joint criminal enterprise and not a legitimate counterterrorist operation aimed at retaking Croatian territory from Serb rebels enraged Croatian officials and put the Račan government in a particularly precarious position. If the government acted on the indictments—in line with its obligations to the ICTY—and arrested the suspects, it not only would anger Croatian nationalists but would have a hard time explaining this move to the Croatian public, which understood Operation Storm to be the final act of Croatia's liberation against Serb rebels and therefore the military maneuver that had made today's independent state of Croatia possible. To criminalize Operation Storm was, in effect, to criminalize the Croatian state itself. At the same time, if the government ignored the ICTY indictments or refused to act on them, it feared angering international friends, freezing international aid and putting a stop to Croatia's dream of joining the EU, the ultimate prize for ICTY cooperation.

The Račan government, therefore, was in a serious bind. It did not help that the ruling coalition was beginning to fall apart at the seams. The second largest coalition partner, the HSLS, was showing signs of internal strain, as HSLS leader Budiša was moving the party further to the right, competing for Tuđman's HDZ voters, while other HSLS officials preferred to maintain a more centrist position. This ideological and strategic split clearly played itself out in the parliament during the debate about what to do with the ICTY indictments. Budiša directed his party MPs to vote against cooperation with the ICTY, but half of his parliamentary delegation sided with Račan and the other half resigned to protest Račan's decision to arrest the generals, leading to a major intercoalition showdown.[43]

The nationalists threatened to hold street protests once again. They invoked powerful symbols of the Croatian war, such as the siege of Vukovar, to stress the heroism and sacrifice of Croatian war heroes. A coalition of veterans' groups issued a statement claiming that the ICTY indictments threatened the very survival of the Croatian state and that the government's decision to cooperate

---

42. The strongly worded indictment read, in part, "Between 5 August 1995 and 15 November 1995, Croatian forces committed numerous acts of killing, arson, looting, harassment, terror and threat of physical harm to person and property. By these acts, Croatian forces intimidated and coerced Krajina Serbs into leaving their villages, hamlets and homes." ICTY, *Prosecutor vs. Ante Gotovina*, case no. IT-01-45-I, June 8, 2001.

43. B92, July 8, 2001.

indicated it was not protecting Croatian national values but instead had "bargained and betrayed all values achieved in the Homeland War."[44]

In the light of all this domestic turmoil, Prime Minister Račan called for a vote of confidence in the government and with the support of the HSLS splinters won a surprising victory. However, even though he won over his nationalist opponents, Račan made clear that he in effect agreed with their objections to the ICTY indictments and that any cooperation with the tribunal would be reluctant at best.[45] He even enunciated his objections to the indictments in a letter to ICTY prosecutor Del Ponte. The objections focused on the ICTY's use of command, as opposed to individual, responsibility for any war crimes carried out during Operation Storm, as well as on the general interpretation of the operation as somehow criminal rather than strategic and defensive.[46]

Although his opposition to the indictments was clear, Račan still decided to cooperate with the ICTY and arrest the generals. He explained this apparent inconsistency in purely instrumental terms. He argued that Croatia had a legal obligation to cooperate with the tribunal and that the country's application to the EU would be sidelined if Croatia refused to cooperate with The Hague. He warned that "to turn down the request from The Hague would be to plunge Croatia into the abysses of the Balkans conflict."[47] Furthermore, there was increasing concern that political instability would hurt the Croatian economy, especially its booming tourist sector.[48]

The Croatian government's strategy was multifaceted. While Račan focused on international rewards, Croatian president Mesić argued that individualization of crimes in fact would serve to preserve the legacy of the homeland war, not taint it. In his address to the nation, he said, "The government did the only thing it could do and made the only decision possible....The fact that crimes were committed during the Homeland War on the Croatian side casts a shadow on the entire war and all its participants, as long as those responsible for the crimes are not indicted and convicted."[49] In a statement that he later repeated many times, Mesić said, "The Croatian nation should not and will not be a hostage to those who bloodied their hands, bringing shame upon Croatia's name—no matter what credits they might have otherwise."[50]

44. Cited in Peskin and Boduszynski, "International Justice," 1141 n. 51.
45. International Crisis Group, "Croatia."
46. Ibid.
47. "Croatia in Turmoil over Extraditions," BBC News, July 8, 2001.
48. "Political Pitfalls for Croatia's Economy," BBC News, July 9, 2001.
49. B92, July 8, 2001.
50. Carlotta Gall and Marlise Simons, "Croatia in Turmoil After Agreeing to Send 2 to Tribunal," *New York Times,* July 9, 2001.

The Croatian government's decision to arrest and transfer the two generals met with instant international praise. United States officials promised to step up their international support to Croatia.[51] Chris Patten, the EU's commissioner for external relations "applauded the decision of the Croatian Government" and "urged the people of Croatia to support that decision, difficult though that may be for many of them to do: it is the only course of action open to their government if it is serious about Croatia's European future and international commitments."[52] International actors reiterated Prime Minister Račan's position that acts of international justice were important internationally; they were European and would take Croatia into Europe's fold. Transitional justice was once again placed in the service of the Croatian state and its European strategy. Račan also used it domestically, as his victory in the parliament over nationalist opponents consolidated his hold on power and marginalized his major coalition rival, HSLS. In this case, transitional justice was used to both obtain international legitimacy and deal with domestic political opponents.

Transitional justice was also used to further perpetuate inaction at home. After scoring international and domestic points, Račan failed to follow through on his international promises. As stated earlier, he in effect sided with the nationalists' critique of ICTY indictments and also failed to arrest Gotovina, who quickly went into hiding, remaining at large for more than four years. General Ademi, on the other hand, surrendered to the tribunal in July 2001.[53] Ademi's surrender placated the international community for the time being and greatly helped the Croatian government, which could point to him as a sign of Croatian cooperation. At the same time, the government could ignore the fact that the slow move to arrest Gotovina, a much more popular Croatian war hero than Ademi, most likely helped him escape. For Croatian nationalists, Gotovina became an almost mythical figure, with a vast network of supporters who helped provide him refuge.

To sum up, Prime Minister Račan used transitional justice as a rhetorical tool to score international points without alienating domestic constituencies. As he told the parliament just before the July 2001 confidence vote, "It is hard for one nation to face dark pages of its history—even harder for a small nation. But we have to give a chance to the world to respect us, while also fighting for our truth."[54] Constantly in fear of vocal nationalists, right-wing parties, and remnants of Tuđman's HDZ, Račan was worried that his communist background would

---

51. Peskin and Boduszynski, "International Justice," 1129.

52. EU press release, Speech/01/338, July 10, 2001.

53. Ademi is an ethnic Albanian, and as a non-Croat outsider he never enjoyed the kind of popular support in Croatia that Gotovina did.

54. Quoted in "Government in Croatia Survives Vote on Generals," *New York Times*, July 16, 2001.

make him vulnerable to charges of patriotic deficit and would ultimately lead to electoral defeat by right-wing parties, if not an actual coup.[55] He then tried to overcompensate for this "communist mortgage," a politically lethal label in virulently anticommunist Croatia, by placating the nationalists whenever they raised objections regarding issues of justice.[56] In fact, by siding with the nationalists' arguments against the ICTY, Račan ensured that they would continue to have a powerful voice in all future debates about transitional justice in Croatia.[57] Račan, in the words of his allies, "had neither a vacuum nor a mop" with which to clean up Croatian nationalists.[58]

This inability of Račan's government to make a serious break with the past, acting out of necessity only when international pressures became unbearable, was evident in all consequent crises that would come with each new ICTY indictment.[59] Račan's cautious dance, however, did not impress either his supporters or his opponents. He was too scared to be bold with nationalists and he took moderates for granted, so he ended up without the support of either bloc. In addition, he lost many friends in the international community who had no patience with his continual equivocating on the issue of justice and international cooperation.

Unusual Suspect: A Croatian Hard-Liner's U-Turn

The November 2003 parliamentary elections shook up the Croatian government. Račan's SDP suffered significant losses, and the HDZ had enough parliamentary seats to set up a ruling coalition with Ivo Sanader as prime minister. Even though Račan's SDP had enough potential coalition partners to form a government, however unstable, there is evidence that Račan decided to pass on the 2003 elections and hand over the reign to Sanader and the HDZ, mostly because he did not want to be the one to have to arrest Gotovina. Račan's apparent calculation was that Gotovina's imminent arrest would destabilize Sanader's government and Račan could then walk in, the major international headache resolved.[60]

---

55. Ivo Josipović (Zagreb Law School professor and Croatia's premier expert on war crimes legislation), in interview with author, November 28, 2005, Zagreb.

56. Ivica Đikić (war crimes investigative reporter for *Feral Tribune*), in interview with author, November 4, 2005, Zagreb.

57. Peskin and Boduszynski, "International Justice," 1130.

58. Josipović, interview.

59. It was perhaps most pronounced in the case of general Janko Bobetko, an eighty-three-year old former army chief of staff and hero of the Croatian homeland war, indicted in September 2002 for crimes against Serb civilians in 1993.

60. Đikić, interview.

Although the international community expressed some concern at the return of the HDZ to power and expected Sanader, a hard-liner on the issue of international justice, to be even more reluctant to cooperate with the ICTY than a weakened Račan had been, he surprised almost everybody—in Croatia and abroad—with his businesslike approach to ICTY cooperation and a renewed energy to bring Croatia closer to Brussels by way of The Hague.

When in February 2004 the ICTY indicted Croatian generals Ivan Čermak and Mladen Markač for crimes against humanity committed during Operation Storm, the Sanader government's reaction was markedly different from its predecessor's. For one, both Čermak and Markač immediately surrendered to the tribunal. This was followed by the transfer of six other ICTY indictees, Bosnian Croat military and political leaders, who flew from Zagreb to The Hague on April 5, 2004, two weeks before the European Commission was to issue an opinion on Croatia's application for EU membership.[61] There were other visible changes in the way Croatia was approaching cooperation with the ICTY. The Croatian Department for Cooperation with the ICTY was moved from under direct government's control to the Justice Department, a structural change intended to "move cooperation from the political to the purely legal sphere."[62]

The 2004 surrenders and the role of Sanader's government in providing documentary evidence to the Hague tribunal led ICTY chief prosecutor Carla Del Ponte to make a statement that reverberated across the country: "Croatia is now cooperating fully with the Tribunal."[63] Del Ponte's statement was significant in itself, but it was particularly important for Croatia a year before the start of negotiations for EU membership. In November 2004, however, Del Ponte revised her assessment, this time stating that Croatia would be considered fully compliant only after it transferred fugitive Ante Gotovina to The Hague.[64]

Domestically, however, Sanader's shift in strategy was presented not only as good for the Croatian EU bid but also as a comprehensive strategy that helped the ICTY indictees themselves. Urging suspects to surrender voluntarily and assisting ICTY investigations meant that the "Croatian government is convinced of [the suspects'] innocence and will provide all the legal, technical and other means for their defense," according to Croatian justice minister Vesna

61. Human Rights Watch, "World Report 2005: Croatia," New York, January 13, 2005.

62. Author's interview with staff of the Department for Cooperation with the ICTY, November 16, 2005, Zagreb.

63. International Criminal Tribunal for the Former Yugoslavia, "Carla Del Ponte's Address to the UN Security Council, June 29, 2004," press release, June 30, 2004.

64. International Criminal Tribunal for the Former Yugoslavia, "Carla Del Ponte's Address to the UN Security Council, November 23, 2004," press release, November 23, 2004.

Škare-Ožbolt.[65] Indeed, the Sanader government identified a four-prong domestic strategy of cooperation with the ICTY, which involved "protecting the historical truth about the homeland war, helping suspects, allowing suspects to defend themselves while on bail, and finally transferring ICTY cases to Croatian courts."[66] In other words, the Sanader government managed to turn cooperation with the ICTY, the issue that had caused such great problems for Prime Minister Račan, into a win-win situation for Croatia—scoring international points for cooperation while ensuring that the public interpretation of the Croatian past would remain ideologically intact.

Things were only to get better for Croatia. On December 7, 2005, General Ante Gotovina, one of the three men most wanted by the Hague tribunal,[67] was arrested in the Spanish Canary Islands after a massive international manhunt. Even though public opinion surveys pointed to the general sense of "unfairness" at Gotovina's arrest,[68] in a sharp difference from the public outcry that followed Norac's arrest in 2001, only about five hundred people protested Gotovina's arrest in Zagreb, and about fifty thousand people gathered in Split—a far cry from the hundreds of thousands that had held Croatia hostage just four years earlier.

The Croatian government's reaction was ecstatic. Not only was the government vindicated in its claims that Gotovina was not hiding on Croatian territory—a claim Sanader's government had been trying to prove to the ICTY prosecutors for years—but his arrest closed the final chapter of Croatia's relationship with the ICTY. With his arrest, there were no more formal obstacles to Croatia's EU accession.

But equally significant for the Croatian government, with the last Croatian suspect in custody, Croatia could begin the comprehensive project it had long hoped for: to individualize alleged crimes against non-Croat populations and exonerate the Croatian state. And indeed, on January 10, 2006, Prime Minister Ivo Sanader met with defense lawyers of all indicted Croatian generals to discuss a joint strategy for their defense before the ICTY. The government also hired respected Croatian lawyers and historians to work together on the defense project, whose main purpose was to refute the ICTY prosecution's claim that

---

65. "Croatian Generals to Surrender," BBC News, March 8, 2004.

66. Staff of the Department for Cooperation with the ICTY, interview.

67. The remaining high-profile suspects still at large at the time were Bosnian Serbs Ratko Mladić and Radovan Karadžić. Karadžić was arrested in July 2008.

68. In an opinion survey conducted immediately upon Gotovina's arrest, 61 percent considered the arrest "bad news." The same number felt the ICTY indictment of Gotovina was "unfounded." United Nations Development Program (UNDP), "Transitional Justice: Assessment Survey of Conditions in the former Yugoslavia," Belgrade, 2006. Another opinion poll put the number of Croatian citizens opposed to Gotovina's arrest at 47 percent. *Večernji list*, December 8, 2005.

1995's Operation Storm was a "joint state criminal enterprise aimed at removing the entire Serb population from Croatia.[69] Finally, in June 2006, the Croatian parliament adopted a comprehensive Declaration on Operation Storm, which qualified the operation as legitimated by international law, as well as "victorious," "international," "antiterrorist," "decisive," "unforgettable," and "final."[70] Slaven Letica, the parliament MP who submitted the declaration for consideration, argued that the ICTY concept of joint criminal enterprise would have a negative impact on the international legitimacy of the Croatian state and on the Croatian national consciousness but would also allow Serb refugees to ask for reparations.[71] Most important, the declaration stated:

> It is the duty of the Croatian parliament, Croatian expert community, Croatian scientific and educational institutions and media to over time turn "Operation Storm" into a battle that must not and will not be forgotten: into a decisive, glorious, victorious battle of the Homeland War, that will become part of the Croatian "useful past" for future generations. Preserving the memory of "Operation Storm" should also include the right of all scientists, journalists, human rights activists and others to substantively and freely investigate the dark side of this and all other operations: violations of war and humanitarian law, crimes, human casualties and suffering....."Operation Storm"...should be remembered in history not only as victorious and decisive, but also the "last Croatian battle.[72]

The significance of this statement was that it further affirmed Operation Storm—the military action that rid Croatia of its entire Serb population—as the foundational battle of the war, the battle that made Croatia. It made it official Croatian policy to treat the operation historically as glorious and victorious and not as controversial and problematic. However, it left open the possibility that individual crimes had been committed—as a matter not of state policy but of individual personal responsibility.

Thus the clearest evidence of Croatia's cooperation with the ICTY—the arrest of Ante Gotovina—was used to buttress Croatian nationalist claims and exonerate the Croatian state from charges of ethnic cleansing or other serious war crimes. International justice here did not serve the purpose of opening up the debate about

---

69. Željka Vujčić, "Croatia: Gotovina's Last Battle?" *Transitions Online* 1, no. 17 (2006), http://www.tol.cz.

70. Croatian Parliament, *Deklaracija o Oluji* [Declaration on Operation Storm], *Narodne novine*, no. 76/2006, June 30, 2006.

71. Humanitarian Law Center, "Tranziciona pravda u post-jugoslovenskim zemljama: Izveštaj za 2006. godinu" [Transitional Justice in Post-Yugoslav States: 2006 Report], Belgrade, 2007, 35.

72. Croatian Parliament, *Deklaracija o Oluji*.

the past, but in effect it closed it. Since Gotovina's transfer to The Hague was the last requirement Croatia had to fulfill on its path to the EU, international actors no longer had much leverage on influencing Croatian debates about past crimes. By fulfilling international institutional requirements, Croatia in fact managed to use them to perpetuate nationalist mythology and advance its state interests. At the same time, instrumental compliance allowed Croatia to reclaim its international legitimacy as a global citizen and to elevate its international reputation and status.

The Challenge of Domestic Trials

In addition to cooperating with the Hague tribunal, Croatia was under pressure from international promoters of transitional justice to rigorously prosecute war crimes in front of its own courts.[73] However, Croatia's track record in prosecuting war crimes has been the subject of great concern for organizations of international justice.[74]

Ethnic bias, unprofessional court proceedings, willingness to prosecute non-Croats while offering immunity to Croatian suspects, trials in absentia,[75] lack of witness protection, and poor legal representation of victims have continued to plague Croatian domestic war-crimes trials even as the government steps up its cooperation with the Hague tribunal.[76] The status of Croatian domestic trials is especially critical during the so-called ICTY completion strategy, by which the Hague tribunal plans to transfer remaining cases to local courts as the tribunal winds down its operations by 2010.

Blatant ethnic bias in prosecutions has been aptly documented by both local and international human rights organizations.[77] Many Croatian Serbs have been

---

73. Author's interview with staff of the Croatian Helsinki Committee for Human Rights, November 8, 2005, Zagreb.

74. Human Rights Watch, "Croatia: EU Must Address Domestic War Crimes Trials," December 20, 2004, http://hrw.org/english/docs/2004/12/20/croati9917.htm; Human Rights Watch, "Justice at Risk: War Crimes Trials in Croatia, Bosnia and Herzegovina, and Serbia and Montenegro," vol. 16, no. 7(D) New York, October 13, 2004; Thierry Cruvellier and Marta Valiñas, "Croatia: Selected Developments in Transitional Justice," International Center for Transitional Justice, New York, December 2006.

75. Trials in absentia have been a persistent problem in Croatia. Croatia's chief war-crimes prosecutor opposes such trials, but they nevertheless continue to take place. At the end of October 2007, nineteen of the twenty-three defendants on trial in absentia were Serbs. Human Rights Watch, "Overview of Human Rights Issues in Croatia," New York, January 31, 2008.

76. Centre for Peace, Nonviolence and Human Rights, "Monitoring of War Crimes Trials: Annual Report 2005," Osijek, Croatia, 2005.

77. Of 3,666 people charged with war crimes since 1991, 3,604 were prosecuted for involvement in aggression against Croatia (i.e., they were ethnic Serbs), while only 62 were members of the Croatian armed forces. See Human Rights Watch, "Overview." Profound ethnic bias has been reported by

prosecuted on far weaker charges than ethnic Croats have been.[78] In many cases, Serb defendants have been convicted even when evidence of guilt was clearly lacking.[79] At the same time, trials of Croats accused of war crimes are far more likely to result in acquittals. After many years of careful monitoring of domestic trials, the OSCE issued a blunt statement: "At all stages of procedure from arrest to conviction, the application of a double standard against Serb defendants and in favor of Croat defendants continues as a general rule."[80]

A famous case that captured public attention in both Croatia and Serbia was the *Lora* case, when eight members of the Croatian military police were accused of torture and killing of Serb detainees in the Lora military prison in Split in 1992.[81] The lengthy trial was mired in controversy from the beginning. For example, the suspects were welcomed by loud applause from the public at the start of the trial. Even in the face of abundant evidence of the officers' guilt, including first-person witness accounts, the presiding judge addressed the accused by their first names, shook their hands when they entered the courtroom, appeared to mock the testimony of a witness, and routinely made inflammatory anti-Serb ethnic statements and praised the accused for their patriotism and service in the homeland war.[82] In November 2002, all the accused were acquitted,[83] a verdict that caused great outrage in Serbia but also serious alarm within international

---

international organizations throughout the past decade. For some illustrative data, see "Key Findings of the 2005 Progress Report on Croatia," European Union, November 9, 2005. In the year 2002, for example, 83 percent of Serb defendants were found guilty of war crimes, while only 18 percent of Croatian defendants were convicted. Conversely, 17 percent of Serb defendants were acquitted or the prosecution was dropped, while 82 percent of Croats were found not guilty or the charges were dropped. See Organization for Security and Cooperation in Europe, "Background Report: Domestic War Crimes Trials in 2002," Zagreb, March 1, 2004. In 2004, Croatian courts prosecuted only two cases of war crimes carried out by Croats against the Serbs. See Human Rights Watch, "World Report 2004: Croatia," New York, January 13, 2005. Of the only five new war-crimes indictments issued in 2005, all were against Serb suspects. See Organization for Security and Cooperation in Europe, "Background Report: Domestic War Crimes Trials in 2005," Zagreb, September 13, 2006.

78. For example, Croatian prosecutors have indicted Serbs for minor acts such as the theft of flour, plates, or tapestry from a house (charged as pillage) or the knocking out of a tooth (charged as an inhuman act). Human Rights Watch, "Broken Promises: Impediments to Refugee Return in Croatia," vol. 15, no. 6(D), New York, September 3, 2003.

79. For a particularly egregious case of ethnically biased prosecution and conviction, see Human Rights Watch, "Croatia: The Case of Ivanka Savić," Briefing Paper, New York, July 19, 2004.

80. Organization for Security and Cooperation in Europe, Status Report no. 13, Zagreb, December, 2003.

81. Testimonies of Lora survivors are detailed in a documentary *Lora: Testimonies,* produced by Factum Agency, Zagreb.

82. B92, November 22, 2002. Also Amnesty International, "A Shadow on Croatia's Future."

83. In explaining his decision to acquit, the judge stated that had the witness been tortured as much as he claimed, "not even Rambo would have survived." Quoted in Drago Hedl, "Croatia: Lora Retrial Eases Pressure on Sanader," IWPR, May 27, 2004.

justice organizations.[84] Croatian veterans and nationalists were pleased, but the verdict came at the cost of a huge embarrassment to the Croatian government at a time when Croatia was trying to prove to the ICTY that its courts were fully capable of conducting war-crimes trials without the intervention of The Hague.

Perhaps in response to increasing international criticisms of the way it was conducting its war-crimes trials, but primarily in fulfillment of EU requirements for judicial reform in preparation for EU accession, Croatia restructured its judiciary and created specialized domestic war-crimes chambers.[85] The October 2003 law provided for the creation of four district courts as "special courts" for the prosecution and trial of war-crimes cases.[86]

The international reaction to the creation of specialized war chambers has been largely encouraging, but serious concerns remain. One of the main concerns was the inclusion in 2004 of command responsibility in the Croatian penal code, a legal move that continues to be bitterly resisted by Croatian judges because its rigorous application may end up implicating the Croatian state in crimes against humanity.[87] The concept of command responsibility remains problematic even for leading Croatian legal experts, who argue that from a strict legal perspective command responsibility shows "neither a clear causal link of responsibility nor a clear showing of guilt."[88] However, as the leading Croatian international legal expert said, "Command responsibility may be important and necessary for Croatia for moral reasons.... There are great moments in history for which law has no clear answer."[89]

There is some evidence, however, that the creation of specialized war-crimes chambers has somewhat professionalized Croatian prosecution of war crimes. For example, the infamous *Lora* case was retried in the county court of Split in September 2005, after the Croatian Supreme Court annulled the acquittals in

---

84. Amnesty International, "A Shadow on Croatia's Future"; Human Rights Watch, "Justice at Risk."

85. Organization for Security and Cooperation in Europe (OSCE). "Background Report 2005."

86. Croatian Parliament, *Zakon o primjeni Statuta Međunarodnoga kaznenog suda i progonu za kaznena djela protiv međunarodnoga ratnog i humanitarnog prava* [Law on the Application of the Statute of the International Criminal Court and on the Prosecution of Criminal Acts against the International Law on War and Humanitarian Law], *Narodne novine,* no. 175/2003, November 4, 2003.

87. Ivo Josipović, ed., *Responsibility for War Crimes: Croatian Perspective* (Zagreb: University of Zagreb, 2005); Cruvellier and Valiñas, "Croatia."

88. Croatian legal experts specifically object to Article 7(3) of the ICTY statute, which states: "The fact that any of the acts referred to in articles 2 to 5 of the present statute was committed by a subordinate does not relieve his superior of criminal responsibility if he knew or had reason to know that the subordinate was about to commit such acts or had done so and the superior failed to take the necessary and reasonable measures to prevent such acts or to punish the perpetrators thereof."

89. Josipović, interview.

August 2004. In March 2006, all eight accused were convicted and sentenced to six to eight years in prison.[90] In 2005, the supreme court reversed 60 percent of all war-crimes verdicts.[91] In 2006, Croatian war-crimes chambers took up several important cases of war crimes committed by Croat nationals against Serbs. In addition, the Croatian Supreme Court has increasingly refused trials in absentia and reversed such convictions. The supreme court is getting more aggressive in reviewing past convictions. However, ethnic bias in prosecutions remains, with Serbs still forming the vast majority of domestic prosecutions and convictions. Continuing monitoring of war-crimes cases still demonstrates an inconsistent approach toward Croat and Serb suspects, especially in terms of indictment, prosecution, conviction, and sentencing.[92] Trial observers have also noted an unusually high percentage of repeated trials. Between 2002 and 2007, more than half of war-crimes trials had to be repeated because of judicial incompetence or reluctance to issue an unpopular sentence.[93] Indictments of Croatian suspects have often been so vague as to be easily defeated in trials, and prosecutors have been reluctant to pursue cases of providing shelter to fugitive war-crimes suspects.[94] Perhaps the most persistent problem is the continued predominance of trials in local courts where the crimes occurred rather than in the four specialized war-crimes chambers, which remain understaffed and to which war-crimes cares are rarely referred.[95] This practice is also in clear violation of the 2003 law.[96] Since most domestic war-crimes trials end up in local courts, there have been multiple problems with judicial professionalism and impartiality.[97] For example, in November 2005, the Osijek city mayor and member of parliament Ante Đapić held a press conference and publicly disclosed the names of nineteen witnesses prepared to testify in the trial held in front of the Osijek court. The names were then repeated in the media, creating an atmosphere of insecurity and hostility for potential witnesses who wanted to come forward.[98]

---

90. Humanitarian Law Center, "Successful Retrial for Case Lora," March 3, 2006.

91. United Nations Development Program, "Transitional Justice."

92. Human Rights Watch, "Human Rights Report: Croatia," New York, January 11, 2007.

93. Centre for Peace, Nonviolence and Human Rights, "Monitoring of War Crimes Trials: Report for January–June 2008," Osijek, Croatia, September 26, 2008.

94. Ibid.

95. Humanitarian Law Center, "Transitional Justice."

96. Centre for Peace Nonviolence and Human Rights, "Monitoring 2008."

97. For example, many judges in local courts who end up with war crimes cases are experts not in criminal but in civil law, which makes them professionally unsuitable to conduct these kinds of cases. Ibid. For examples of blatant ethnic bias in the case of Mihajlo Hrastov, a Croat accused of crimes against ethnic Serbs, see Human Rights Watch, "Overview."

98. Documenta, "Povodom objavljivanja imena potencijalnih svjedoka u istrazi zločina nad civilima u Osijeku 1991" [Regarding the Disclosure of Names of Potential Witnesses in the Investigation of Crimes against Civilians in Osijek in 1991], press release, December 27, 2005.

Domestic war-crimes trials have also been heavily influenced by the Croatian parliament. For example, the parliament directly injected itself into the high-profile trial of Branimir Glavaš, a sitting member of the Croatian parliament, once a high-ranking official in the HDZ and wartime commander of the city of Osijek defense forces. In 2006, Glavaš and six other suspects were accused of torturing and killing Serb civilians in Osijek in 1991. In an extraordinary decision, the parliament voted not to strip the accused of his parliamentary immunity, a necessary step to begin proceedings against him and determine his police custody. The parliament's decision allowed Glavaš, the accused mastermind of the massacre, to be released on bail pending trial, while his six coconspirators remained in jail.[99] This decision by the parliament seriously undermined the legal process and, according to Croatian human rights groups, threatened to undermine trust in the Croatian judiciary more generally.[100] The Glavaš case caused further embarrassment for the Croatian government when in September 2008, after two years of proceedings, the judge threw out the case because of defense delays and ordered it to begin anew. Human rights groups called the declared mistrial an obstruction of justice and a sign of the declining authority of domestic war-crimes trials.[101] The politicization of the Glavaš case was seen by Croatian transitional justice activists as a harsh blow because they considered the case the most significant domestic war-crimes trial Croatia had conducted since the end of the war.[102]

Problems like these have attracted the attention of European Union representatives, who issued a stern letter to the Croatian government listing complaints about the conduct of domestic war-crimes trials. The letter warned that such conduct would cause Croatia significant problems in making the judicial and legal reforms necessary for Croatia's European integration.[103] Croatia, however, has much more leeway in its approach to justice locally, as the EU has attached no conditions for progress on domestic war-crimes trials comparable to the ones on cooperation with the ICTY.[104] Croatia has brushed off international criticism

---

99. One of the memorable statements made during the parliament deliberations on the Glavaš case was by an independent MP, Ivan Lončar, who argued that Croatians are a "tragic" people, akin to Jews and Kurds, and as such should not be the subject of any war crimes prosecution. Humanitarian Law Center, "Transitional Justice," 36.

100. Croatian Helsinki Committee for Human Rights, "Izjava o odluci Sabora RH o ukidanju pritvora Branimiru Glavašu" [Statement on the Decision of the Croatian Parliament to Release Branimir Glavaš], press release, January 14, 2008.

101. Documenta, "Konferencija za tisak povodom odluke suda da suđenje za zločine nad civilima u Osijeku odgodi na neodređeno vrijeme" [Press Conference Regarding the Court Decision to Postpone Indefinitely the Trial for Crimes against Civilians in Osijek], press release, September 3, 2008.

102. Humanitarian Law Center, "Transitional Justice," 9.

103. B92, September 5, 2008.

104. Human Rights Watch, "Croatia: EU Must Address Domestic War Crimes Trials."

of its domestic trials and has gone to great pains to demonstrate how substantially different (more democratic, more European) it is from its immediate neighbors, Serbia and Bosnia, when it comes to the quality of its domestic transitional justice.[105]

What Croatian domestic trials experience indicates is that changing entrenched institutional biases and obstacles is very difficult, even in the face of international pressure. However, in Croatia, the overriding elite strategy of integrating Croatia into the European Union was so strongly shared by most political actors that the government moved aggressively to change and improve its justice institutions and reshape them to make them more internationally acceptable, if still substantively problematic.

Official Truth Telling: "The Truth Is in Croatia's Favor"

Transitional justice theory and recommendations from flagship transitional justice organizations such as the International Center for Transitional Justice frequently stress the need for official truth telling to follow or complement any judicial—international and domestic—processes.[106] Either in the form of truth commissions or memorial or documentation centers, official truth telling is recommended to create a historical transcript of past events that can be useful in avoiding manipulation of history by both supporters of the perpetrators and vengeful victims groups.

In Croatia, official truth-telling projects got off to a rough start. In 2005, a group of historians prepared a history textbook supplement for the Podunavlje region, an area in Croatia that had suffered greatly during the war and had slowly begun to incorporate some returning Serb refugees. Even before the textbook supplement was published, its content was leaked to the Croatian press, who attacked the supplement for "twisting the historical truth about the Serbian aggression" and "an attempt to equate the responsibility for the war."[107] According to the supplement authors, the outcry was even more prosaic: the critics objected to two pictures—one of Slobodan Milošević "smiling" and the other of

---

105. Vlado Rajić, "Uravnilovka boraca za ljudska prava" [Leveling On the Part of Human Rights Defenders], *Vjesnik,* October 16, 2004.

106. For example, see Priscilla B. Hayner, *Unspeakable Truths: Confronting State Terror and Atrocity* (New York: Routledge, 2001).

107. Documenta, "Jedna povijest, više historija" [One History, Many Histories], http://www.documenta.hr.

Krajina Serbs leaving their burned-down homes after Operation Storm.[108] The Ministry of Education pulled the plug on the project and deemed it "unacceptable" for adoption. The authors then offered it to a human rights group for publication and distribution if some schools still decided to adopt it. In April 2007, during the Croatian public schools' textbook adoption period, members of the Croatian Academy of Arts and Sciences and a number of historians wrote an open letter to the prime minister, speaker of the parliament, and Ministry of Science, Education, and Sport, as well as the parliament's Council for Education, Science, and Culture in which they argued that "history textbooks should be guided by concerns for the national and state interests as well as scientific and pedagogic standards."[109] This academic pressure on the public education curriculum drew sharp criticisms from the human rights community, but to not much effect. The supplement was never adopted.

Croatia's real test of official truth telling, however, came in March 2005, when the government-sponsored Croatian Memorial and Documentation Center on the Homeland Defense War was opened, with the mandate to collect and process documentation on the 1990s war.[110] The center was defined as a "public scientific institute," with plans to carry out research into various war-related topics.[111] However, the center—the only *official* institution in Croatia with the comprehensive mandate to study events of the past war—opened with a clear ideological point of view. The center's director stated in an interview that the mass flight of Serb civilians after Operation Storm, which resulted in hundreds of dead and hundreds of thousand displaced, was "coordinated by Croatian Serb leadership, and was not the result of Croatian attack and intimidation."[112] The documentation center indeed was set on creating a historical transcript of the war, but this transcript would be strictly in line with the Croatian official interpretation of the conflict. As the director of the center said, "The Center needs to show the truth to the people, because the truth is in Croatia's favor."[113] Indeed, according to the center's director, it was important for Croatia to have such an institution so that the

108. Author's interview with coauthor of the supplement, November 8, 2005, Zagreb.

109. Documenta, "Izjava za javnost u povodu najave izlaska udžbenika za povijest za 8. razred osnovnih škola" [Press Statement Regarding the Announcement of the Publication of Eighth Grade History Textbooks], press release, April 24, 2007.

110. In fact, the initial impetus for the creation of the Center came from the Croatian Rights Party (HSP), an extreme right-wing profascist party. However, the HSP proposal was overambitious; it would have included a museum of the homeland war in addition to the center, so it was scrapped to create a more modest institution.

111. *Hrvatski vojnik*, February 7, 2006.

112. Author's interview with the director of the Croatian Memorial Documentation Center, November 23, 2005, Zagreb.

113. Ibid.

"scientific method" could be used to create a history of the Croatian war, which had so far been created by the "media and the ICTY," both "focusing disproportionately on Croatian war crimes, not crimes against Croats."[114]

The interesting twist presented by Croatia's only official truth-telling research center points to another paradox of domestic adoption of international transitional justice models. An institutional model designed and supported by international justice actors is used domestically to quite different ends—to perpetuate nationalist mythologies and certify the official interpretation of the violent past.

Domestic Demand from Below

There are a number of reasons why dealing with the past was so controversial in Croatia. As in Serbia, the social demand for transitional justice from below has been consistently low. The very character of the Croatian war as understood locally has made accepting international justice demands difficult. The 1991–95 war is generally referred to in Croatia as the "homeland war," a war of independence, or a state-building war. It is the war that finally made Croatia independent from communist rule but more importantly from the Yugoslav federation, which was historically perceived as a Serb-dominated autocracy that crushed Croatian national interests. Critical to this nation-building myth is both suffering (victimization of the cities of Vukovar and Dubrovnik) and triumph (Operation Storm). The Declaration on the Homeland War, passed by the parliament in October 2000, is the clearest example of Croatian official understanding of the 1990s war. The declaration states, "The Republic of Croatia led a just and legitimate, defensive and liberating, and not aggressive and occupational war against anyone, in which she defended her territory from the great Serbian aggressor within its internationally recognized borders."[115]

The Croatian desire for independence is also rooted in a conflicted historical memory of the previous Croatian independent state, a Nazi puppet creation that existed during World War II and that carried out numerous atrocities against non-Croat minorities and other political enemies, including a full-scale Holocaust of Croatian Jews.[116] While the legacy of that independent Croatia looms large in contemporary debates about statehood, even for Croatian antifascists the

---

114. Ibid.

115. Croatian Parliament, *Deklaracija o domovinskom ratu* [Declaration on the Homeland War], *Narodne novine,* no. 102/2000, October 13, 2000.

116. Ivo Goldstein and Slavko Goldstein, *Holokaust u Zagrebu* [Holocaust in Zagreb] (Zagreb: Novi liber, 2001).

creation of a truly independent, modern, and democratic Croatia of the 1990s represented a momentous historical event.

But the focus here really is on state formation, on Croatia's historical dream of having an independent state. In the contemporary Croatian national mythology, the independent, sovereign state guarantees that Croats will be safe from harm and will be protected from the outside by Croatian military and Croatian police. In today's Croatia, the state is intact, it is untouchable and unquestionable, and its existence and importance are not open for discussion.[117] As one political analyst noted, "Croats don't believe in Jesus Christ, but they believe in the Croatian state."[118] Some have interpreted this role of the state in Croatia's contemporary politics as an "obsession," which defines a particular type of politics in which the health of the state is much more important than the human rights of its citizens, and where non-Croatian minorities—mainly Serbs—were defined as standing in the way of Croatian statehood and so needed to be, if not physically eliminated, then at least removed from Croatian territory.[119]

What further complicates the Croatian political narrative about the recent past is that the purpose of the Yugoslav wars of the 1990s was not the acquisition of territory but the ethnic cleansing of territory already under control in pursuit of ethnically pure states. In other words, the war crimes committed were not a consequence of the war but its principal strategy: violence had to be used to force population expulsions.[120] If the Croatian war is interpreted in this way, the independent state of Croatia was in fact created through a criminal enterprise; Croatia's independence is rooted in a war crime. Obviously this is an interpretation of the recent past that the Croatian citizenry would forcefully deny. Recent public opinion surveys of attitudes toward the past in Croatia confirm that domestic demand for transitional justice efforts, if they involve revaluation of the homeland war, remains consistently low.[121]

As in Serbia, the character of the crimes committed directly influenced Croatian social and political response. Crimes committed against non-Croats were interpreted domestically as crimes against either domestic insurgents or "terrorists" (Croatian Serbs) or "foreign enemies" in an internationalized war setting (Bosnian Muslims). This war context and the victims' dislocation—either physical

---

117. Đikić, interview.

118. Author's interview with member of the Serbian Democratic Forum, November 3, 2005, Zagreb.

119. Ivo Banac (professor emeritus of history at Yale University, independent MP in the Croatian parliament, and president of the Croatian Helsinki Committee for Human Rights), in interview with author, November 24, 2005, Zagreb.

120. Ibid.

121. United Nations Development Program, "Transitional Justice."

or political—made seeking justice for the victims much more difficult to promote than if the atrocities had been committed by Croats against other Croats.
This fact was intensified by the nature of the postwar settlement, which solidified
ethnic divisions and divided Croatian Serbs and Croats and Bosnian Croats and
Muslims into segregated ethnic enclaves, without much encouragement to come
together as a community.[122]

In fact, ethnic separation and refugee return remain major human rights
problems facing the country. The pace of return of Serb refugees who fled or
were forced out of Croatia during the war has been exceptionally slow, with no
more than 40 percent of the refugees returning home.[123] Human rights groups
have documented patterns of hostility toward returning Serbs, such as intimidation and violence, and inadequate efforts by the state to prevent these incidents.
The refugees also face the practical difficulties of repossessing their homes and
land or accessing funds for reconstruction assistance.[124] This vulnerable social
and political position makes it very hard for victim groups to stake a strong claim
for transitional justice.

A vivid example of the difficulty of breaking through the dominant Croatian
narrative about the past is the huge controversy that erupted in 2001 with the
airing of the documentary *Storm over Krajina,* which documented war crimes
against Serb civilians in the aftermath of Operation Storm in 1995. Even though
the events of August 1995 were familiar to the Croatian public, the documentary
showed images of the devastation for the first time on Croatian national television.[125] What followed the broadcast was a series of attacks against the filmmakers,
including death threats and public condemnations by all major political parties
and political figures such as then prime minister Račan, as well as a debate in the
parliament.[126] A poll conducted after the documentary was aired found that only
51 percent of the public believed the claims of Croatian war crimes presented
in the film. Although 73 percent of the surveyed public agreed in general with
investigating all war crimes, including Croatian crimes, a majority of the public
also believed that the documentary was anti-Croatian and should not have been

---

122. Vukovar, Croatia, and Mostar, Bosnia provide well-documented examples of ethnic segrega-
tion. For an in-depth ethnographic analysis of the problems of reconciliation in postwar Vukovar,
see Kruno Kardov, "Remember Vukovar: Memory, Sense of Place, and the National Tradition in
Croatia," in Ramet and Matić, *Democratic Transition in Croatia.*

123. Human Rights Watch, "Overview."

124. Ibid.

125. Author's interview with the producer of the documentary, November 16, 2005, Zagreb.

126. The events that followed the broadcast, including the fatal car crash of one of the filmmakers
under still unresolved circumstances, are recounted in Boris Rašeta, ed., *Oluja nad Hrvatskom [Storm
over Croatia]* (Beograd: Samizdat B92, 2003).

broadcast.[127] The scandal reverberated throughout Croatia, and as a consequence of the controversy, Croatian national television has refused for years to air any more documentaries that show evidence of Croatian war crimes. In March 2007, Croatian national television broadcast a documentary about the *Lora* case by the same filmmakers. This time, the post-broadcast roundtable included Croatian generals and the presiding judge of *Lora* case who gained notoriety during the *Lora* proceedings, as well as Croatian right-wing journalists, in an effort to provide "balance" against the negative tone of the film.[128]

To sum up, Croatia, in every sense, is a state "forged in war."[129] This is why international justice norms and institutions are perceived in Croatia as questioning the very legitimacy of the conflict by indicting participants in the homeland war. Transitional justice, in other words, is questioning the historical basis on which the contemporary Croatian state is founded. It challenges and even criminalizes the Croatian state itself and thus is literally incompatible with contemporary Croatia's understanding of its past, present, and future.

The Power of Old-Regime Spoilers

Old-regime loyalists and supporters of the war project were many and varied in Croatia. They were mostly grouped among Croatian right-wing parties— Tuđman's HDZ and the more extreme right HSP, war veterans associations,[130] and the Catholic Church. However, in many ways, their power to destabilize the country was overestimated and overplayed by successive Croatian governments, who made critical decisions about Croatia's transitional justice projects in an effort to appease this vocal but increasingly marginalized coalition.

Prime minister Račan, in particular, consistently made attempts to appease the nationalists by touting a hard line on international justice or forming a coalition with the nationalist HSLS, which was used to give the government a right-wing shield. Old-regime spoilers did indeed put up a public show of strength in 2001 during the Mirko Norac crisis, detailed earlier in the chapter, but with each consequent ICTY indictment, the protesters drew fewer and fewer crowds. Today, although right-wing nationalists and war veterans are vocal and continue to be a

---

127. *Jutarnji list,* October 4, 2001.

128. B92, March 1, 2007.

129. Marcus Tanner, *Croatia: A Nation Forged in War* (New Haven: Yale University Press, 1997).

130. Notable veterans associations are the Committee for Defending the Dignity of the Patriotic War, the Association for the Protection of Homeland War Values, and the Croatian Association of Disabled Veterans of the Homeland War.

disruptive force in all venues where Croatian crimes are being discussed,[131] their actual political strength is weakening. In many ways, Croatia is going through a conflict between war veterans who do not want to forget about the war and the rest of society that does.[132]

The first move that significantly limited the power of old-regime spoilers occurred in September 2000. In response to the first government arrests of Croatian nationals accused of committing war crimes, a group of twelve generals published "open letters to the public" blaming the Croatian government for "undermining the legitimacy of the homeland war" and calling for the government to resign. However, in a shocking rebuttal to the nationalists, president Mesić responded by promptly retiring seven of the twelve generals still serving, for "politicizing the army."[133] Mesić's action was widely approved by the public, but more significantly it immediately demonstrated the government's resolve to limit the power of old-regime loyalists by removing them from positions of authority and denying them access to means of violence. This move was strikingly different from Serbian president Koštunica's decision to co-opt former military personnel in the hope of avoiding a coup, a decision that preserved Serbian old-regime loyalists in positions of power and in control over the monopoly of force. By contrast, Mesić's quick reaction of calling the nationalists' bluff provided the Croatian government with a sense of confidence that even if the government continued to make unpopular choices—such as arresting Croatian war heroes—their supporters would not be able to mount a serious countergovernment insurgency from within the government itself or within the military or secret service, as had been the case in Serbia. Government confrontation with the nationalists would continue to be unpleasant, "but it would not be civil war."[134]

Finally, the old-regime loyalists themselves were beginning to change. While the largest political party loyal to the previous regime, the HDZ, had unvarnished nationalist credentials and was consistently a force against transitional justice institutions, it had slowly begun to change its image from a crude nationalist to a modern right-wing party, in the mold of West European conservative groups. This change was intensified when Ivo Sanader took over the party, as he himself, a bona fide nationalist, was firmly committed to polishing up his party and

---

131. A round table on monitoring war-crimes trials that the author attended at the Zagreb Law School on November 10, 2005, was interrupted by right-wing journalists and veterans who complained that discussing Croatian war crimes was a national shame and embarrassment. In the face of their increasingly disruptive behavior, the organizers were forced to end the round table.

132. Kruno Kardov (University of Zagreb sociology professor), in interview with author, November 10, 2005, Zagreb.

133. Voice of America, September 29, 2000.

134. Đikić, interview.

making it more of an acceptable partner in international negotiations—all part of the Croatian EU strategy. Even more extreme parties were having a makeover. The extreme right-wing HSP, which made international headlines by using fascist iconography of black shirts and Nazi hand salutes throughout the 1990s, was moving toward more conventional politics.[135] The HSP refocused on dealing with corruption as its main political platform. And in one of the more memorable recent political images in Croatia, HSP leader Anto Đapić made a much-publicized visit to Israel to show off his party's "postfascist" rebirth.[136]

To sum up, unlike Serbian old-regime spoilers, who merged seamlessly into the democratic government, Croatian old-regime loyalists remained vocally present but politically marginalized. This distinct and isolated position in contemporary Croatian politics eased the Croatian government's hand in continuing and intensifying its cooperation with international justice institutions, as well as opening up more domestic transitional justice processes. Croatian elites in many instances gave the reactionaries too much credit for their power to destabilize Croatia. However, prompt government action and internal changes within the right wing de facto prevented the spoilers from derailing Croatia's resolve to get to Europe by complying with international requirements, the most significant of which was Croatia's respect of international justice institutions.

Croatian Elite Strategies

As in Serbia, the Croatian domestic political landscape can be crudely grouped into norm resisters, instrumental norm adopters, and true believers in ideas and institutions of transitional justice. While each coalition had distinct preferences in the way it approached dealing with Croatia's past, what made Croatia much different from Serbia was the overarching shared strategy of Europeanizing Croatia—a vision that was shared by virtually all segments of Croatian society and the political elite. This shared goal in the end superseded any ideological differences Croatian elites may have had about the legacy of the Croatian war and allowed Croatia to pull all societal resources into achieving the national mission—bringing Croatia into the EU fold.

---

135. Apparently trying to buttress its image as a nonfascist party, HSP created a film about the history of the party, which somewhat amusingly states that the Nazi puppet state of independent Croatia "was not independent as it depended on fascist Germany." Robert Bajruši, "Čačić i Đapić razbijaju duopol HDZ-a i SDP-a [Čačić and Đapić Breaking the Duopoly of HDZ and SDP], *Nacional*, December 18, 2006.

136. This about-face, however, did not prevent Đapić from publicly outing twenty individuals who had cooperated with the ICTY, at a press conference in 2005.

Croatian norm resisters included members of Tuđman's HDZ party, other smaller nationalist parties, the military, and the Catholic Church, as well as most of the Croatian media. Most pronounced public displays of rejecting international justice occurred in the early 2000s, when the Hague tribunal first began indicting Croatian nationals for war crimes. In fact, rejecting the possibility that Croatian citizens could be guilty of war crimes was for a long time part of official legal policy. Milan Vuković, former president of the Supreme Court of Croatia and a current member of its constitutional court, famously declared that as a matter of law, Croats could not have committed war crimes because they had waged only a defensive war.[137] Croatian norm resisters have consistently been very vocal and in many ways prevented or at least significantly slowed down Croatia's transitional justice processes. Unlike those in Serbia, however, Croatian norm resisters were never in full control of government after Tuđman's death and Croatia's first democratic elections. By the time the HDZ came back to power in 2003, it was led by a moderate leader who made it his goal to rid the party of its reactionary image and work full force toward taking Croatia into Europe by way of respecting international institutions and demands.

Therefore, the interesting aspect of the Croatian elite strategy is that the real political fights occurred within the second bloc, the instrumental adopters, who in different party incarnations dominated Croatian politics after 2000. The Račan government, as described in earlier sections of the chapter, walked a tightrope between appeasing nationalist constituencies suspicious of Račan's communist background and pleasing Croatia's international sponsors who demanded that Croatia deliver on its promises of respecting international justice requirements. But it is really the Sanader government that has most clearly used the instrumental adoption approach.

The return of HDZ to power in 2003 with Sanader as prime minister caused alarm among international actors, as well as domestic proponents of transitional justice. This was after all the same Sanader who as a fiery nationalist had given one of the strongest anti-ICTY speeches at the right-wing rally in 2001.[138] This was the same HDZ that had once been led by Franjo Tuđman, under whose leadership so many Croatian atrocities against non-Croat populations occurred.

---

137. Drago Hedl, "Croatia: Impunity Prevails," *Transitions Online* 8, no. 12 (2005), http://www.tol.cz.

138. Sanader was one of the main speakers at the pro-Norac rally in Split in February 2001. His speech was especially feisty and amounted to a threat to the Račan government: "The government has two options: to step down and call an election or organize its own counter-protest, in which case we shall all go to Zagreb." Quoted in "Croatian Rally Protests U.N. and Demands Early Elections," *New York Times*, February 12, 2001.

However, Sanader quickly proved his skeptics wrong. Unlike Račan, who was in constant fear of the right wing and felt insecure with his own political biography, Sanader had unquestionable nationalist credentials, and his credibility with the nationalists was not at stake; he could easily cash in on his nationalist political capital. His strategy was to maintain tough language on international justice by praising ICTY indictees as Croatian war heroes while at the same time working behind the scenes to fulfill ICTY obligations. Since he did not have to placate the Croatian right wing, Sanader could focus on appeasing the international audience. He firmly held on to his nationalist base and even managed to clean up the HDZ a bit by removing the most extreme wing of the party, as well as disassociating himself from the party's previous unsavory coalition partners, such as the extremist HSP. In a series of savvy political stunts with wide international appeal, he made overtures toward Croatia's beleaguered Serb minority. In a Croatian miniversion of the "Sadat goes to Jerusalem" moment, Sanader made a historic visit to the Serbian Orthodox Church to pay his respects on Orthodox Christmas Day, January 5, 2004. Moves like these, which scored Sanader great points with international observers, were something his predecessor, Račan, would never have been able to get away with domestically.

The great political mystery of contemporary Croatia is what caused Sanader's startling U-turn from a fierce nationalist into a moderate pro-internationalist statesman. One answer is that he realized early on that his best chance of political survival lay in being the prime minister who would take Croatia into the EU. He also wanted to become a statesman of an EU country.[139] By putting all his political eggs in one basket, Sanader focused intently on doing whatever it took to make Croatia's European dream a reality. Since the EU had made it clear that the road to Brussels led through The Hague, Sanader decided that international justice would be a fast ticket to the place where he wanted Croatia to be. Ignoring international requirements, he feared, would place Croatia in Europe's waiting room, in the dreaded group of European losers (such as Serbia and Bosnia)— and that was unacceptable.[140] Finally, Sanader made many friends in the international community, especially among central European conservatives in Germany and Austria. His election advertisements even showed him in the warm embrace of Edmund Stoiber, leader of the German Christian Social Union of Bavaria. His increasingly close relationships with European conservative parties played a role in socializing Sanader, as his friends were placing persistent pressure on him to speed up cooperation with the ICTY as a way to obtain European favors.

---

139. Vesna Teršelič (director of Documenta, Croatia's leading transitional justice NGO), in interview with author, November 9, 2005, Zagreb.

140. Đikić, interview.

Croatia's political environment was further shaped by the presence of a heterogeneous group of true believers in the ideas and institutions of transitional justice, a cross-section of political elites that included Croatian president Stjepan Mesić, as well as a number of Croatian human rights groups and activists.

Like the public at large, Croatia's civil-society sector had to deal with the paradox of Croatia's status as both the victim and the perpetrator of atrocities committed during the wars in Croatia and Bosnia. Most human rights organizations dealt with this problem by acknowledging the right of Croatia to defend itself from aggression by the Yugoslav army and Serbian forces while at the same time condemning all atrocities, including ones committed against Croatian Serbs, documenting them, and also opposing Croatian involvement in the Bosnian war. In addition, some Croatian organizations viewed dealing with the recent past in the context of reexamining Croatia's fascist and antifascist World War II legacy.[141]

While Croatian NGOs have compiled documents and gathered victims' testimonies, including a comprehensive oral history project, they have decided not to establish more formal transitional justice mechanisms, such as a truth commission.[142] This decision is partly rooted in a shared sense that the Croatian parliament would never ratify such an institution,[143] and public surveys have consistently shown no public support for this move.[144] In addition, the few NGOs that persistently advocated investigations of abuses and justice for victims have been vilified in the press in much the same way as in Serbia.[145] In fact, the position of the Croatian NGOs is in some ways worse than that of the Serbian groups, as they have consistently been less well funded by international sponsors, who looked at Serbia and Bosnia in the 1990s as Balkan hot spots that needed to be supported. Croatian civil society has been left to fight for transitional justice alone, a consequence of the international community's general on-and-off focus on Croatia as a regional problem that needs to be addressed.

But it is really the support of Croatian president Mesić for transitional justice that made Croatian true believers serious stakeholders in the process of facing the past. The evolution of president Mesić from a high-level communist official in the former Yugoslavia to a distinguished HDZ nationalist in Tudman's

---

141. Teršelič, interview. There is also an increased media interest in Croatia's complicity in the Holocaust, as part of a larger project of dealing with the past. Author's interviews with director of the Open Society Institute Croatia, November 24, 2005, Zagreb, and coordinator of the Zagreb Law School's Digital Documentation on War Crimes, November 3, 2005, Zagreb.

142. Documenta, http://www.documenta.hr.

143. Croatian president Mesić, however, was more open to a truth-telling project.

144. Cruvellier and Valiñas, "Croatia."

145. The Croatian Helsinki Committee for Human Rights, the Center for Peace, and Documenta have been the most active.

government, to a lefty populist, antiglobalization statesman, and finally to a regional leader focused on ridding Croatia of its fascist heritage in many ways is an illustration of how far Croatia has come in the decade since the war ended. Mesić is widely respected in the region and internationally, but more strikingly he has consistently managed to win presidential elections since 2000 even though many of his public statements and initiatives continue to fly in the face of much of Croatia's national narrative about its past and the institutionalized public discourse about the homeland war. In the words of Mesić's senior adviser, "Mesić is the voice of Croatia that the world would like to have, but this is not the Croatia a significant number of Croatians want to have."[146]

Like Prime Minister Sanader, Mesić had the benefit of flouting bona fide nationalist credentials as a former high-ranking member of the HDZ. While he was a communist, he made a famous statement that he planned to be "the last president of Yugoslavia," so his desire for the Yugoslav breakup and the independence of Croatia was clear from the outset. Because of this strong nationalist background he did not have to constantly work on placating the right wing but could gradually turn to the left and slowly build a legacy of progressive public statements that focused on Croatia's place in Europe, its antifascist legacy, and recognition of crimes committed and their just punishment.[147] Since he was elected president in 2000, he has persistently argued that unless Croatia faces its past, it cannot claim to be a European liberal democracy.[148]

In his weekly addresses to the nation, Mesić has taken on a mission, a "permanent campaign"[149] to educate the Croatian public and implore them to reject Croatia's fascist legacy, which was getting whitewashed and normalized in the new Croatian state. For example, in the first five years of Tuđman's regime three thousand antifascist monuments from World War II were destroyed, leaving Croatia with no serious monuments of antifascism left. Also famous from this period was Tuđman's statement that he was "happy his wife [was] neither Jewish nor Serb."[150]

The normalization of Croatian fascism significantly dropped after the democratic transition, but ambiguity concerning its legacy still remains. For example, in May 2008, a massive rock concert by the extreme nationalist singer Marko Perković Thompson at the main Zagreb public square ended with a fascist hand

---

146. Tomislav Jakić (president Mesić's foreign policy adviser), in interview with author, November 22, 2005, Zagreb.

147. His powerful early speech renouncing Croatia's fascist legacy was delivered in front of the Israeli Knesset on October 31, 2001. The text of this speech is available at http://www.predsjednik.hr.

148. Jakić, interview.

149. Ibid.

150. Diana Jean Schemo, "Anger Greets Croatian's Invitation to Holocaust Museum Dedication," *New York Times*, April 22, 1993.

salute, while fans wearing fascist insignia chanted "death to Serbs," all to no government condemnation. Instead, the city of Zagreb sponsored the event and the police inspector who filed criminal charges against the fans for inciting violence was suspended.[151] It is in this context that president Mesić has made constant appeals to his citizenry to celebrate antifascist traditions, resist chauvinism, and respect international law as the foundation of the liberal democratic order Croatia wants to join.[152]

In an address in 2002, Mesić, using rhetoric similar to that of Serbia's pro-international reformers, claimed that nationalist mobilization against the ICTY was "anti-European and anti-democratic." He stressed that Croatia had a strong democratic order; it was firmly dedicated to individualizing culpability for war crimes and would "build its future in the company of the democratic world and united Europe."[153] As Serbian reformers had emphasized, adopting international norms and institutions of transitional justice was justified in the name of European identity and desired membership in the elite club of liberal democracies.

Mesić also spoke the language of true transitional justice believers. At an international conference on transitional justice organized by Croatian human rights groups, he said, "We must know the truth; truth needs to be established and determined, truth needs to be faced, whatever it might be, and regardless of whether it will please all; there is only one truth."[154] The Croatian president also made some stunning personal gestures in the pursuit of justice. Mesić is the only Croatian politician to have issued an official apology to victims of Croatian war crimes.[155] He also embraced the Croatian and regional civil-society sectors and frequently participated in NGO and academic initiatives aimed at bridging the ideological and political divide among countries of the region[156]—all behaviors quite unprecedented for a former communist and nationalist politician. Finally, he also volunteered to be a witness at The Hague in a few trials, most famously in the trial of Slobodan Milošević. But much more significantly and to great public

151. Documenta, "Otvoreno pismo protiv dvosmislenog odnosa vlade spram ustaštva" [Open Letter against Government's Hypocritical Relationship with the Ustashe Legacy], press release, undated, http://www.documenta.hr.

152. Ivica Đikić, *Domovinski obrat: Politička biografija Stipe Mesića* [Patriotic Turnover: Political Biography of Stipe Mesić] (Zagreb: VBZ, 2004).

153. Mesić's address to the nation, September 25, 2002, http://www.predsjednik.hr.

154. Mesić spoke at the International Conference "Establishing the Truth about War Crimes and Conflicts," February 8–9, 2007, Zagreb. Transcript available at http://www.documenta.hr.

155. "In my name, I also apologise to all those who have suffered pain or damage at any time from citizens of Croatia who misused or acted against the law." Quoted in "Presidents Apologise over Croatian War," BBC News, September 10, 2003.

156. For example, Mesić was very involved in the Balkan Lustration Project. See http://www.lustration.net.

controversy in Croatia, he handed over classified information about Tihomir Blaškić, a Bosnian Croat suspected of war crimes in Bosnia, to the ICTY. However, even with his significant support of justice processes, Mesić consistently approached them as issues of individual responsibility. Individual perpetrators of war crimes needed to be vigorously pursued, he argued, in order to avoid placing collective responsibility for crimes on the Croatian state.[157] In other words, while Mesić did believe in the ideas and institutions of transitional justice, his support was guided by the overarching goal of preserving the sanctity of the Croatian state.

It is difficult to measure the extent to which Mesić's public statements have had a real impact on changing Croatia's public discourse and shared understanding of the war. However, it is evident that, even though Mesić has no executive power and has been criticized for being all rhetoric and no action, his support of both international and domestic justice processes has served to open up rhetorical and normative space for a changed discourse in Croatia, which in turn has made contemporary debates about the past possible.[158] Unlike true believers in Serbia, which is badly "in search of its own Mesić,"[159] those in Croatia can channel transitional justice initiatives through to their chief statesman.

To sum up, the Croatian transitional justice experience points to the strength of instrumental adopters of international norms and institutions. While different segments of society and the political elite had different reasons to accept international demands in the field of transitional justice, they all shared a grand national strategy. All major political stakeholders saw Croatia's future in Europe, and they were all willing to manipulate the domestic political environment in order to achieve this goal. While nationalist norm resisters were vocal and multiple, they became increasingly marginalized politically by pragmatic instrumental adopters from a succession of different Croatian governments. Finally, Croatia's true believers in civil society had a powerful ally in the Croatian president, who supported transitional justice efforts as a way to individualize crimes and absolve the Croatian state.

---

157. Representative of this approach is Mesić's public statement on July 8, 2001, http://www.predsjednik.hr.

158. Opinion polls on Croatians' attitudes toward transitional justice show somewhat more favorable results than comparable polls in Serbia. In a poll conducted in 2007, 76 percent of the respondents agreed that individual accountability for war crimes committed on all sides was important. However, when asked what the concept "facing the past" meant for them personally, 30 percent held a negative view of the concept, 41 percent were indifferent, and only 23 percent thought "facing the past" was a positive thing. Results available at http://www.documenta.hr.

159. Goran Svilanović (former foreign minister and president of the Civic Alliance of Serbia), in interview with author, September 26, 2005, Belgrade.

Conclusion

The Croatian strategy of instrumental adoption of international norms and institutions of transitional justice has served the Croatian state very well. As a reward for Croatia's renewed compliance with the international tribunal, the ICTY agreed to transfer some of its caseload to Croatian domestic courts. This was a move Croatia had long demanded, arguing that it was now a consolidated democracy based on the rule of law, capable of adjudicating its own war crimes.

However, it was only with the arrest in December 2005 of Ante Gotovina, the last Croatian suspect wanted by the ICTY, that Croatia officially fulfilled its last obligation toward the Hague tribunal.[160] Croatia's international sponsors generously rewarded this development. In October 2005,[161] the chief prosecutor of the Hague tribunal had stated that Croatia was "cooperating fully" with the ICTY, which immediately triggered the beginning of accession negotiations between Croatia and the EU.[162] Cooperation with international institutions of transitional justice, therefore, led Croatia to its ultimate prize—a real possibility of EU membership.

In many ways, this path was much easier for Croatia than for Serbia, as international actors focused exclusively on Croatia's institutional cooperation with the ICTY—and even this was in the end reduced to the transfer of a single individual—while giving Croatia much more leeway to conduct its domestic affairs as it saw fit. The consequence of this was that Croatia's transitional justice experience has been Janus-faced—proactive internationally and lackluster, if not quite reactive, domestically. And in fact, as soon as Gotovina was transferred to The Hague, the international pressure on Croatia, already suffering from an "attention span deficit" began to ease.[163] Now that Croatia has already received the most important carrot—EU candidacy—international actors increasingly have less leverage in influencing its domestic policies. The prevailing public attitude in Croatia is that transitional justice processes ended with Gotovina's arrest and it is now time for Croatia to move on to other, more pressing issues such as economic reform, foreign investment, and general adjustment to European markets and institutions.[164] Since Gotovina's arrest and the EU accession talks have been interpreted in Croatia as great national triumphs, in some ways the final fulfillment of international obligations has served to close further domestic debate about war crimes in Croatia.

---

160. All that remains is documentary support and facilitation of ICTY investigations.
161. This is when the ICTY prosecutor was presented with evidence that Gotovina was in Spain.
162. Council of the European Union, untitled press release, 12514/1/05, October 3, 2005.
163. Author's interview with OSCE Croatia War Crimes Unit staff.
164. Đikić, interview.

The disparity between Croatia's international image as a country that has come to willingly face its past and cooperate with international justice institutions and the domestic justice failings that are continuing to plague its domestic trials for war crimes indicates that in those states that adopt justice mechanisms in the pursuit of international legitimacy, we can expect shallow or instrumental compliance with international norms. States like Croatia may fulfill their international obligations and may be rewarded for doing so, but that may be at the expense of a serious domestic debate about crimes of the past and deeper normative and behavioral shifts.

What Croatia's experience also indicates is the extent to which norms and institutions of transitional justice can be used to service the state and, conversely, how the narrative of the state can help push forward transitional justice processes. What made Croatian transitional justice efforts seem so focused was the fact that all the Croatian elites used the grand narrative of Croatia as a European state to spearhead their policy shifts, even when these changes at first appeared unpopular domestically. This self-identity of the Croatian state as a European state, defined in many ways in opposition to Serbia and to lesser extent to Bosnia, superseded and overpowered existing nationalist narratives. Unlike Serbia, where the state self-identity revolves around the nation first and around European membership second, in Croatia there existed a wide social pact among almost all significant political groups that joining the EU was the single most important national strategy. This political and social consensus allowed Croatian elites to move fast in fulfilling international requirements, even when their substance went against widely shared national beliefs and understandings about Croatia's past. Transitional justice was effectively presented to the population as a necessary step on the road to Europe. In the words of Jadranka Kosor, Croatia's deputy prime minister, "facing the past for us means preparing for our European future."[165] Transitional justice, therefore, is widely understood as Croatia's "international obligation," proving the country's character as a democracy based on the rule of law with functioning institutions. It is not, however, interpreted in moral terms, as simply the right thing to do.

Croatia's transitional justice strategy therefore allowed Croatian elites to have the best of both worlds. They could prove to the international community that they respected international rules and were happy to play by them. At the same time, the domestic aspect of the transitional justice strategy managed to preserve almost intact the Croatian national understanding of the character of the war and Croatia's role in it.

---

165. Ms. Kosor spoke at the International Conference "Establishing the Truth about War Crimes and Conflicts," February 8–9, 2007, Zagreb. Conference transcript at http://www.documenta.hr.

4

WHO LIVES IN YOUR NEIGHBORHOOD?

Bosnia is in many ways a perfect laboratory for studying the effectiveness, consequences, and potential of transitional justice to bring justice to victims and reconciliation to broken communities. It is the country that suffered more than any other in the Yugoslav conflict. Its population was decimated, its cities and villages ravaged. The war left a traumatic imprint on Bosnian society, which is still, more than a decade after the war ended, trying to come to grips with what has happened to their country.

Bosnia's experience with transitional justice, however, has been much more complicated than promoters of international justice had expected. Bosnian transitional justice efforts have reflected a classic dilemma: although the country has an incredibly high demand and need for justice, it has suffered from incapacity to deliver it.[1] International justice institutions such as the ICTY have received a decidedly mixed response from Bosnian citizens, with each group—Bosniacs, Serbs, and Croats—finding different reasons to be disappointed. Domestic war-crimes trials are nascent and still heavily influenced by international justice experts, while any attempt at creating a Bosnian truth commission has been put on hold, a consequence of low domestic interest, lackluster international support, and the Bosnian federal bureaucratic maze.

In analyzing the transitional justice experience in Bosnia, this chapter proceeds as follows. First, it outlines international goals and expectations for transitional

---

1. Mark Freeman, "Bosnia and Herzegovina: Selected Developments in Transitional Justice," International Center for Transitional Justice, New York, October 2004.

justice in Bosnia, expressed in and after the Dayton Peace Accords. Then it looks at specific international transitional justice mechanisms carried out in Bosnia—international and domestic trials and truth-telling projects—and their domestic political effects. The chapter then analyzes specific domestic political conditions—domestic demand from below, the power of old-regime spoilers, and competing elite strategies—that led to Bosnia's piecemeal adoption of international transitional justice models. The chapter concludes by analyzing the consequences of using transitional justice as a pathway to creating a strong unitary state in light of winding down international involvement in Bosnia.

Bosnia in the Dayton Straightjacket

Bosnia was a country clearly in need of justice. The Bosnian war (1992–95) was one of the most brutal conflicts in recent memory, a harrowing succession of violence and massacres that reminded Europe of its worst nightmares. What made the Bosnian war so horrendous, besides the enormity of human suffering, misery, and death, was the fact that before neighbors, friends, relatives, and schoolmates turned on one another, Bosnia had been a functioning multiethnic society. It prided itself on a long history of multiculturalism, with the region's four major religions—Islam, Christian Orthodoxy, Catholicism, and Judaism—coexisting in peace, with even a degree of mutual appreciation. The city of Sarajevo demonstrated its acceptance of a variety of faiths by the cathedrals, churches, mosques, and synagogues lining the once leafy but since the war often barren streets of the Bosnian capital. Bosnia also prided itself on a high prewar intermarriage rate, often used as an indicator in measurements of ethnic relations and ethnic proximity.[2] None of these assets, however, prevented the bloodbath that ensued. As the former Yugoslavia began to disintegrate in 1991, the Bosnian leadership was becoming nervous about what it perceived as Serbia's quest for Yugoslav dominance. Observing the war in neighboring Croatia between Croatian troops and Croatian Serb rebels, the Bosnian ruling elites calculated that declaring independence and obtaining international recognition would prevent the war and would spare Bosnia Croatia's fate. However, immediately upon Bosnia's declaration of independence in April 1992, Bosnian

---

2. A demographic analysis of the 1981 federal census data concluded that "if children of mixed marriages were included, over half the population of Bosnia had a close relative of a different nationality." Quoted in Steven L. Burg and Paul Shoup, *The War in Bosnia-Herzegovina: Ethnic Conflict and International Intervention* (Armonk, NY: M.E. Sharpe, 1999), 42. Also see Tone Bringa, *Being Muslim the Bosnian Way: Identity and Community in a Central Bosnian Village* (Princeton: Princeton University Press, 1995).

Serb troops, with logistical and weapons support from the Milošević-dominated Yugoslav army, began the siege of Sarajevo. During the four-year siege, up to ten thousand people were killed from sniper attacks, shelling, land mines, or starvation and exposure.

And while the world's attention, but not much action, was focused on the suffering of Sarajevo, the war raged on in other parts of Bosnia.[3] Almost no city, town, or community in the country remained unscathed. Villages were burned, great numbers of civilians were deported or massacred, thousands went missing, never to be found, entire settlements were wiped out, and many centuries-old, internationally protected architectural treasures were destroyed.[4] The horror culminated in July 1995, when Serb forces organized the single worst atrocity in Europe since World War II, the massacre at Srebrenica, where seven thousand Bosniac boys and men were executed over a period of five days in the presence of powerless or uninterested United Nations troops deployed to guard the city as a save haven.

The Srebrenica massacre, today legally classified as genocide by the ICTY,[5] sped up the lackluster international action to end the Bosnian war. After a few days of NATO bombing, the Serbs were ready to negotiate. In November 1995, the United States brought the warring parties together in Dayton, Ohio, and hammered out a compromise deal that would carve Bosnia into two halves—the Republika Srpska (RS) (Bosnian Serb Republic) and the Federation of Bosnia and Herzegovina (BH), which was divided into ten cantons to preserve a delicate balance of power between Bosniacs and Bosnian Croats.[6]

The Dayton accords did put an end to the war and stopped the continuing brutalization of the Bosnian population. However, by imbuing the two entities with the trappings of statehood, such as control over their police and militaries, the peace deal in effect reasserted and institutionalized the consequences of mass population displacement, or ethnic cleansing.[7] Dayton served as a freeze-frame, acknowledging territorial gains by the three warring groups and solidifying

---

3. Thomas Cushman and Stjepan Gabriel Mestrovic, *This Time We Knew: Western Responses to Genocide in Bosnia* (New York: New York University Press, 1996).

4. Islamic monuments were particularly hard hit. Famous examples include the destruction of the centuries-old mosques in Foča and Banjaluka as well as of the old bridge in Mostar.

5. The precedent-setting case was *Prosecutor v. Radislav Krstić*, Appeals Chamber Judgment, April 19, 2004, para. 39.

6. In addition to these entities, the Brčko District was established in 2000 as a single administrative, self-governing unit.

7. International Crisis Group, "The Wages of Sin: Confronting Bosnia's Republika Srpska," Europe Report no. 118, Sarajevo, October 8, 2001.

them with a constitutional framework.[8] Bosnian Serbs were awarded a significant chunk of territory almost completely devoid of any non-Serbs, while Bosniacs and Croats lived in strained partnership in their own minifederation.

The Dayton constitution for Bosnia was a massively complex document creating layers of overlapping jurisdictions, all in order to prevent any one side from ethnic dominance. It established a central government with a bicameral legislature, a three-member rotating presidency (consisting of a Bosniac, a Croat, and a Serb), a council of ministers, a two-house legislature, and a constitutional court. Two subentities—the Republika Srpska and the BH federation—were given their own parliaments, prime ministers, and ten regional authorities, each with its own police force and education, health, and judicial authorities. The World Bank has estimated that this governing labyrinth uses 50 percent of Bosnia's gross domestic product.[9]

Most important, the Dayton accords made Bosnia an international protectorate, ruled by the Office of the High Representative (OHR) with almost limitless executive powers, with the mandate of not only reconstruction but in effect also state building.[10] The OHR was granted intrusive oversight into almost all aspects of the Bosnian states—organizing elections, appointing and approving local officials, supervising local public administration, human rights monitoring, arms control, composition of the police and the judiciary, and even such mundane tasks as street naming, flag layout, and license plate design. As a consequence of this unprecedented international intrusion, Dayton made Bosnian state institutions so powerless as to be irrelevant, maintained Bosnia's status as a permanent protectorate, and fostered a sense of "political irresponsibility" among Bosnian elites.[11] This is why for many Bosnians their state today feels like not much more than a geopolitical construct of the international community.[12]

---

8. Author's interview with staff of the University of Sarajevo Center for Human Rights, January 20, 2006, Sarajevo.

9. Nicholas Wood, "Fiery Campaign Imperils Bosnia's Progress, Officials Warn," *New York Times,* August 27, 2006.

10. The initial postwar international presence in Bosnia included sixty thousand NATO troops, with almost as many international aid workers, NGO staffers, civilian administrators, and professional consultants. During the most intensive period of international investment in Bosnia (1996–2000), the international community spent tens of billions of dollars for infrastructure reconstruction, refugee return, and economic and structural reforms, as well as the continuing military presence in the country. International Crisis Group, "Ensuring Bosnia's Future: A New International Engagement Strategy," Europe Report no. 180, Sarajevo, February 15, 2007.

11. International Crisis Group, "Whither Bosnia?" Europe Report no. 43, Sarajevo, September 9, 1998.

12. Author's interview with a University of Sarajevo political science professor, January 17, 2006, Sarajevo.

Internationalization of Transitional Justice in Bosnia

In addition to carving up Bosnia's territory and providing it with a political, legal, and military framework, the Dayton Peace Accords also institutionalized international expectations for transitional justice in Bosnia. All state signatories of the accords—including both Bosnian entities—were obligated to "cooperate in the investigation and prosecution of war crimes and other violations of international humanitarian law."[13] The implementation of Dayton "civilian provisions" was handed over to different international organizations, with the OHR as the coordinator of various activities carried out by the OSCE, the UN Mission in Bosnia and Herzegovina, and the UN High Commissioner for Refugees. But most directly, the OHR was to coordinate Bosnia's cooperation with the ICTY, the international community's principal benchmark of transitional justice commitment in the region. Postwar Bosnia also attracted tremendous attention from different international NGOs, which opened local offices throughout Bosnia with the intent of building civil society and contributing to reconciliation.[14] Finally, transitional justice and a general improvement in human rights were conditions placed on Bosnia by the European Commission for any potential Bosnian EU accession bid.[15]

All this international attention directly influenced transitional justice processes in Bosnia by internationalizing them and removing them from local authorities who were judged either too biased or too unprofessional, or both, for the complexities of dealing with Bosnia's traumatic and violent past.[16] In other words, all aspects of transitional justice in Bosnia were to various degrees under the international fold. International justice promoters reacted to this political environment by exerting pressure on Bosnia from within, by working through the de facto government in charge, the OHR.

---

13. Article IX of the General Framework Agreement for Peace in Bosnia-Herzegovina, the Dayton Peace Accords on Bosnia-Herzegovina, http://www1.umn.edu/humanrts/icty/dayton/daytonaccord.html.

14. For a very critical assessment of international NGO activities in rebuilding Bosnia's civil society, see Roberto Belloni, "Civil Society and Peacebuilding in Bosnia and Herzegovina," *Journal of Peace Research* 38, no. 2 (2001): 163–80. On the larger issue of how international peacebuilding in Bosnia resonates locally, see Paula M. Pickering, *Peacebuilding in the Balkans: The View from the Ground Floor* (Ithaca: Cornell University Press, 2007).

15. Office of the High Representative, "Bosnia and Herzegovina: Commission Approves Feasibility Study," November 18, 2003, http://www.ohr.int/other-doc/eu-stmnt/default.asp?content_id=31227.

16. International Crisis Group, "Rule over Law: Obstacles to the Development of an Independent Judiciary in Bosnia and Herzegovina," Europe Report no. 72, Sarajevo, July 5, 1999; Human Rights Watch, "Justice at Risk: War Crimes Trials in Croatia, Bosnia and Herzegovina, and Serbia and Montenegro," vol. 16, no. 7(D), New York, October 13, 2004.

Bosnia and The Hague

As indicated above, the Dayton agreement required cooperation with the ICTY as the appropriate international venue for transitional justice in Bosnia. In the immediate aftermath of the war, all international efforts were directed at the Republika Srpska, where most of the perpetrators of war atrocities had origi-nated.[17] Soon thereafter, however, the ICTY prosecutor indicted a number of Bosnian Croats for crimes against Bosniacs. In 1996, the prosecutor also indicted a number of high-ranking officials in the Bosnian army, a move that was very controversial among the Bosniac population, who maintained that as victims of genocide they should not be punished for the defensive actions of their wartime leaders.[18]

As the location of most of the Balkan war atrocities, and as the country whose population was more devastated than any other during the three years of the conflict, Bosnia was also the country on which most of the ICTY investigations focused. International trials, therefore, were of great significance to Bosnia. And while initially Bosnian citizens followed the ICTY proceedings with great inter-est, as the trials dragged on, seemingly endlessly, the public fascination with the ICTY began to dwindle. But, like everything else in Bosnia, the domestic political effect of the ICTY trials was felt very differently in the two Bosnian entities: the Republika Srpska and the federation.[19]

The Republika Srpska and the ICTY

In the Republika Srpska, even though the parliament passed a law on coopera-tion with the ICTY in September 2001, for a long time there was practically no cooperation at all with the tribunal. RS authorities continuously denied having knowledge of the presence of Radovan Karadžić, Ratko Mladić, or any other Bosnian Serb indictee on RS territory, and they openly opposed and hindered international efforts to arrest the suspects. RS institutions in charge of coop-erating with the tribunal were not only unhelpful in supporting the ICTY but actively worked to undermine its findings.[20]

---

17. Human Rights Watch, "A Chance for Justice?: War Crimes Prosecutions in Bosnia's Serb Repub-lic," vol. 18, no. 3(D), New York, March 16, 2006.

18. Dan Saxon, "Exporting Justice: Perceptions of the ICTY among the Serbian, Croatian and Mus-lim Communities in the Former Yugoslavia," *Journal of Human Rights* 4, no. 4 (2005): 552–72.

19. According to a large-scale survey conducted in 2002, trust in the ICTY is at 51 percent in the federation and only 4 percent in the RS. See International Institute for Democracy and Electoral Assistance (IDEA), South East Europe (SEE) Public Agenda Survey, April 4, 2002, http://www.idea. int/europe_cis/balkans/see_survey.cfm.

20. International Crisis Group, "The Wages of Sin."

International requirements for the RS to cooperate with the Hague tribunal were always complicated by the fact that the Bosnian Serbs for the most part did not act independently of Milošević's Serbia. This meant that some of the alleged perpetrators were Serbian citizens, some were hiding in Serbia, and some were Bosnian citizens hiding in the RS, allowing Serbia to claim deniability about arresting them on its territory. For almost a decade after the conflict ended, both the RS and its patron, Serbia, used this delaying tactic to deflect ICTY pressures. Because of this joint conspiracy of silence that served both states' interests, RS authorities could stall for time, hoping that international pressures would ease. International demands persisted, however, and the OHR made increasingly intrusive demands on the RS leadership to begin cooperation with the ICTY or else be excluded from international reconstruction aid. In addition, the RS was losing support from Serbia, as the succession of Serbian governments made it a priority to work toward integrating Serbia into European institutions, a prerequisite for which was disassociating from RS internal affairs. Over time, therefore, the RS was feeling increasingly isolated from both its friends and its foes. Under such political conditions, appeasing international actors and improving relations with the Bosnian federation was the only viable political strategy.

In 2005, the RS authorities reversed their recalcitrant position and began arresting and transferring Bosnian Serb war suspects to the ICTY.[21] This change of heart with respect to the ICTY also followed a new readiness to bring war-crimes charges against Bosnian Serbs in local courts.[22] This "justice momentum" reflected the diminishing power of extreme nationalist old-regime spoilers in the Republika Srpska, whose influence had been steadily reduced as the OHR fired them one by one from any position of significant authority. It also indicated a growing understanding that the future of the Serb entity was in improving relations with Sarajevo and loosening ties with Belgrade. However, it also demonstrated that RS cooperation with the ICTY was now being "commercialized," as Bosnian Serb authorities calculated what international gains they could reap in return for transferring war-crimes suspects.[23]

---

21. In January 2005, RS authorities transferred Savo Todović, former deputy commander in a detention camp in Foča, to the ICTY. Gojko Janković, also charged in relation to crimes against Bosnian Muslims in Foča, surrendered to RS authorities in March 2005. Finally, Sredoje Lukić, charged with crimes against Bosnian Muslims in Višegrad in 1992, surrendered in September 2005. Human Rights Watch, "Overview of Human Rights Issues in Bosnia and Herzegovina," New York, January 18, 2006.

22. Human Rights Watch, "A Chance for Justice?"

23. Author's interview with staff of the Heinrich Boell foundation, January 18, 2006, Sarajevo.

The Bosnian Federation and the ICTY

The relationship of the Bosniac-Croat federation with the Hague tribunal has also been rocky. This Bosnian entity had its own set of political complexities to deal with, such as multiple layers of contradictory interests involving the federation's antagonistic relationship with the Republika Srpska and the unresolved tensions between Bosniacs and Croats within the federation. As a result, both Bosniacs and Croats used ICTY proceedings to make political claims about their relative power and authority in the state. For Bosnian Croats, ICTY indictments of high-profile Croat wartime leaders such as Tihomir Blaškić and Dario Kordić manifested their position of vulnerability as a minority in Bosnia and were used to justify their attempts to secede from the legal and constitutional structures of the Bosnian state.[24]

For the Bosniac majority, however, the establishment of the ICTY in 1993 was seen as a welcome development, as the next best thing in the absence of an international military intervention to stop the Bosnian bloodshed. The expectation was that the ICTY would focus its efforts on prosecuting mostly Serb and perhaps some Croat perpetrators of war crimes against Bosniacs. This all changed with the ICTY's first indictment of Bosniac generals and members of the Bosnian army for crimes committed against Serbs.[25] The public reaction among Bosniacs was anger, resentment, and a reaffirmation of the position that victims of genocide could not be accused of war crimes that were reactive or defensive.[26]

Perhaps the clearest illustration of the many conflicting narratives of the Bosnian past and its adjudication in The Hague is the case of Naser Orić. In April 2003, NATO forces arrested Orić, a Bosniac wartime commander, and flew him to The Hague to face charges of war crimes against Bosnian Serbs.[27] Orić was one of the most fascinating characters of the Bosnian war—a wartime hero for some Bosniacs, a traitor to others,[28] and a war criminal to Bosnian Serbs, who repeatedly claimed that Orić was responsible for the massacre of two thousand Serbs in the village of Kravica, an event Serbs sometimes referred to as their own

---

24. International Crisis Group, "Turning Strife to Advantage: A Blueprint to Integrate the Croats in Bosnia and Herzegovina," Europe Report no. 106, Sarajevo, March 15, 2001.

25. The case was about alleged war crimes committed by the Bosnian army at the Čelebići Prison Camp.

26. Illustrative of this position is the interview with the defense attorney of one of the Bosniac suspects in Nerzuk Ćurak: "Intervju Dana: Edina Rešidović" [Interview of the Day: Edina Rešidović], *Dani*, December 7, 1998.

27. He was accused of the murder of seven and the torture of many more Bosnian Serbs in the Serbian villages surrounding Srebrenica in 1992 and 1993.

28. The Bosnian press repeatedly ran stories of Orić's apparent abandonment of Srebrenica in 1995, which made the Serbian massacre of Bosniacs possible. B92 network, April 11, 2003, http://www.b92.net. He was also accused of ties with organized crime.

Srebrenica.[29] His arrest and transfer to The Hague enraged many Bosniacs, who accused the ICTY of trying to create a false "ethnic balance" of suspects at the tribunal.[30]

Survivors of the Srebrenica massacre were especially bitter. In a much-repeated statement, one of the "Mothers of Srebrenica," an organization that represented survivors of the massacre, claimed that Orić's arrest was "shameful." "They arrested him just a few days after we buried 600 murdered Srebrenica residents....Orić is not a war criminal, but a man who defended his own people."[31] The Bosniac political leadership was equally enraged. Sulejman Tihić, leader of the major Bosniac political party, Party of Democratic Action (SDA), and a member of the Bosnia-Herzegovina presidency, said that Orić would prove his innocence, since the "truth is that he had defended the unarmed people in Srebrenica from the aggressors who wanted to destroy them."[32] His Bosniac supporters even held a protest demonstration outside the ICTY, with placards that read, "If he is guilty, then so am I—so are we all."[33] Predictably, Bosnian Serbs welcomed Orić's arrest while still displaying disappointment at the scope of the indictment.[34]

If Orić's indictment was controversial, his sentence was even more so. In July 2006, he was sentenced to two years in prison but was immediately released for time served. In justifying the sentence, the judges said the "abysmal conditions" of Srebrenica—a city surrounded by Serbian troops and overwhelmed with starving refugees—had led to such a breakdown of law and order that Orić could not be held accountable for crimes by his troops.[35] Orić enjoyed a hero's welcome back in Bosnia, including from then president of the Bosnian rotating presidency, Sulejman Tihić, who congratulated Orić on "courage and persistence" during his ordeal.[36]

Orić's release, however, only served to further entrench Serb and Bosniac ethnic positions. The president of the Republika Srpska complained that the lenient sentence was a "reward for war crimes against the Serbs" and a clear manifestation

29. These charges, however, were never proven by ICTY investigators, and Orić was not charged for the Kravica killings.

30. Amra Kebo, "Bosnian Fury at Orić Arrest," IWPR, April 14–18, 2003. For an illustrative commentary in the Bosnian press, see Senad Avdić, "Naser u Haagu" [Naser in The Hague], *Slobodna Bosna*, April 17, 2003.

31. Quoted in Kebo, "Bosnian Fury."

32. Quoted in Kebo, "Bosnian Fury."

33. Chris Stephen, "Orić Makes First Appearance," IWPR, April 7–11, 2003.

34. "Naser Orić u Hagu" [Naser Orić in The Hague], *Reporter*, April 16, 2003.

35. Marlise Simons, "Muslim Freed after Conviction," *New York Times*, July 1, 2006.

36. S. R., "Tihić čestitao Oriću na hrabrosti i izdržljivosti" [Tihić Congratulates Orić on Courage and Perseverance], *Oslobodjenje*, July 7, 2006.

of political influence on the ICTY. Srebrenica survivors, however, were relieved by his release but still bitter about his indictment in the first place.[37] "He defended the defenseless and this is why he was indicted," was one of the reactions by the Mothers of Srebrenica.[38]

For Bosnian Serbs, therefore, Orić's lenient sentence gave further fuel to the claim that the ICTY was an anti-Serb body, influenced by international actors with an anti-Serb agenda. The Orić case and the support he continued to have among Bosniac elites were also used by Bosnian Serb leadership to accuse their Bosniac counterparts of "extremism,"[39] a charge that was then used to justify continuation of the Republika Srpska's autonomous status. It made Bosnian Serbs and their political entity further distrust international actors and strengthened their calls for independence and self-rule within Bosnia, positions that flew in the face of international and Bosniac plans for the future of the country. On the other hand, Bosniac elites used the ICTY opinion that leniency was warranted for crimes committed under terrible circumstances as a confirmation of their long-standing argument that as victims of genocide, Bosniacs should be judged differently than their Serb and Croat counterparts. The Orić case, therefore, served as a bargaining chip between Serb and Bosniac elites, who each took what they wanted from the process to pursue their national claims.[40]

The Hague: The Letdown of High Expectations

The Orić case, however, was just one of the hundreds of Bosnian cases brought before the ICTY. It is therefore worth examining more systematically the extent to which the ICTY fulfilled many international and local expectations as a major institution that would bring justice to Bosnia.

As indicated earlier, Bosniac elites and victims' groups welcomed the ICTY enthusiastically, hoping that it would investigate and adjudicate many if not most war crimes committed against the Bosniac population. In that regard, the existence of the ICTY was instrumental in jump-starting the process of transitional justice in Bosnia. Without the ICTY, it is unlikely that Bosnian authorities would

---

37. Sakib Smajlović, "Naser Orić nije trebao dobiti ni dana zatvora" [Naser Orić Should Not Have Been Sentenced to a Day in Prison], *Oslobodjenje*, July 5, 2006.

38. B92, July 1, 2006.

39. O. V., "Čavić optužio SDA da podstiče ekstremizam" [Čavić Accused SDA of Supporting Extremism], *Oslobodjenje*, July 29, 2006.

40. Senad Pećanin, "Naser Orić—moneta za potkusurivanje" [Naser Orić—Bargaining Chip], *BH Dani*, July 7, 2006.

have begun any serious prosecutions of war-crimes trials. The ICTY investigations and indictments also removed from power many old-regime spoilers, preventing them from causing further destabilization of Bosnia. In that sense, the ICTY has served as another agent of lustration in Bosnia.[41]

This is especially the case in the Republika Srpska, which has only recently started its domestic war-crimes trials after direct pressure from the OHR as well as from the ICTY itself, which is beginning to transfer cases to local courts as part of its exit strategy. The ICTY therefore opened possibilities for domestic trials as well as for the special Bosnian War Crimes Chamber, and it has contributed to developing a true legal system in Bosnia that focuses on the individual responsibility of the perpetrators.[42] By doing so, the ICTY has personalized guilt. The first ICTY president, Antonio Cassese, often emphasized this aspect of the ICTY: "If responsibility for the appalling crimes perpetrated in the former Yugoslavia is not attributed to individuals, then whole ethnic and religious groups will be held accountable for these crimes and branded as criminals."[43]

The ICTY has also served an invaluable historical purpose by creating a body of evidence of war crimes committed in the Yugoslav wars that likely would not have been collected in the absence of The Hague proceedings. International trials have also included the first-person testimonies of more than 3,500 witnesses, giving them some public acknowledgment of their loss and suffering.[44]

However, the ICTY has caused great disappointment for both victims and local transitional justice activists in Bosnia. First, ICTY legal proceedings have been staggeringly difficult for the local population to understand and internalize, mostly because the ICTY uses the Anglo-Saxon trial system, which involves guilty pleas and bargaining—concepts very alien and often considered offensive to war-crimes victims and survivors.[45] For many victims, ICTY sentences have been shockingly low, plea bargains overused, and the percentage of acquittals too high.[46]

---

41. For an argument about the positive contribution of the ICTY to democracy building in Bosnia, see Lara J. Nettelfield, "Courting Democracy: The Hague Tribunal's Impact in Bosnia-Herzegovina" (PhD diss., Columbia University, 2006).

42. Author's interview with staff of the Research Documentation Center, January 13, 2006, Sarajevo.

43. Quoted in Payam Akhavan, "Justice in the Hague, Peace in the Former Yugoslavia? A Commentary on the United Nations War Crimes Tribunal," *Human Rights Quarterly* 20 (1998): 737–816, 766.

44. United Nations Development Program, "Transitional Justice: Assessment Survey of Conditions in the former Yugoslavia," Belgrade, June 2006.

45. Institute for War and Peace Reporting, "The Hague Tribunal and Balkan Reconciliation," TU No. 462, July 21, 2006.

46. Staff of the Heinrich Boell Foundation, interview.

An example of an ICTY ruling in which great expectations were followed by bitter disappointment was the reduction of the sentence for Radislav Krstić, the first Bosnian Serb official convicted of genocide in Srebrenica. After the ICTY Appeals Chamber lowered Krstić's sentence from forty-six to thirty-five years in prison, Hajra Ćatić, president of the Srebrenica Women's Association, said:

> We are glad that the genocide charge has remained. Any sentence shorter than a life sentence for a criminal such as Krstić is unacceptable for us. Of course, no one listens to us. We are so disappointed with the Hague Tribunal and unhappy with their sentences. If a criminal who is being tried just admits that he committed crimes, he is forgiven for half [of what he did] and gets a minimum sentence. Thus, we really do not expect justice from them.[47]

Some victims' groups have been even more critical of ICTY sentencing. Reacting to a fifteen-year sentence for Dragan Zelenović, a Bosnian Serb accused of massive atrocities against Bosniacs, Bakira Hasečić, president of the association Women Victims of War said, "The tribunal openly sided with the defense of war criminals."[48] This overwhelming sentiment that the tribunal had turned war criminals into victims themselves was even turned into a popular Bosnian documentary film, *Blind Justice.*[49]

Part of what makes ICTY rulings, which often end in reduced sentences, so controversial locally is that the ICTY did not make it a priority early on to educate the Bosnian public about its proceedings and about international war-crimes jurisprudence. For example, the ICTY waited several years to translate its statute and decisions into the local language, leaving all education to the local media, who reinterpreted the tribunal's work in line with their often ethnically biased preconceptions. In fact, a comprehensive survey conducted in 1999, six years after the ICTY was founded, showed that Bosnian NGOs that worked daily on issues of war crimes and reconciliation were woefully uninformed about the processes of international justice and had many misconceptions about war-crimes law and the role of the ICTY.[50] These problems have begun to be addressed by

---

47. Quoted in Saxon, "Exporting Justice," 564.

48. S. S., "Žrtve izgubile povjerenje u Hag" [Victims Lost Confidence in The Hague], *Dnevni Avaz,* April 5, 2007.

49. One of the three Bosnian filmmakers who produced the film was a former ICTY employee. *Dani,* December 10, 2004.

50. For example, over 60 percent of local NGOs did not know what laws governed war crimes. Over half of the groups did not understand that the NATO-led Stabilization Force (SFOR) did not work directly for the ICTY. Two-thirds of Bosnian NGOs felt that the SFOR was damaging the tribunal's reputation either because of its failure to make arrests or because of the way in which it made arrests, while 60 percent did not think the tribunal was a credible legal institution. Kristen Cibelli and

ICTY outreach offices, but for many Bosnian promoters of transitional justice, the reaction has been too little too late.[51]

The confusion about the ICTY proceedings and their location far away from Bosnian war-crime scenes have further limited the tribunal's impact on the local population.[52] Its decision to prosecute high-ranking perpetrators and leave low-ranking suspects to local courts has also embittered survivors. Victims claim that they would get more satisfaction from prosecutions of direct perpetrators, who still live free and in many cases among the victims, than from trials of party officials, whose responsibility is more removed from their daily experience.[53]

The people of Bosnia have also been bitterly disappointed by the international forces' inability to apprehend the men they hold responsible for the genocide. Even the arrest of Radovan Karadžić in July 2008, while clearly welcome news, did not soothe all victims. Some were jubilant: "We have been waiting for 13 years and we lost hope. Now we know—there is justice," said Kada Hotić, a Srebrenica survivor.[54] Hatidža Mehmedović, another Srebrenica survivor, was more muted, however: "If Karadžić was the political brains behind the war in Bosnia, then Mladić was the butcher who executed his orders. I will not sleep until Mladić is in custody. He is the one with the most blood on his hands."[55] Hasan Nuhanović, another Srebrenica survivor, was even gloomier:

> There are literally thousands of war criminals still at large in Bosnia. They live in our neighborhood and they also have to be arrested. This arrest came thirteen years late! Listen, this man means nothing to me to be honest. There will never be satisfaction for me or other Srebrenica genocide survivors. We will have to live with our pain until the end of our lives.[56]

This broadly shared view of justice denied or, at the very least, justice decades delayed has further played into the view of the ICTY as an ineffectual institution with a huge budget and not much to show for it. Bosnian sociologists have

---

Tamy Guberek, "Justice Unknown, Justice Unsatisfied? Bosnian NGOs Speak about the International Criminal Tribunal for the Former Yugoslavia," unpublished manuscript, Tufts University, 2001.

51. Staff of the Heinrich Boell Foundation, interview.

52. Freeman, "Bosnia and Herzegovina," 2 n. 6.

53. Author's interview with the president of the Bosnian Constitutional Court, January 12, 2006, Sarajevo.

54. Quoted in Jenny Booth, "World Reaction to Radovan Karadžić's Arrest," Times, July 22, 2008.

55. Quoted in Dan Bilefsky, "Bosnia Fugitive Is Hero to Some, Butcher to Others," New York Times, August 5, 2008.

56. Quoted in Sebastiaan Gottlieb, "Disbelief in Bosnia over Karadžić Arrest," Radio Netherlands Worldwide, July 23, 2008. Mr. Nuhanović unsuccessfully sued the Dutch government for failing to protect the Srebrenica enclave.

argued that the popular disillusionment with the ICTY has contributed to further retraumatization of the population, who are continuing to be prey to nationalist ideologies that are in abundant supply.[57]

In some ways, the disappointment with the ICTY is the result of greatly overstated expectations that both international actors and the local population had of this institution. As the only institution of transitional justice in the country for a long time, the ICTY was locally perceived as the place to go to get some kind of acknowledgment of individual suffering and loss. Since the atrocities committed in Bosnia were so numerous and horrific, it was clearly not possible for an international court in the Netherlands to address each individual grievance. Finally, the disappointment with the ICTY felt widely in Bosnia across all sections of society has to do with one of the paramount paradoxes of transitional justice—there can never be appropriate punishment for crimes of such magnitude. This is why some ICTY officials have been advocating less of a focus on victims and more on ensuring that the trial process runs as fairly as possible.[58]

The widespread criticisms of the ICTY within Bosnia have also been used to absolve domestic elites of their role in the lackluster process of transitional justice in the country. This has especially been the case in the Republika Srpska, where the police have consistently refused to act on arrest warrants for war crimes issued by cantonal or district courts.[59] To a great extent, this political environment of obstruction has contributed to fewer prosecutions at The Hague. However, since the ICTY is the most visible institution of transitional justice in Bosnia, the blame for underperformance has been laid squarely at the door of the tribunal.

Bosnian political elites used the ICTY's sinking reputation to further advance their local agendas. The Bosniac leadership made repeated claims that the persistent obstruction of transitional justice by the Republika Srpska was a confirmation of the entity's political immaturity, isolationism, extremism, and harboring of war criminals. Sulejman Tihić, SDA leader and former president of the Bosnian collective presidency, said that the Republika Srpska should be eliminated "due to its repeated violations of international justice."[60]

---

57. Staff of the University of Sarajevo Center for Human Rights, interview.

58. Author's interview the senior ICTY official in Bosnia, who requested anonymity, January 13, 2006, Sarajevo.

59. Human Rights Watch, "Still Waiting: Bringing Justice for War Crimes, Crimes against Humanity, and Genocide in Bosnia and Herzegovina's Cantonal and District Courts," New York, July 9, 2008.

60. D. R., "Krajnje vrijeme da međunarodna zajednica preispita postojanje RS" [It Is High Time for the International Community to Reexamine the Existence of the RS], *Nezavisne novine*, June 11, 2004.

Bosniac elites also used the ICTY's diminishing popularity to push for relocating the justice process from the international sphere back to Bosnia, to localize justice.[61] This push was made easier by the increasing international unease with the huge cost and underperformance of the ICTY. These criticisms were leveled most strongly by the United States under the Bush administration, which voiced its hostility toward institutions of international justice most loudly with its obstruction of the International Criminal Court. Bosniac elites played off this decreasing international appetite for endless funding of a bloated international institution such as the ICTY to revisit calls for a stronger Bosnian national judiciary and establishment of Bosnian national institutions to process war crimes.[62] They used the decreasing legitimacy of an international justice institution to argue for a general diminishment of international rule in Bosnia and return of sovereignty to Bosnian institutions.

International Justice and Genocide

The Bosniac leadership has always argued that Bosnian Serbs and Serbian forces committed genocide in Bosnia. However, legally classifying the conflict as genocide was important for a number of reasons. It clearly defined the character of the war as not a civil war or international conflict or territorial dispute but a determined effort by one side (Serbs) to eliminate Bosniacs as a people on the territories Serbs controlled or fought to control. Calling the conflict genocide also defined Bosnia internationally as a "victim state," entitling it to generous international economic and political aid and securing sustained international support, partly out of a sense of shared guilt for not preventing atrocities in the first place. Politically, qualifying the conflict as genocide made calls for a unitary Bosnia stronger, diminishing the standing of the autonomous Republika Srpska as the entity that carried out the ultimate act of evil. Finally, treating the war as genocide had significant precedent-setting legal repercussions, as Bosnia sued the state of Serbia for reparations for genocide in front of the International Court of Justice, the first time one nation had sued another over claims of genocide.[63]

---

61. Rubina Čengić, "Suđenje za ratne zločine postaće naša realnost" [War Crimes Trials Will Become Our Reality], *Nezavisne novine*, July 17, 2004.

62. Mirza Čubro, "Odlaskom stranih sudija i tužilaca neće se urušiti BiH" [Departure of Foreign Judges and Prosecutors Will Not Destroy BH], *Nezavisne novine*, April 17, 2005.

63. *Application of the Convention on the Prevention and Punishment of the Crime of Genocide (Bosnia and Herzegovina v. Serbia and Montenegro)*, filed in the ICJ Registry on March 20, 1993. The Bosnian genocide case, in fact, was the most complex case in the sixty-year history of the ICJ, set up by the United Nations to adjudicate disputes between nations.

Even though the ICTY and the ICJ were separate tribunals, a genocide conviction of an individual in front of the ICTY would strengthen the Bosnian case in front of the ICJ.

The ICTY passed its first genocide conviction in 2001, in the case against Bosnian Serb commander Radislav Krstić, who was accused of supervising the Bosnian Serb massacre of Bosniacs in Srebrenica in 1995. Upholding the genocide sentence, the ICTY Appeals Chamber stated:

> By seeking to eliminate a part of the Bosnian Muslims, the Bosnian Serb forces committed genocide. They targeted for extinction the 40,000 Bosnian Muslims living in Srebrenica, a group that was emblematic of the Bosnian Muslims in general.... The Appeals Chamber states unequivocally that the law condemns, in appropriate terms, the deep and lasting injury inflicted, and calls the massacre at Srebrenica by its proper name: genocide. Those responsible will bear this stigma, and it will serve as a warning to those who may in future contemplate the commission of such a heinous act.[64]

The genocide conviction caused great alarm in Serbia, where the government feared it would bolster Bosnia's case in front of the ICJ.[65] In contrast, Bosniac leaders were quick to applaud the ICTY ruling as a final determination that Bosnian Serb forces had committed genocide against Bosniacs. The conviction also "showed the truth, justice and confirmed the character of the Bosnian war," said top Bosniac leader Sulejman Tihić.[66] The Bosnian press hailed the verdict as "historic"[67] and predicted that it would influence the ICJ verdict so that "generations of Serbians would pay reparations to Bosnia."[68] Not all Bosniacs, however, were happy with the ruling. The fact that the appeals chamber lowered Krstić's sentence from forty-six to thirty-five years in prison struck Srebrenica survivors as profoundly unjust. Other survivors worried that the genocide verdict would be used for political purposes by the Bosniac elites to create a "cult of the victim" that had been developing in Bosnia since the end of the war.[69]

---

64. *Prosecutor v. Krstić*, Appeals Chamber Judgment, April 19, 2004.

65. B92, April 19, 2004.

66. Ibid.

67. Danka Savić and Nidžara Ahmetašević, "Posljedice presude o genocidu bit će ogromne i dalekosežne" [The Consequences of the Genocide Verdict Will Be Great and Long-Term], *Slobodna Bosna*, April 22, 2004.

68. Mirha Dedić, "Generacije Srbijanaca mogle bi plaćati ratnu odštetu Bosni i Hercegovini" [Generations of Serbians Could Be Paying War Reparations to Bosnia and Herzegovina], *Slobodna Bosna*, April 29, 2004.

69. Emir Suljagić, "Genocid!" [Genocide!], *BH Dani*, April 23, 2005.

Although the Krstić case was of great interest to Bosnians, it was the Bosnian lawsuit in front of the ICJ that truly captured the imagination of the Bosnian people. The genocide case, as it was popularly referred to, was much more often discussed in the Bosnian media and by Bosnian officials, and its progress was generally of much more interest to the Bosnian public, than the often-tedious trials of individuals in front of the ICTY. For many Bosniac leaders, the genocide case was also the real test of international justice. As the former Bosnian foreign minister, Muhamed Šaćirbegović, said, "Now that the process has reached its conclusion, it is time to see if international justice is really attainable or is an empty phrase."[70]

The ICJ case was important for Bosnia as a way for the world to acknowledge the character and magnitude of Bosnian suffering and loss. In his opening statement in front of the ICJ, Bosnian legal representative Sakib Softić said that Serbian violence "destroyed the character of Bosnia and Herzegovina and certainly destroyed a substantial part of its non-Serb population." He said that Serbian leaders took the Bosniac population "on a path to hell, a path littered with dead bodies, broken families, lost youths and lost futures." Since many Serbs continued to deny that war crimes had occurred, the purpose of the ICJ suit was to put an end to "the falsification of history."[71] For Bosniacs, therefore, the genocide case was instrumental in putting forward "the Bosniac" truth, implicitly confirming their long-held claims of being the true victims of the Balkan wars, a fact they felt the Dayton agreement did not acknowledge. But even more than providing an accurate historical transcript, the genocide case was important for Bosniac leaders because it provided an opportunity to correct the injustices of Dayton by rewriting the Bosnian constitution and getting rid of the Republika Srpska as a political entity "founded on genocide."

The expectation that the ICJ would rule in Bosnia's favor was a foregone conclusion in the Bosnian press. The media competed in calculating the amount of reparations Serbia would pay, and they often quoted the number given by Francis Boyle, University of Illinois law professor and senior adviser to the Bosnian legal team, who repeatedly claimed that Bosnia would receive $100 billion in reparations.[72]

In such a media environment, the February 2007 ruling came as a huge shock to the Bosnian public. In the longest ruling in the ICJ's history, the court found

70. S. S., "Pravda je na našoj strani" [Justice Is on Our Side], *Dnevni avaz*, February 11, 2007.

71. Quoted in Marlise Simons, "Bosnia's Genocide Case against Serbia Starts," *New York Times*, February 28, 2006.

72. Sead Numanović, "Počinje historijski proces protiv agresorske SCG" [The Historic Trial against Aggressor Serbia-Montenegro Begins], *Dnevni avaz*, February 26, 2006.

that Bosnian Serb forces, not Serbia proper, had committed genocide in Bosnia. Furthermore, the ICJ determined as the only "confirmed" case of genocide the massacre at Srebrenica, disputing Bosnian claims that the genocide had begun in 1992 in eastern Bosnia. The ICJ ruling found a direct link between Serbia and the Bosnian Serbs but failed to determine that it was Serbia that ordered the killings of Bosniacs. The Serbian state, therefore, was found not guilty of committing genocide, but the court declared it responsible for failing to prevent the genocide from happening. Predictably, the ruling came as a relief to Serbia, which was spared from paying large reparations, but it was a bitter disappointment for Bosniac leaders and war survivors, who were already becoming disillusioned with the idea of international justice. Bosnian outrage was even further inflamed a few months later when evidence emerged that the ICJ was unable to access secret documents that more firmly connected Serbia to orders for genocide. These documents were apparently provided to the ICTY by the Serbian government but on condition that the ICTY not share them with the ICJ in the genocide case.[73]

"I am speechless," said Fadila Efendić, whose son and husband were killed in Srebrenica. "We know that Serbia was directly involved. We saw Serbian troops shell us and kill our sons and husbands. We saw them commit genocide here." The Croat member of the Bosnian presidency, Željko Komšić, said he was shocked. "We must respect the court's ruling, but I know what I will teach my children," he said.[74] The ruling was also loudly criticized by Bosnian academics, who called it political, unjust, and unfair and an encouragement to criminals and criminalized states worldwide.[75] Once again an international justice institution had been used to settle local political accounts. Haris Silajdžić, Bosniac member of the BH presidency and president of the Party for BH issued a statement calling for a constitutional restructuring of Bosnia that would "annul the results of genocide."[76] Silajdžić also argued that, at the very least, the RS should lose authority over its police forces as a result of the ICJ ruling. He also suggested that the Republika Srpska (Serb Republic) should change its name to the Republic of Serbs, Croats, and Bosniacs.[77]

---

73. Marlise Simons, "Genocide Court Ruled for Serbia without Seeing Full War Archive," *New York Times*, April 9, 2007; Simon Jennings, "Secrecy and Justice at the ICTY," IWPR, May 14, 2008.

74. Quoted in Nicholas Wood, "Bosnian Muslims View Ruling as Another Defeat," *New York Times*, February 27, 2007.

75. Zdravko Grebo, University of Sarajevo law professor and director of Center for Interdisciplinary Studies, interviewed in *Oslobodjenje*, March 3, 2007. Nerzuk Ćurak, University of Sarajevo political science professor, interviewed in *Dani*, March 2, 2007.

76. "Presuda Suda u Hagu je pobjeda BiH [Hague Court's Decision is a Victory for BH]," *Dnevni avaz*, March 6, 2007.

77. Senad Pećanin, "Ko je ovdje lud?" [Who Is Crazy Here?], *BH Dani*, April 6, 2007.

The Bosnian population had great expectations from both Hague tribunals—ICTY and ICJ—and hoped these institutions would bring acknowledgment of their suffering and provide some measure of justice to victims. However, the bureaucratic nature of the courts, the legalization of truth seeking, the displacement of the process from Bosnia to a foreign country, the inability of the ICTY to prosecute the most-wanted targets, and the stinging defeat in the genocide claim all contributed to the widespread popular feeling that the opportunity for justice in Bosnia had been lost. Domestic elites in Bosnia used this sinking reputation of international justice institutions to push for more localized justice efforts, a reinforced national judiciary, and—more generally—a stronger unitary Bosnian state, with diminishing dependence on the international community.

The Uneven Promise of Domestic War-Crimes Trials

Domestic trials for war crimes in Bosnia were seriously compromised and the justice system in Bosnia severely impaired for many years after the end of the war. Many legal professionals were killed or displaced, institutions were physically destroyed, and the postwar Bosnian constitutional framework was a maze of bureaucratic complexity.[78]

The Bosnian judiciary in both entities was greatly influenced by extreme nationalists. The quality and professionalism of investigators and judges were questionable, and domestic trials were marred by ethnic bias, poor case preparation, witness intimidation, underutilization of evidence generated by ICTY investigations, and a complete lack of cooperation between the two Bosnian entities.[79] Because of these profound problems, the Bosnian justice system had a very limited impact on transitional justice processes in Bosnia.

The problems with the Bosnian domestic war-crimes trials have been many and serious, especially in the Republika Srpska, where the first domestic war-crimes trial against a Bosnian Serb was held in 2003,[80] almost eight years after the end of the war, while numerous investigations and prosecutions were carried

---

78. Organization for Security and Cooperation in Europe, "War Crimes Trials before the Domestic Courts of Bosnia and Herzegovina: Progress and Obstacles," Sarajevo, March 2005, 4.

79. International Crisis Group, "Courting Disaster: The Misrule of Law in Bosnia and Herzegovina," Europe Report no. 127, Sarajevo, March 25, 2002; Freeman, "Bosnia and Herzegovina." For a particularly egregious example of a compromised domestic war-crimes prosecution, see Human Rights Watch, "The Trial of Dominik Ilijašević," Balkans Justice Bulletin, January 15, 2004.

80. The precedent-setting case was the indictment of a Serb in Banja Luka for the 1995 murder of an ethnic Croat Catholic priest in the town of Prijedor.

out against non-Serbs for crimes against Serbs.[81] The total number of domestic prosecutions in the RS is very low. By March 2008, only 18 indictments had been issued and 7 verdicts rendered.[82] While trials in the Bosniac-Croat federation have been more numerous (144 verdicts in the same period) and somewhat less biased because of the multiethnic composition of judging panels, hundreds of suspects have remained at large in parts of Bosnia where the suspects' ethnic group was in the majority.[83] This has largely been the result of local police reluctance to arrest suspects and the lack of political will in the community to prosecute war crimes.[84]

To correct the significant justice deficiency of the local Bosnian courts in dealing with war-crimes cases, and as part of the international community's exit strategy from Bosnia, the ICTY and the Office of the High Representative in 2005 established a special War Crimes Chamber.[85] The principle guiding the establishment of the WCC is that "accountability for war crimes is ultimately the responsibility of the Bosnian people."[86] Located structurally within the State Court of Bosnia and Herzegovina, the WCC was designed to try the most serious war-crimes cases within Bosnia.[87] In addition to its internally generated caseload, the chamber was to process cases of lower- and mid-ranking suspects as part of the ICTY's completion strategy. Initially, the WCC was to be staffed by both international and local judges and prosecutors, while over time the composition would change to include majority local staff.[88]

The establishment of the Bosnian War Crimes Chamber was also significant internationally, as it was the latest in a series of hybrid tribunals supported by the international justice community as a way to correct institutional deficiencies of

---

81. For example, in 2002, the district prosecutor in Srpsko Sarajevo sought approval from the ICTY for trials against 416 Bosniacs. "Podignute optužnice protiv 416 Bošnjaka" [Indictments Issued against 416 Bosniacs], *Glas javnosti,* April 9, 2002. Also in 2002, the district court in Banja Luka prepared cases against 300 Bosniacs and Bosnian Croats and 12 Bosnian Serbs. Milorad Labus, "U Banjoj Luci pod istragom tri stotine Hrvata i Bošnjaka" [Three Hundred Croats and Bosniacs under Investigation in Banja Luka], *Slobodna Dalmacija,* March 22, 2002.

82. Human Rights Watch, "Still Waiting."

83. Ibid.

84. Human Rights Watch, "Justice at Risk."

85. International Criminal Tribunal for the Former Yugoslavia, "Joint Preliminary Conclusions of OHR and ICTY Experts Conference on Scope of BiH War Crimes Prosecutions," press release, January 15, 2003; UN Security Council, "Security Council Briefed on Establishment of War Crimes Chamber within State Court of Bosnia and Herzegovina," press release SC/7888, October 3, 2003.

86. Office of the High Representative, "War Crimes Chamber Project: Project Implementation Plan," Registry Progress Report, Sarajevo, October 20, 2004, 4.

87. The War Crimes Chamber, together with the Organized Crime and General Crime Chambers, operates within the Criminal Division of the State Court of Bosnia.

88. Human Rights Watch, "Justice at Risk."

purely local and purely international trials.[89] Therefore, the significance of the Bosnian WCC was both substantial (to improve on justice processes currently under way in Bosnia) and institutional (as a real-world test case of the latest trend in transitional justice models).[90]

International justice organizations welcomed the establishment of the WCC as a corrective to problematic local trials and slow and distant ICTY proceedings. The hope was that the WCC proceedings would resonate more deeply with victims in Bosnia not only because they would take place in Bosnia and within the domestic justice system but also because they would involve mid- and low-level direct perpetrators of war crimes, something the victims had long demanded.[91] It was also assumed that the WCC's international staff would be able to carry out "expertise transfer" and contribute to the capacity building of Bosnian war-crimes law experts and institutions.[92]

After two years of setup, the WCC began work in March 2005 and has since seen a steady increase in its caseload and in legal proceedings, such as the taking of statements, searches, and archive research. As of January 2009, seventy-five cases were in trial or on appeal, with twenty-two cases completed.[93]

The manner in which the WCC was established, however, caused great alarm among Bosnian transitional justice promoters. Even though constitutionally the WCC was to be a national Bosnian institution, it was founded by two international institutions—OHR and ICTY—and was overstaffed by international lawyers, with few Bosnian legal experts.[94] But perhaps the most criticized aspect of the WCC was its role as a replacement for the ICTY, as a way for the international community to "defund" the ICTY by starting a new, cheaper, justice institution.[95]

International justice organizations were also critical of the way in which the WCC was set up. Amnesty International, for example, complained that the WCC was based on short-term planning aimed at the "quickest and cheapest possible

---

89. Other recent applications of the hybrid model are Regulation 64 panels in Kosovo, the Special Panels for Serious Crimes in East Timor, and the Special Court for Sierra Leone.

90. Human Rights Watch, "Narrowing the Impunity Gap: Trials before Bosnia's War Crimes Chamber," vol. 19, no. 1(D), New York, February 12, 2007.

91. Experts assess the total number of perpetrators of war crimes who may need to be prosecuted to be as high as ten thousand. Author's interview with WCC prosecutor's staff, January 23, 2006, Sarajevo.

92. Human Rights Watch, "Looking for Justice: The War Crimes Chamber in Bosnia and Herzegovina," vol. 18, no. 1(D), New York, February 7, 2006.

93. Updated information available from the Court of Bosnia and Herzegovina, http://www.sudbih. gov.ba/?opcija=predmeti&jezik=e.

94. The international staff presence at the WCC is slated to expire by the end of 2009.

95. The WCC currently functions on approximately 6 percent of the funds considered essential for the operation of the ICTY. Human Rights Watch, "Looking for Justice."

withdrawal of the international community from the ICTY."[96] Most of the criticism was aimed at WCC funding, as it would drain almost all international aid for justice institutions and leave district and cantonal courts that still processed the majority of war crimes cases without any financial support.[97] Bosnian human rights NGOs have also criticized the apparent lack of victim and civil-society participation in the WCC setup.

There have also been concerns about the way in which the WCC carries out its mandate, which has threatened to erode Bosnian confidence in the institution. Special areas of concern are the prosecution's case selection criteria, broad use of closed sessions, lack of transparency, and poor public outreach and communication.

According to the WCC's mandate, it is to prosecute cases determined to be "highly sensitive," leaving other "sensitive" cases to district and cantonal courts. The determination of a case as highly sensitive, however, is at the prosecutor's discretion and has been applied inconsistently, causing great confusion among the victims and the Bosnian public at large.[98] This lack of clear prosecutorial strategy has contributed to very critical reviews of the WCC in the Bosnian press.[99] It has also been used by political elites in the Republika Srpska, who have exploited the public confusion about the WCC strategy to accuse the chamber of anti-Serb bias, since more than 90 percent of WCC cases have involved Serb defendants.[100] Victims' groups in the BH federation, who were disappointed that not enough was being done to prosecute perpetrators of crimes against them, have also heavily criticized the chamber.[101]

Another issue that has caused public outcry is the prosecutorial use of plea bargains or grants of immunity to lower-level suspects in exchange for testimony. These provisions were introduced to Bosnian case law by the OHR through the adoption of the new Criminal Procedure Code in 2003 and have no background

---

96. Amnesty International, "Bosnia-Herzegovina: Shelving Justice—War Crimes Prosecutions in Paralysis," EUR 63/018/2003, London, November 12, 2003.

97. Since the WCC will handle only the most sensitive cases, it is estimated that it will likely not prosecute more than a few hundred cases, leaving thousands of others to district and local courts. Human Rights Watch, "Still Waiting."

98. Mirela Huković Hodžić, "Justice far from Public Eyes," Balkan Investigating Reporting Network (BIRN), December 25, 2006.

99. Sarajevo's Centre for Investigative Journalism detailed problems with international judges, witness protection, prisons, and the chamber's low profile in Bosnia in an eleven-part series, "Waiting for Justice," available at www.cin.ba. See also Alison Freebairn and Nerma Jelačić, "Bringing War Crimes Justice Back Home," IWPR, November 26, 2004; Beth Kampschror, "Questions Raised over Sarajevo Court Readiness," IWPR, July 23, 2004; Beth Kampschror, "High Hopes for Bosnian Court," IWPR, March 5, 2005.

100. BIRN, Justice Report, September 8, 2006.

101. Human Rights Watch, "Narrowing the Impunity Gap."

in prior Bosnian jurisprudence.[102] As in the case of the ICTY's use of the same prosecutorial tools, they have been met with great disappointment, even hostility, by Bosnian war victims' and human rights groups. The WCC has also been harmed by unresolved regional legal relationships in regard to extraditions of war-crimes suspects, since Croatia and Serbia have continually refused to extradite their citizens to Bosnia for prosecutions.[103] Finally, the WCC promise of expertise transfer has so far been disappointing, as no institutional mechanism has been set up for collaboration between WCC judges and courts at the state and entity levels.[104]

The WCC's poor public relations strategy, its "communication problem,"[105] has resulted in the fact that Bosnian citizens are very poorly, if at all, informed of the chamber's work.[106] The WCC has no regular press briefings, deliberations are closed to the public, press releases are often delayed, and the WCC public schedule is often incorrect and hard to follow.[107] This inconsistent media strategy and general lack of transparency have greatly damaged the WCC's legitimacy with the Bosnian public.[108] Finally, the reputation of the WCC was not helped by a high-profile embarrassment in May 2007, when Radovan Stanković, the first indictee to be transferred from the ICTY to Bosnia, escaped while being transferred to a hospital.[109]

Despite all these problems, the international community has accepted the WCC as a necessary, albeit temporary institution, since the ICTY's closure is imminent and the Bosnian local justice system is still weak and unprofessionalized.[110] For many observers, this indicates that the international community is using this new institution as an easy way out in the face of both local and international disappointment with transitional justice processes in Bosnia. In other words, if the WCC fails, international actors can claim plausible deniability; they can argue that they have given the institution their best effort but that it failed because of domestic incompetence.[111]

---

102. Ibid.
103. WCC prosecutor's staff, interview.
104. Human Rights Watch, "Narrowing the Impunity Gap."
105. Author's interview with staff of OSCE Sarajevo, Rule of Law unit, January 19, 2006, Sarajevo.
106. Huković Hodžić, "Justice far from Public Eyes."
107. Human Rights Watch, "Narrowing the Impunity Gap."
108. Author's interview with staff of the Center for Investigative Reporting, January 12, 2006, Sarajevo.
109. Stanković was serving a twenty-year sentence for crimes against Bosniac civilians in the Foča area. He was convicted by the WCC in November 2006.
110. Freeman, "Bosnia and Herzegovina."
111. Staff of the Heinrich Boell foundation, interview.

The international focus on the WCC has left trials at the local level almost completely in the shadows, and this is where many problems loom large. As many as several thousand cases are lingering unresolved in front of the cantonal courts in the BH federation and the district courts in the Republika Srpska. These trials face a plethora of obstacles: lack of adequate prosecutorial staff who specialize in war-crimes legislation, poor cooperation between prosecutors and police in the two entities, limited witness protection, lax enforcement of suspects' attendance at trial, inadequate defense lawyers' training, and many other issues documented by human rights observers.[112] In fact, some local courts have not tried a single case, more than a decade after the war ended, and those that have remain almost completely shielded from public view.[113]

International human rights observers have warned that Bosnia is in danger of developing a two-tiered war-crimes justice system in which prosecutions take place at the international level and in the WCC, while lower-ranked cases remain in limbo in front of local courts.[114] If this problem persists, it will create an impunity gap for thousands of direct perpetrators of war atrocities, delegitimize transitional justice efforts, and perhaps even lead to further political instability in Bosnia.[115]

To sum up, the Bosnian experiment with domestic war-crimes prosecution has been mixed. International actors aggressively promoted the WCC for a number of reasons. International justice experts wanted to correct for the deficiencies of Bosnian domestic trials and the ICTY and also to put the newly developed hybrid model to use in a real political environment. Donor states, mostly the United States, supported the WCC as a cheaper and more manageable alternative to the bloated and expensive ICTY. Victims' groups within Bosnia were encouraged by the domestic location of war-crimes trials, and promoters of transitional justice welcomed the opportunity for international justice expertise transfer to the local Bosnian legal community. However, a very slow pace of WCC cases, unclear and inconsistent prosecutorial strategy, and the low involvement of Bosnian civil society in the proceedings have all considerably dampened the initial enthusiasm for this new transitional justice institution.

Finally, Bosnian domestic elites have used the WCC to renew calls for strengthening Bosnian national institutions, to show institutional and governing independence from the OHR and international community, and to make a claim for

---

112. Human Rights Watch, "Still Waiting."

113. Ibid.

114. United Nations Development Program, "Solving War Crime Cases in Bosnia and Herzegovina: Report on the Capacities of Courts and Prosecutor's Offices within Bosnia and Herzegovina to Investigate, Prosecute and Try War Crimes Cases," Sarajevo, August 13, 2008.

115. Human Rights Watch, "Still Waiting."

a sovereign Bosnian state with a strong central structure. However, they have wanted to do it on the international dime. The WCC experience therefore serves as another example of the deep paradoxes and contradictions of Bosnian society, a particular love-hate relationship with the international community.[116] It also points to the inconsistencies of international approaches to transitional justice, guided in the Bosnian case mostly by donor state ideological positions (U.S. opposition to international courts), budget concerns, and a feeling of deep distrust in local political elites. Like other transitional justice models, domestic trials in front of the War Crimes Chamber have been fundamentally shaped by international and domestic political strategies and bargains.

Truth Seeking in Bosnia

The Bosnian Truth Commission: Dead on Arrival

Most transitional justice literature recommends that countries coming out of violent conflict institute parallel mechanisms of dealing with the past, to capture both justice and truth.[117] In Bosnia, however, projects for war-crimes trials and a truth commission developed on quite separate tracks and in many ways were quite exclusive of each other.

As in the case of the War Crimes Chamber, the idea for a Bosnian truth and reconciliation commission originated internationally. Discussions about establishing a truth commission for Bosnia first emerged in 1997 at a conference of Bosnian religious leaders organized by the United States Institute of Peace (USIP).[118] The idea was picked up by Bosnian NGOs, and in 2000 the Association of Citizens for Truth and Reconciliation, the seed of the future Bosnian TRC, was established. The USIP sponsored a proposal for a truth commission that aimed to "establish the facts about the nature and scale of past violations and serve as a safeguard against nationalist or revisionist accounts."[119] The ambitious project also recommended reparations to victims, comprehensive legal and institutional reforms, and providing a platform for victims to directly address their grievances, as well as general attempts at promoting national reconciliation and tolerance.

---

116. Staff of the University of Sarajevo Center for Human Rights, interview.

117. Robert I. Rotberg and Dennis F. Thompson, *Truth v. Justice: The Morality of Truth Commissions* (Princeton: Princeton University Press, 2000).

118. Jakob Finci (director of the Association of Citizens for Truth and Reconciliation), in interview with author, January 13, 2006, Sarajevo.

119. Freeman, "Bosnia and Herzegovina," 7.

Problems first arose when members of the rotating Bosnian presidency insisted on maintaining the authority to appoint members of the commission. In fact, Bosnian national leaderships expressed great willingness to support the TRC but only because they felt it was a good vehicle to tell their side of the story.[120] Bosnian civil society reacted by rejecting the TRC proposal, and they rightly feared that all three nationalist leaders wanted to plant a fuse in the TRC so that they could kill it when it stopped serving their nationalist interests.

The second obstacle to the TRC came from the ICTY in 2000. ICTY officials viewed the TRC as both a funding competitor and a redundant institution to the tribunal that would use up all ICTY witnesses. They also argued that persistent ethnic tensions in Bosnia were not conducive to a truth commission and that international attention should be placed on punishment for war crimes and not the search for truth.[121] Over time, however, with the change of leadership at the ICTY, the tribunal became more open to the possibility of a TRC for Bosnia, but it still insisted on limiting its mandate. In 2001, then ICTY president Claude Jorda gave a speech in Sarajevo, arguing that the activities of a TRC in Bosnia should complement, not conflict with, ICTY proceedings. He also identified four areas of activity more suited to a truth commission: dealing with lower-ranking perpetrators, victim reparations, historical analysis, and "the work of undiluted memory." He insisted, however, that no truth-seeking mechanism in Bosnia should replace war-crimes prosecutions.[122]

After several months of follow-up negotiations, a law to establish the TRC was drafted. The law provided for a seven-member commission, made of Bosnian experts and assisted by an international advisory board. Its mandate would be to examine events in Bosnia and the former Yugoslavia from the elections of November 19, 1990, to the conclusion of the Dayton agreement on December 14, 1995. The purpose of the TRC would be to shed light on the nature, causes, and extent of human rights violations committed during the conflict.[123] The proposed TRC would work for two years, would not carry out any investigations that would duplicate ICTY efforts, and would have no courtlike attributes or powers and would provide no amnesty. In other words, it was designed to be a truth-seeking and not a judicial body.[124]

---

120. For example, Bosnian Serb leader Dragan Kalinić initially enthusiastically supported the TRC as an institution "that would finally help the Serbs tell their story." Finci, interview.

121. Ibid.

122. Freeman, "Bosnia and Herzegovina," 7.

123. Neil J. Kritz and Jakob Finci, "A Truth and Reconciliation Commission in Bosnia and Herzegovina: An Idea Whose Time Has Come," Association of Citizens for Truth and Reconciliation, Sarajevo, 2000.

124. Freeman, "Bosnia and Herzegovina."

However, the Bosnian TRC never came into being. There was never even a true debate about the merits of establishing a TRC for Bosnia. Different Bosnian national governments refused to introduce the draft law to the parliament for debate, fearing that calls for reconciliation with their former enemies would cost them votes. The lack of Bosnian state institutions also contributed to the project's stalemate. The project initiators insisted that the TRC should be an official, state-sponsored institution to give it power, authority, and legitimacy. However, the absence of strong Bosnian national institutions, uncertainty about the future of the Bosnian federation, and the internationalization of the Bosnian state all presented obstacles to the creation of the Bosnian truth commission.

Different Bosnian human rights groups also adamantly opposed this project. Mirsad Tokača, director of the very well-respected Research Documentation Center, was almost enraged by very idea of the TRC:

> The idea that they should come to our country and tell us that we need a commission on the South African model is nonsense, especially given that we are at a critical juncture in the work of the Hague tribunal. Institutions of justice are crucial for the future of this country, but there are too many killers here. The question now is what kind of mechanism is needed to assist the acceptance of the truth; the problem is not so much how to reach the truth as how to have it accepted given that so much of the evidence has already been established....I do not need the pretense that what happened was some infringement of human rights— what occurred here was genocide. If the proposed commission, whatever its name is, does not deal with such issues, what else could it do?![125]

But perhaps most damningly, Bosnian victim groups also expressed hostility to the TRC idea, partly because they were not adequately consulted in its setup but mostly because they feared the TRC would be no more than "a debate club with amnesty." As the mother of a Srebrenica victim said, "I don't have anybody to reconcile with. I don't want to forget what happened to me."[126] Emir Suljagić, one of the few male survivors of the Srebrenica genocide, now a respected Bosnian journalist, gave perhaps the clearest explanation for why he was against reconciliation:

> I feel the way a Holocaust survivor would have felt if the Nazis had reinvented themselves....I never wronged anyone. I did nothing wrong.

---

125. Quoted in Emir Suljagić, "Genocid nije u brojevima [Numbers Do Not Make Genocide]," *Dani*, December 23, 2005.

126. Quoted in Nicholas Wood, "Bosnian Jew Promotes Inquiry into Causes of the 1990's War," *New York Times*, April 4, 2004.

Reconciliation means we have to meet halfway, but that's offensive. I was wronged and almost my entire family was killed. I care about justice and truth.[127]

In light of the myriad of institutional, political, and psychological obstacles outlined above, it was almost certain that the Bosnian TRC would never see the light of day, despite great efforts by its main promoter, Jakob Finci.[128] The failure of this institution to hit the ground despite international efforts by organizations such as the USIP and ICTJ is an illustration of great difficulties international models of transitional justice are faced with in complex political environments, where different political stakeholders use them or undermine them for quite local political agendas.

The Sarajevo Truth Commission

In 2004, victims' groups and politicians from the Republika Srpska demanded that the parliament of Bosnia and Herzegovina set up a commission to investigate the fate of Serb victims of the siege of Sarajevo. The Bosnian Council of Ministers delayed a full discussion on this proposal for more than two years, arguing instead for a statewide commission. In reaction to the council's delays, Bosnian Serb representatives boycotted the parliament in May and June 2006. Under Serb pressure, the council finally appointed the commission in June 2006 but with a changed mandate—it was to investigate all victims of the Sarajevo siege, not only ethnic Serbs. The commission was placed under the jurisdiction of the Ministry of Human Rights and Refugees.[129]

The commission's composition, however, created waves of domestic political controversy. In the BH federation, the public objected to a Bosnian Serb commissioner who had been removed by the OHR from membership on the Srebrenica commission in 2004. In the Republika Srpska, objections were raised to the appointment of a Bosniac member, president of the Bosnian Commission for Missing Persons, for alleged lack of objectivity.[130]

Members of the commission insisted that their mandate did not include the broader questions of war responsibility and war onset but only practical details

---

127. Quoted in Tim Judah, "The Fog of Justice," *New York Review of Books,* January 15, 2004. Suljagić's harrowing first-person account of the Srebrenica massacre is published in Emir Suljagić, *Postcards from the Grave* (London: Saqi Books, 2005).

128. Wood, "Bosnian Jew Promotes Inquiry."

129. Mirna Buljugić, "No Progress for Sarajevo Truth Commission," BIRN, February 20, 2007.

130. Humanitarian Law Center, "Tranziciona pravda u post-jugoslovenskim zemljama: Izveštaj za 2006. godinu" [Transitional Justice in Post-Yugoslav States: 2006 Report], Belgrade, 2007, 35.

about the fate of the victims. They could not agree, however, on whether they should also investigate the material damage done to the city during the siege. Reports also leaked to the media of the commissioners' wrangling over the lack of financial compensation for their work.[131] Bosnian human rights groups also criticized the commission's plan to research the fate of the victims according to their ethnicity. Under the commission's action plan, it would investigate whether victims of the Sarajevo siege belonged to eleven distinct ethnic and religious categories.[132] In addition, ostensibly to eliminate bias, researchers were to work in multiethnic pairs.[133]

These structural and personnel problems paralyzed the work of the commission, which has in effect ceased to exist, as it did not produce any report by the expiration date of its mandate in June 2007.[134] The commission also lost political clout, since Bosniac and Croat representatives never showed much interest in the research body initiated by the Republika Srpska. Bosnian Serb representatives, on the other hand, lost interest in the project when it was expanded to include victims of all ethnic groups, not just the Serbs.[135]

The Republika Srpska Comes Clean?:
The Srebrenica Report

Authorities in the Republika Srpska have for a long time either denied that any massacre ever took place in Srebrenica or seriously deflated the number of victims. For example, in September 2002, the RS Government Bureau for Liaison with the ICTY issued a report about the 1995 "events in Srebrenica." Against the overwhelming evidence of a massacre of thousands of Bosniacs collected by ICTY investigators, the RS report claimed that only 100 Bosniacs were unlawfully killed, while 1,900 died "in combat or from exhaustion."[136]

This continuing denial caused great strain on interentity relations in Bosnia, as acknowledging the Srebrenica genocide became in many ways a focal point for Bosniacs, who were in constant search of acknowledgment and recognition of their suffering at the hands of Serbs. Acknowledging the massacre was also

131. Buljugić, "No Progress for Sarajevo Truth Commission."
132. The ethnic options were Serb, Croat, Bosniac, Jewish, Gypsy, Montenegrin, Albanian, Slovenian, Macedonian, undecided, and other; religious options were Orthodox, Catholic, Muslim, Jew, Jehovah's Witness, Adventist, Cosmopolitan, Buddhist, Atheist, undecided, and other.
133. Buljugić, "No Progress for Sarajevo Truth Commission."
134. "Muslimani koče istinu" [Muslims Blocking the Truth], Glas javnosti, October 12, 2007.
135. Humanitarian Law Center, "Tranziciona pravda," 25.
136. Human Rights Watch, "World Report 2003: Bosnia and Herzegovina," Washington, DC, January 14, 2003.

important for victims for practical reasons, as until their loved ones were officially pronounced dead, they could not claim their benefits, remarry, or in any
way move on with their lives. This issue became so toxic politically that in 2003
the internationally appointed Bosnian Human Rights Chamber ordered the RS
to disclose the full truth about the Srebrenica massacre in a report. The chamber found that the failure of RS authorities to inform the victims of the fate
and whereabouts of their missing loved ones violated Article 3 of the European
Convention for the Protection of Human Rights and Fundamental Freedoms as
well as the victims' Article 8 right to respect for their private and family lives.[137]
The chamber also ordered the Republika Srpska to pay more than $2 million in
compensation to the victims and to use the money to build a memorial at the
grave site where families of the victims planned to bury their relatives' remains
once they were finally identified.[138]

In April 2004 the commission issued its interim report, but it listed only the
personnel and institutional problems that prevented it from carrying out its
research. Bosnia's high representative, Lord Paddy Ashdown, reacted by replacing
a few commission members deemed "obstructionist" and ordered the commission to go back to work. In June 2004 the commission published its final report,
which, while short of calling the Srebrenica massacre "genocide," still for the first
time unambiguously stated that on July 10–19, 1995, several thousand Bosniacs
had been "liquidated in a manner which represents a grave violation of international human rights." The report also stated that the perpetrators "undertook
measures to cover up the crime" by removing bodies from the killing sites.[139] The
commission also disclosed thirty-two previously unknown locations of mass
graves, a development that would allow for new exhumations and possible iden-
tifications of the victims, something the survivors had long hoped for.[140] In one
of the clearest statements of repentance by Bosnian Serbs since the end of the
war, the report's conclusion stated "that some members of the Serb people committed a crime in Srebrenica in July 1995." This finding, the report said, might
help bring perpetrators of other war crimes in Bosnia to justice.

But perhaps the most striking result of the Srebrenica report was the turnaround in the rhetoric of the Bosnian Serb hard-line nationalist leadership. RS
president Dragan Čavić read excerpts from the report on RS public television and
indicated that his government would begin to revise its previously recalcitrant

---

137. Human Rights Chamber of Bosnia, Cases Nos. CH/01/8365 et al.
138. Daniel Simpson, "Bosnian Serbs Told to Pay $2 Million for Srebrenica Massacre," *New York
Times,* March 8, 2003.
139. The report is available on the OHR's website, www.ohr.int.
140. Four of the sites were declared "primary" and twenty-eight "secondary" (containing bodies
that had been removed from other sites in order to hide them from international investigators).

position on crimes committed by Serbs during the war. "After years of prevarication, we will have to finally face up to ourselves and to the dark side of our past. We must have the courage to do that."[141]

In November 2004 the report was followed by a public apology of RS officials to victims of war crimes committed by Bosnian Serb forces. The Bosnian Serb government's statement said it "sympathizes with the pain of relatives of the Srebrenica victims and expresses sincere regrets and apologies over the tragedy which has happened to them."[142]

In October 2005 the commission completed its work by turning over to the Bosnian War Crimes Chamber the list of Bosnian Serb troops suspected of involvement in the Srebrenica massacre. The list included 19,473 civilians and armed forces members, of whom 17,074 were named, and for the first time it detailed the extent to which Bosnian Serb forces and institutions were involved in the massacre. The report stated that 17,342 soldiers had participated in the capture of Srebrenica and in the subsequent killings, suggesting the vast extent of the preparation involved in the Srebrenica operation.[143]

The public impact of the Bosnian Serb admission of guilt for the Srebrenica tragedy has, however, been more mixed. Even though the president of the Republika Srpska, Dragan Čavić, publicly described the massacre as "a black page in the history of the Serb people,"[144] he subsequently declined to attend a burial ceremony for hundreds of Srebrenica victims and has not discussed the issue since. This behavior has only confirmed what Bosniac victims and many international observers suspected—that the sole impetus for this about-face in the Republika Srpska came from international actors, mostly the OHR and the European Union, who put increasing pressure on the RS to face up to its past or else meet with further international isolation. For some Bosnian transitional justice activists, this made the entire report appear meaningless.[145] In the words of one survivor of the events at Srebrenica, "It is shameful and the final proof that his confession of guilt for the murder of our loved ones was not heartfelt acceptance of the truth, but the result of international pressure."[146]

---

141. Quoted in Nicholas Wood, "Bosnian Serbs Admit Responsibility for the Massacre of 7,000," *New York Times*, June 12, 2004.

142. Quoted in Nicholas Wood, "Bosnian Serbs Apologize for Srebrenica Massacre," *New York Times*, November 11, 2004.

143. Nicholas Wood, "More Prosecutions Likely to Stem from New Srebrenica Report," *New York Times*, October 6, 2005.

144. "Srebrenica Victims Laid to Rest," BBC News, July 11, 2004.

145. Author's interview with staff of the Research and Documentation Center, January 13, 2006, Sarajevo.

146. Agence France-Presse, July 9, 2004.

In many ways, the great international attention put on the Srebrenica report let Bosnian Serb authorities off the hook, as they felt their transitional justice job was done. And even some Srebrenica survivors objected to the fact that most of the international attention focused on Srebrenica while in fact the Bosnian genocide had begun in 1992, with the horrible crimes of Serbian troops against Bosniacs in eastern Bosnia in cities such as Bijeljina and Prijedor. But because Srebrenica was such a paradigmatic image of the Bosnian genocide and had become a familiar name internationally, attempts at truth finding in other regions of Bosnia remained unfulfilled.[147]

To sum up, truth-seeking projects in Bosnia have been sporadic, unfocused, and mostly internationally driven. In the political environment permeated by ethnic politics, attempts at truth finding were drowned in national calls for sovereignty or were used to deflect international pressure—all ends far removed from the substance and expectations of international transitional justice norms.

Domestic Demand from Below

By contrast with Serbia and Croatia, public demand for transitional justice in Bosnia was always high.[148] Even though divided into ethnic entities with limited interaction, the population of Bosnia still nominally lived in one country. Therefore, victims' groups' demands for justice could still be passed on to state authorities and could shape the national debate about the past. And although the pace of refugee return was disappointingly slow, some regions of Bosnia were more successful than others at integrating refugees back into their communities, achieving some, albeit still woefully inadequate, degree of multiethnic coexistence.[149] This continuing presence of victims and survivors in the same state and sometimes in the same communities with perpetrators made calls for justice in Bosnia much more vocal and urgent than in either Serbia or Croatia.

This strong demand for justice also led to the professionalization of victims' groups and their integration into the larger Bosnian civil society. This was perhaps most clearly the case with the female survivors of the Srebrenica massacre, who formed a number of different groups, commonly known as "mothers of

---

147. Emir Suljagić, in interview with author, January 19, 2006, Sarajevo.

148. According to a comprehensive United Nations survey, as many as 84 percent of Bosnian citizens supported efforts to bring perpetrators of war crimes to justice. United Nations Development Program, "Transitional Justice in Bosnia and Herzegovina: Situation Analysis and Strategic Options," Sarajevo, 2005.

149. International Crisis Group, "The Continuing Challenge of Refugee Return in Bosnia and Herzegovina," Europe Report no. 137, Sarajevo, December 13, 2002.

Srebrenica," and raised a consistently loud voice in all discussions about transitional justice in Bosnia. But while the demand for transitional justice consistently remained high in Bosnia, the definition of justice varied from group to group, and like so much in the Bosnian postwar environment, was deeply rooted in ethnic politics.

The first problem was that public stories about the war within Bosnia were incommensurable. In a continuation of the wartime narrative, Bosnian Serbs held that they had fought in the Bosnian war in self-defense against the expansionist and Islamicist tendencies of the Bosniac majority. They did not believe that their troops had committed atrocities on a large scale, and they certainly did not believe they had committed genocide. They perceived international justice as victor's justice and the ICTY as an anti-Serb institution, an extended arm of the great powers. In fact, they believed that it was the Serbs who were the greatest victims of the Bosnian war.[150] And because the war did affect the Bosnian Serb population in very real ways—they suffered significant losses and were victims of terrible atrocities and revenge killings—the shared understanding of the past for Bosnian Serbs was in direct opposition to what institutionalized models of transitional justice were trying to achieve. Transitional justice, in other words, was causing cognitive dissonance in the Republika Srpska. Bosnian Serb truth was simply incompatible with Bosniac and Croat truths about the war, victims, perpetrators, and justice.

The Bosniacs' demand for transitional justice revolved around the shared understanding that they were victims of genocide, not just war crimes. The focus on genocide profoundly shaped the Bosniac narrative about the past and about what needed to be done to address it. In many ways, the collective nature of the crime—the attempt to eliminate an entire ethnic group—made the responses to the crimes and the desire for justice also appear to be group rather than individual in nature. In other words, Bosniacs felt that they had been harmed as a group, not only as individuals, and that they had also been harmed by a group (Serbs), not only by individual direct perpetrators. This understanding of the conflict, crimes, and grievances directly shaped the type of transitional justice model the Bosniac population was interested in. It also explains why the genocide case in front of the ICJ caught the public imagination so much more than the individual cases before the ICTY.

The narrative of Bosniacs as victims of genocide also influenced inter-Bosniac debates about transitional justice. A particularly interesting example of this debate was the deep controversy about the exact number of victims of the Bosnian war.

---

150. Results of the UNDP opinion poll conducted in 2005. United Nations Development Program, "Transitional Justice in Bosnia and Herzegovina."

In December 2005, the Sarajevo-based nongovernmental organization Research and Documentation Center (RDC) published the results of its four-year, internationally sponsored project to determine the actual number of war-related deaths in Bosnia and name all the victims. The findings of the research put the number of war deaths at an estimated 102,000, of which 65 percent were Bosniacs, 30 percent Serbs, and 5 percent Croats and "others."[151] While this number was consistent with previous scholarly research,[152] it was significantly less than the 200,000 or 300,000 figures given consistently since the end of the war as historical "facts" by Bosniac leaders, national and international media, foreign leaders, and international organizations.[153]

The publication of this revised number caused great consternation among Bosniac elites, who immediately attacked the project's methodology, findings, sources of funding, and researchers' integrity.[154] Bosniac newspapers ran commentaries arguing that the RDC numbers served the agenda of "many who want to deflate the number of Bosniac victims."[155] Leading Bosniac genocide scholars (and top-ranking SDA officials) argued that the number dramatically deflated Bosniac casualties, as it did not take into account "total demographic losses" that would include thousands of children that were never born, as well as victims who died of poor health or stress brought on by the war.[156] As such, the RDC project undermined the genocidal character of the Bosnian war. The project leaders defended their work:

> Genocide is not a question of numbers; it is a matter of the identity of the victims, the way in which they died, and when they died.... A myth about the victims is a myth against the victims: it is the greatest

151. The actual number of reported deaths in the RDC database changes daily as new entries are added and duplicates deleted. For example, on the day of author's visit to the RDC in January 2006, the number stood at 94,450. The project leaders estimated that the number would go up to 102,000 to account for the margin of error, mostly missing victims whose deaths were never reported or noted, which was often the case when entire families were wiped out.

152. Demographics experts working for the ICTY had earlier arrived at a figure of 102,622. See Ewa Tabeau and Jacub Bijak, "War-Related Deaths in the 1992–1995 Armed Conflicts in Bosnia and Herzegovina: A Critique of Previous Estimates and Recent Results," *European Journal of Population* 21, nos. 2–3 (2005): 187–215, 206.

153. Bosnian reporters credit Alija Izetbegović, Bosnia's wartime leader, with the first mention of this figure in 1993, at a press conference held during the Geneva negotiations. Suljagić, "Genocid nije u brojevima."

154. Mirsad Tokača, project leader, also reported death threats after the report was published. Author's interview with staff of the Research and Documentation Center.

155. Almasa Hadžić, "Licitiranje bh. žrtvama" [Auctioning BH Victims], *Dnevni avaz*, January 28, 2006.

156. Author's interview with the director of the Institute for War Crimes Research, January 12, 2006, Sarajevo.

disservice we can do to them. Changing the numbers will not change the nature of what happened.[157]

Although one would have expected that the reduced number of victims would have been welcome news to Bosniacs, this controversy put on display the way in which debates about the past are used for today's political gains. In many ways, the Bosniac academic and political elites wanted to keep the number of victims high for shock value and to stir up nationalist sentiment come election time. For example, human rights activists have noted that the debate about numbers and exhumations of Bosniac graves always happen on the eve of elections.[158]

For Bosniac elites, the controversy over the war dead was justified in the name of the Bosniac national interest; high numbers served to recognize Bosniac victimization, something the elites felt was not recognized by the Dayton accords. In other words, the elites mythologized the number of Bosniac victims in an attempt to shape Bosniac national consciousness around the concept of a victim.[159] In the blunt words of Emir Suljagić, Bosniacs internalized the cult of victimhood so much so that "they have become like Serbs."[160]

To sum up, while domestic demand from below was high in Bosnia, the three ethnic groups had different narratives about past events that would be subject to transitional justice processes. Transitional justice projects therefore became an obstacle to the ethnonationalist elites in Bosnia. They had the potential to destroy mythologized interpretations of the past on which the nationalist elites had to depend if they were to remain in power.

Old-Regime Spoilers in the Neighborhood

The Dayton peace process stopped the Bosnian war and Serbian expansion in its tracks. Dayton's focus on ending the war and preserving the Bosnian state meant, however, that wartime institutions and personnel would remain frozen in time while the international community's high representative would carry out piecemeal reforms over many years.

This decision was particularly significant for the Republika Srpska, where virtually all of the wartime apparatus of force—police officers, military personnel,

---

157. Mirsad Tokača, leader of the RDC project, quoted in Suljagić, "Genocid nije u brojevima."
158. Author's interview with the director of the Helsinki Committee of Bosnia, January 17, 2006, Sarajevo.
159. Staff of the University of Sarajevo Center for Human Rights, interview.
160. Emir Suljagić, interview.

intelligence services—remained unchanged. Considering the huge number of Bosnian Serbs who were in some way involved in the war-crimes enterprise, it is reasonable to assume that thousands of war-crimes suspects roamed Bosnia, some living next door to their victims' families.[161] In the words of a Bosnian Serb human rights activist, "We live with the former war criminals, we see them every day in the streets."[162]

The delayed police reform was especially problematic because it meant that the same forces that had committed war crimes would be in charge of arresting potential suspects. The continued presence of war-crimes suspects in the local administration of the Republika Srpska, many of whom have been indicted by the ICTY, has been a serious impediment to the return of non-Serb refugees to the RS.[163] By authoritative reports, the police forces of Republika Srpska still contain as many as one thousand direct perpetrators of the Srebrenica massacre.[164]

A succession of Bosnia's high representatives has avoided tackling this problem. To some extent the international community tied its own hands in this regard as the Dayton accord allowed all three unreformed wartime nationalist political parties—SDS, SDA, and HDZ[165]—to participate fully in Bosnia's postwar elections, thereby legitimating them as genuine political actors. The international reliance on unreformed nationalist parties has in some ways been inevitable, as these parties still clearly enjoy the overwhelming support of their respective electorates, mostly by continuing to stir nationalist sentiments of victimization or threat. However, Lord Paddy Ashdown, the high representative who more than any of his predecessors or successors believed in direct and intrusive action by the international community in Bosnia, made it a direct policy of his office to make Bosnia's nationalist parties international partners. Ashdown's bet was that a full package of comprehensive reforms of the economy, police, military, and judiciary he wanted to implement in Bosnia could be successfully sold to the Bosnian public only by their trusted nationalist leaders. This approach yielded some short-term gains, mostly by having nationalist parties all sign on to Ashdown's centerpiece reform agenda "Jobs and Justice" and agree to draft

161. Mirsad Tokača, director of the Sarajevo Research and Documentation Center, estimates that between three thousand and five thousand direct perpetrators could potentially stand trial. In Allan Little, "Karadžić's Broken Bosnia Remains," BBC News, September 17, 2008.

162. Branko Todorović, director of the Helsinki Committee for Human Rights in Bijeljina, Republika Srpska. Quoted ibid.

163. International Crisis Group, "War Criminals in Bosnia's Republika Srpska: Who are the People in Your Neighbourhood?" Europe Report no. 103, Sarajevo, November 2, 2000.

164. Suljagić, interview.

165. Stranka demokratske akcije (Democratic Action Party), Srpska demokratska stranka (Serbian Democratic Party), and Hrvatska demokratska zajednica (Croatian Democratic Union), respectively.

legislation on unifying the customs services, carrying out tax reform, subordinating entity armies under the state civilian-led command, and establishing a state intelligence agency.[166] However, the long-term implication of such an approach was to further empower old-regime elites. They appeared inevitable and indispensable and the only legitimate representatives of the citizenry still immersed in their own past ethnic grievances. This approach also further marginalized Bosnia's moderate forces, whose poor showing in elections made them unattractive for the OHR to deal with.

Ashdown's pact with nationalists also did not move Bosnia's stalled police reform.[167] This was a necessary first step that would open the path to more arrests and prosecutions of war-crimes suspects, but it was also one of the reforms required by the EU for any potential Bosnian accession bid. The nationalist parties signed on to the reform plan but then failed to implement it. The opposition to police reform was most acute in the Republika Srpska, whose leadership made public statements opposing any further reform of RS police.[168] RS leaders justified their continuing opposition to reform as an issue of RS sovereignty. It was clear, however, that the great number of perpetrators of war crimes among police forces would be exposed if the police were to be radically reformed and merged with the other entities, a factor that made this a politically hot issue Bosnian Serb elites were not prepared to deal with. After directly tying Bosnia's potential EU accession negotiations with police reform, the Bosnian parliament finally signed the reform bill in April 2008, after four years of contentious debate.[169]

The continuing power of criminalized wartime nationalist parties and the absence of lustration in the police forces have persistently hindered progress in the field of transitional justice. Even more significantly, the normalization of war criminals into postwar Bosnian political and administrative structures has further fueled interethnic distrust, making attempts at reconciliation seem that much more difficult to attain. In the words of Emir Suljagić, Bosnian journalist and survivor of the Srebrenica massacre, "What kind of a state officer can a former camp guard be?"[170]

---

166. International Crisis Group, "Bosnia's Nationalist Governments: Paddy Ashdown and the Paradoxes of State Building," Europe Report no. 146, Sarajevo, July 22, 2003.

167. OHR had more success with reforming the Bosnian military. See International Crisis Group, "Ensuring Bosnia's Future."

168. Ibid.

169. "Police Law Moves Bosnia toward EU," BBC News, April 11, 2008.

170. Emir Suljagić, in interview with author.

Bosnian Elite Strategies

Unlike Serbia and Croatia, who emerged from the war as mostly ethnically homogeneous states, postwar Bosnia was divided territorially, ethnically, and politically. As a consequence, ethnic divisions dominated the Bosnian political landscape, with national agendas guiding all political strategy. The ethnification of Bosnian politics also directly influenced elite transitional justice strategies. While Bosnian ethnic elites mostly resisted transitional justice norms, over time they began to use transitional justice institutions instrumentally, as tools that could help them achieve international legitimacy. This was especially the case in the Republika Srpska, where there was a dramatic change from complete resistance to the somewhat instrumental adoption of international justice mechanisms. Finally, what further distinguished Bosnia from its neighbors was that international actors, so omnipresent in Bosnia, represented the clearest true believers in transitional justice. This is why, like almost everything else in Bosnia, transitional justice was under the international community's spell, making Bosnia move where nationalist elites would stall but at the same time making justice appear less local.

Bosnia's norm resisters included all three top national elites and their respective political parties. The Bosnian Serb elites resisted any attempts at transitional justice for the longest time, and as discussed earlier in this chapter, persistently refused to cooperate with the ICTY or open up domestic war-crimes trials. This resistance was rooted primarily in the Bosnian Serb interpretation of the Bosnian war as a civil war for political dominance of the newly independent state and not aggression or genocide. In fact, Bosnian Serb elites throughout the war and its aftermath played on the population's insecurities and portrayed Bosniacs as an ethnic majority with expansive and dominating aspirations.[171] The permeating presence of direct perpetrators of war atrocities within the Republika Srpska's governing structures further committed the Bosnian Serb leadership to resisting any attempt at transitional justice.

Like all nationalisms, Serbian and Bosniac nationalisms played off and reinforced each other. Every new war-crimes denial by a Bosnian Serb leader was used by the Bosniac elites as proof that the Republika Srpska had emerged out of the war unreformed, an entity created through genocide and urgently in need of abolishment. Calls for the abolishment of the RS in turn further strengthened Bosnian Serb nationalists, who began advocating for a referendum on the full

---

171. For example, see RS prime minister Milorad Dodik's op-ed in *Nezavisne novine*, September 11, 2006.

autonomy of the Republika Srpska from the Bosnian state.[172] These calls have acquired increasing resonance since Kosovo's unilateral declaration of independence in February 2008.

From a political standpoint, Bosnian Serb elites resisted mechanisms of transitional justice, including trials at The Hague, because they feared that these processes only strengthened majority Bosniac calls for the abolishment of the Republika Srpska. The more Bosnian Serbs were found guilty of horrible atrocities, including genocide, the less leverage the Republika Srpska had in negotiations for the future constitutional order of the Bosnian state.[173]

In this political context, the Bosnian Serb elites feared that transitional justice processes would further remove the RS from its ultimate goal, which was a political future with Serbia and away from the Bosnian federation, which they felt looked at them as enemies within and not as fellow citizenry. Over time, however, Serbia's feelings for the Republika Srpska began to cool off, as first Milošević's and then Koštunica's governments continued to rhetorically emphasize ethnic support while in fact removing Serbia further and further from direct mentorship of their Western client state. This change in Bosnia's relationship with Serbia influenced Bosnian Serb political strategy, as without Belgrade sponsorship, the Republika Srpska stood to gain more politically by fostering stronger ties with Sarajevo and the international community. In fact, Dragan Čavić, SDS leader and onetime president of the Republika Srpska, made it one of his major campaign goals to foster "international affirmation and respect of the Republika Srpska."[174] This explains the slow transformation of Bosnian Serb norm resisters into somewhat instrumental adopters of transitional justice, beginning with the release of the Srebrenica report in 2004 and leading to the arrests of war-crimes suspects and their processing before RS courts starting in 2005.

As discussed earlier in the chapter, Bosniac elites enthusiastically supported and pushed for transitional justice processes as long as they did not accuse Bosniac troops of complicity in alleged atrocities. Once Bosniac war heroes stood accused of war crimes, first in front of the ICTY and later before the Bosnian WCC, Bosniac elites joined Bosnian Serbs in decrying international justice as a politically motivated charade.[175]

---

172. Nicholas Wood, "Early Results of Bosnia Vote Reinforce Ethnic Split," *New York Times*, October 3, 2006.

173. This is what RS prime minister Milorad Dodik had in mind when he said in a TV interview that he was "sick and tired" of the politics of Bosniac leaders, "which makes fools of us so that we look like war criminals.... That is all over." Quoted in Wood, "Fiery Campaign."

174. D. Risojević, "Građani znaju kome mogu vjerovati" [Citizens Know Whom to Trust], *Nezavisne Novine*, September 29, 2006.

175. Vedrana Živak, "Izjednačavanje zločina" [Equating Crimes], *Oslobodjenje*, June 1, 2005.

Transitional justice, however, proved an excellent opportunity for the Bosniac elites, and especially the ruling SDA, to continue to use the past for their own political and electoral gains, making them at the same time both resisters and instrumental adopters of transitional justice norms and institutions. As long as the SDA kept the memories of horrible atrocities alive in the public imagination, it continued to present itself as the protector of Bosniacs and could count on majority Bosniac electoral support.[176] War-crimes trials, debates about numbers of victims, exhumations of grave sites, and public memorials all served this political purpose. Even the arrest of Radovan Karadžić could be put to this use. Reacting to the news of the arrest, Haris Silajdžić, chairman of the BH presidency, said, "The genocidal project initiated by those two men [Karadžić and Mladić] should not be left to live."[177] Predictably, RS politicians reacted to accuse the Bosniac leadership of hegemonic intentions. Mladen Bošić, president of the Serbian Democratic Party, described statements such as Silajdžić's as "political orgies that indicate a Karadžić trial would turn into a trial of Republika Srpska."[178]

Transitional justice in Bosnia was also used to further advance the Bosniac nationalist elite concept of Bosnia as a nation-state, with Bosniacs as the "foundational people," relegating Serbs and Croats to the status of a minority. Making Bosnia into a unitary state would also elevate Bosniacs into an unquestionable majority with veto powers in such important matters as control of the military, police, and intelligence services.[179] Furthermore, slowly moving transitional justice processes from the international community's fold into Bosnian national institutions, such as the War Crimes Chamber, strengthened Bosniac calls for independence and sovereignty from the international community and especially from the OHR.

For their part, the Bosnian Croat leadership and the HDZ party elite used transitional justice mechanisms to memorialize crimes against the Croat minority, as they had long claimed that Croatian victims had remained unrecognized by Bosniacs, Serbs, and the international community.[180] At the same time, they used this focus on victims to minimize many documented Croatian war crimes against

---

176. Suljagić, interview.

177. Quoted in Jusuf Ramadanović, "Reactions to Karadžić Arrest Show Depth of Political Fissure in BiH" *Southeast European Times*, July 23, 2008.

178. Ibid.

179. Author's interview with a retired general of the Bosnian army, January 14, 2006, Sarajevo.

180. Croatian member of the BH presidency Ivo Miro Jović even lodged an official complaint with the ICTY for underprosecution of crimes against Croats. A. Omeragić, "Jović nezadovoljan procesuiranjem ratnih zločina nad Hrvatima" [Jović Dissatisfied with Prosecutions of War Crimes against Croats], *Oslobodjenje*, July 5, 2006.

other Bosnian ethnic groups.[181] In other words, Bosnian Serbs and Croats used transitional justice to strengthen the autonomy of their territories at the expense of national institutions. Bosniacs, on the other hand, used transitional justice processes to strengthen the unitary state at the expense of local autonomy.

Furthermore, again in a sharp difference from Serbia and Croatia, the international community's robust presence in Bosnia made international organizations, primarily the OHR, local political stakeholders with their own strategies of transitional justice. The OHR's strategy, however, was inconsistent, and it changed over time from an almost exclusive focus on forcing Bosnian entities to cooperate with the ICTY to an equally strong push for making the Bosnian War Crimes Chamber the primary location of justice processes. Paddy Ashdown, Bosnia's high representative from 2002 to 2006, in fact hailed the opening of the WCC as "Bosnia's great step towards full statehood." Ashdown was especially proud that Bosnia would be the first state in the region that could fully process war crimes cases, making international trials obsolete.[182] It was therefore in the interest of the OHR to strengthen domestic Bosnian institutions of transitional justice, as that would also be a sign of the success of the multiyear, multibillion-dollar OHR mission, which was increasingly being criticized for not having much to show for its efforts a decade after the war ended.[183]

Finally, Bosnia had its share of civil-society true believers in the norms and institutions of transitional justice. They were, however, remarkably splintered and lacked a coherent transitional justice strategy.[184] Nongovernmental organizations that focused directly on transitional justice issues—such as the Association of Citizens for Truth and Reconciliation—enjoyed limited support from other human rights groups and lacked a broad civil-society coalition to push their projects forward. They also encountered most resistance from victims' groups, who were opposed to the concept of reconciliation and instead favored justice and adequate punishment for perpetrators.

But most damningly, Bosnian civil society was disempowered by the overwhelming presence of the international community in Bosnia, which took on itself many activities, projects, and missions that in a less internationalized setting would have been squarely in the domain of civil society.[185] This international juggernaut, especially under Paddy Ashdown's administration, created a self-fulfilling cycle of dependency among both the political elites and civil society,

---

181. University of Sarajevo political science professor, interview.

182. A. Šišić, "Bosna i Hercegovina može započeti procesuiranje ratnih zločina" [Bosnia and Herzegovina Can Begin War Crimes Trials]," *Nezavisne novine*, February 26, 2005.

183. Staff of the University of Sarajevo Center for Human Rights, interview.

184. President of the Bosnian Constitutional Court, interview.

185. Belloni, "Civil Society and Peacebuilding in Bosnia and Herzegovina," 165.

which became more marginalized and too dependent on the OHR to solve Bosnia's social problems.[186]

To sum up, each of the many segments of Bosnian society had its own strategy of transitional justice, and these strategies were not fully compatible with one another. The differences were both horizontal—Bosnia's ethnic entities used transitional justice to advance their claims of sovereignty and control—and vertical—transitional justice was used by Bosnian and international actors as a way to assert authority over the Bosnian state.

Conclusion

Postwar Bosnia seemed like a perfect candidate for transitional justice. The memory of the brutal conflict was still fresh. The victims shared the same state with the perpetrators, and the need for reconciliation seemed urgent if the Bosnian state was to survive. The international community was deeply involved and poured what sometimes seemed like endless funds into postwar Bosnia's reconstruction, including the Bosnian War Crimes Chamber, an ambitious project that was to test the latest transitional justice trend, the hybrid tribunal.

All this interest in Bosnian reconstruction and postwar reconciliation, however, produced decidedly mixed results. Bosnia's post-Dayton ethnic matrix was a straightjacket that channeled all aspects of Bosnia's political life, including all its transitional justice efforts. The political uncertainty of the Bosnian state—an international protectorate with unclear future status—made major Bosnian political actors, domestic as well as international, use transitional justice projects to put forward different kinds of claims about Bosnian statehood. Transitional justice was used to strengthen state institutions but also to weaken and delegitimize the noncooperative Bosnian Serb entity, Republika Srpska, in order to make calls for a unitary and centralized Bosnian state more acceptable and legitimate.

Using transitional justice was an especially convenient way to advance political claims about restructuring the Bosnian state because, on the face of it, transitional justice was a noncontroversial endeavor. All Bosnian political actors could agree that they wanted justice, truth, and some form of reconciliation in order to move Bosnia forward. However, as their understandings of the past were at variance, so were their ideas for the future. Bosnian political actors could never

---

186. Željko Kopanja, a leading Bosnian Serb war-crimes investigative reporter, in an interview in *Start*, April 3, 2007.

quite agree on the final goal of Bosnia, on whether "Bosnia had a point."[187] This political uncertainty, along with mutually exclusive political strategies, stalled transitional justice projects and put them fully in the service of political goals unrelated to the purpose of transitional justice norms. This is why transitional justice in Bosnia was removed from the domain of human rights promotion into the domain of politics, where it quickly became an obstacle to ethnonationalist elites. In this complex context, ethnic politics remained the key that the Bosnian national elites used to open up transitional justice processes.[188]

All of this produced in the traumatized Bosnian population an overwhelming feeling of disappointment with the international community, of justice denied and truth untold. And while transitional justice projects were implemented with great enthusiasm and much support, it remains unclear whether the commitment to these projects will remain once the international community finally leaves Bosnia, something it has been eager to do for years. The signing of the EU SAA with Bosnia in June 2008 puts more pressure on European institutions to monitor Bosnian transitional justice processes. However, as the examples from Serbia and Croatia show, the mechanistic approach the EU has adopted in this area does not provide much confidence that Europe will have the patience and attention to detail required to guide Bosnia in dealing with its past.

That Bosnia desperately needs justice and the type of acknowledgment of past abuses that brings dignity to the victims and lays the foundation for a just social order has always been clear. What is much less clear, however, is who exactly will deliver justice to Bosnia in the absence of the state and the diminishing involvement and waning interest of the international community. The architects of the Dayton accords have long used Bosnia as an example of a successful power-sharing constitutional model that ended the horrific war and brought sustainable peace.[189] However, Bosnia can just as easily be used as an example of how not to partition a country, as federalizing Bosnia only reinforced and solidified ethnic divisions, making truth and justice that much more difficult to bring to life.[190]

Finally, transitional justice projects in Bosnia were all carried out or discussed in the context of a highly internationalized state. Bosnia was de facto ruled by

---

187. University of Sarajevo sociology professor, interview.

188. University of Sarajevo political science professor, interview.

189. For example, see the op-ed piece on the tenth anniversary of the Dayton accords by Carl Bildt, the former prime minister of Sweden, EU cochairman of the Dayton Peace Conference, and the first international high representative in Bosnia, *International Herald Tribune*, November 20, 2005.

190. For example, in light of the unraveling situation in Iraq, there have been many warnings not to use Dayton as a model for Iraq. See, for example, Roger Cohen, "In Recasting Bosnia, Some Lessons for Iraq," *International Herald Tribune*, November 19, 2005; Peter Beinart, "War Torn," *New Republic*, October 30, 2006; Don Hays, R. Bruce Hitchner, and Edward P. Joseph, "Bosnia Is No Model for Iraq," *International Herald Tribune*, January 19, 2007.

the international community; it was for all intents and purposes a trusteeship, governed by a present-day version of a viceroy. The international community, in other words, remained the primary focus of power in Bosnia. This absence of a national state and a highly internationalized political context defined all Bosnia's transitional justice efforts as primarily internationally driven, with local ethnic elites using transitional justice to pursue their own national claims. Transitional justice in Bosnia was therefore politicized by the internationalization of the Bosnian state.

HIJACKED JUSTICE BEYOND THE BALKANS

Institutions of transitional justice have become ubiquitous over the past twenty years. Once considered arcane practices or exercises in victor's justice, mechanisms of transitional justice have increasingly become institutionalized as appropriate ways for states to deal with legacies of past violence. From truth commissions in South Africa to international trials at The Hague, from the hybrid court in Sierra Leone to the ad hoc trials of leaders of Iraq or Liberia and the International Criminal Court, transitional justice institutions are now increasingly accepted as necessary mechanisms for states transitioning from an era marred by brutality to a future where disputes are resolved through political deliberation rather than violence.

Transitional justice institutions are promoted by international institutions such as the United Nations, by a myriad of international nongovernmental organizations and human rights groups, and even by military specialists, all of whom believe that transitional justice is a foundation of sustainable postconflict peace and rebuilding in divided societies. Transitional justice today is also discussed as a significant component of regional integration requirements. Because this is a major change in the way international society deals with the legacies of past crimes, we can now begin to consider transitional justice as a new international norm, a set of expectations that transitioning states are required to follow, the violation of which will incur international sanctions.

The way in which this new international norm played itself out in the states and societies it set out to change turned out to be quite different from the expectations of those who promoted it. Instead of adopting international norms and institutions of transitional justice because they serve a desirable social purpose—truth seeking, justice, and reconciliation—domestic political elites have used these models to pursue quite localized political agendas. Institutions of transitional justice have often been used to appease international coercion, to secure international benefits and payoffs, to deal with domestic spoilers, to obtain international club membership, or to resolve political uncertainty. This hijacking of international transitional justice for local political ends is the central concern of this book.

The three cases—Serbia, Croatia, and Bosnia—have provided ample empirical evidence to confirm the main argument of the book: under specific domestic conditions, compliance with international norms becomes a political strategy that allows states to go through the motions of fulfilling international demands while in fact rejecting the profound social transformation these norms require. The empirical cases have also offered avenues for further fine-tuning of the "norm hijacking" approach, especially in the way we measure international pressures for normative compliance, domestic demand for change, and the power of domestic veto players.

Variation in International Pressure

An important lesson from the three empirical cases explored in this book is that the manner and sustainability of international pressures on target states profoundly affect international policy outcomes. As different outcomes in Serbia, Croatia, and Bosnia show, the level of international involvement and the types of international action varied greatly. In Serbia, international actors applied a very direct, almost mechanistic policy of issue linkage, tying Serbian compliance with international transitional justice requirements to any improvement in Serbian international standing (membership in the EU, international loans, or direct investment). In fact, compliance with international justice demands—mostly reduced to cooperation with the Hague tribunal—became the *most significant* measurement of Serbian compliance with international standards and the most important impediment to Serbian advancement on the international stage. The international hard-line stance on Serbia—and the emphasis on coercive techniques to make Serbia comply—in many ways greatly contributed to the hijacking of the international transitional justice norm and institutions by the Serbian elites. Judging that they had no room to maneuver internationally and faced with powerful veto players and spoilers at home, Serbian elites chose to play a two-level game that would simultaneously appease both international and domestic audiences. They adopted a piecemeal approach to cooperation, fulfilling international requirements at the very last minute, while presenting this strategy to the domestic public as a purely benefits-driven arrangement that would not require politics or ideology to change. Coercive international action, therefore, provided an opportunity for domestic elites to hijack international norms and use them to pursue local political agendas.

In Croatia, international pressure was less pronounced. In fact, international actors made a point of protecting Croatian reformist elites from the burden of international sanctions, thus propping them up politically at times of domestic political turmoil. This softer approach allowed reformers to deal more harshly with veto players and spoilers because they had international backing for their action and did not fear a coup or reversal of power, as was the case in Serbia. Since Croatia cared mostly about international legitimacy and joining the society of European states, a favorable international environment and measured international pressure allowed the elites to sail more or less smoothly toward that goal.

International pressure was, in many ways, the strongest in Bosnia, but the types of international action were much different. International actors took over the state and ran it as an international protectorate, making decisions about international justice as part and parcel of running the state. By doing so, they removed the agency of compliance from domestic political actors and detached the transitional justice process from the society that needed it the most. In this case, it was the international actors who hijacked the justice norm and used it as another tool of bureaucratic governance.

But the lessons learned from these cases point to a more general conclusion about the relationship between international pressure and the hijacking of transitional justice. Although the issue-linkage approach taken by international actors in the three cases is a widely used international tool of policy change, it has led to a flood of unintended consequences. First, international actors have abandoned a more nuanced, comprehensive approach to addressing the brutal crimes of the 1990s that would include seriously monitored domestic trials, official truth commissions, investigative reporting, and civil society projects, in addition to transfers of suspects to The Hague. By doing so, the international community has given ruling elites in the three countries an escape hatch not to deal with the legacy of past crimes in a domestic setting but to delegate the problem abroad, to the Netherlands, hoping that it will somehow go away. In fact, since the international community, particularly the European Union, has made it the sole requirement in the international justice area for these countries to transfer suspects to the ICTY, the governments have been unusually willing to send the suspects off to The Hague, achieving two goals at the same time: showing the EU that they are cooperative and worthy of reward while presenting this policy shift to the still powerful nationalist elites as another patriotic sacrifice that former war heroes are making in the service of their country—this time, by trading themselves for future membership in the EU.

This trade-off—suspects for EU talks—has cheapened international justice and clearly has not brought about reckoning with the past. The serious consequence of this approach is that it has done nothing to delegitimize the nationalist ideologies that brought on the conflict in the first place. In fact, it has presented the incredibly significant issue of justice for past abuses as an issue of barter—international membership for transfer of suspects—that has harmed the image of international institutions as bulwarks of human rights and opened the political space for nationalist ideologues to devalue the entire enterprise of justice. The conclusions of my book therefore serve as a cautionary tale for similar international interventions in domestic politics of target states. Issue linkage is a powerful tool for policy change, but it can produce the opposite effect from the one intended if it is not followed by a comprehensive package of broader social transformation rather than mechanistic compliance that ends up being not much more than policy lip service. In extreme cases, issue-linkage policy may collapse, making international actors appear fickle, not serious, and not dedicated to seeing a policy change go through. This international issue-linkage fatigue allows other target states in future policy interventions to try to wait it out, judging that international actors will get tired, distracted, or move on to a new project.

In sum, international pressure varies in its consistency, reliability, and sustainability. International requirements are not always internally coherent and enforceable, nor do they always contain clear sanctions for violations. Different types and degrees of international pressure therefore allow domestic elites to hijack international norms in a variety of ways.

Fickle and Narrow Domestic Demand

The theoretical model presented in this book takes issue with the idea that the demand for normative change comes from below. Specifically, it is a response to the existing assumption in transitional justice scholarship that since victims deserve justice, they will support transitional justice projects if they are properly designed and set up. This assumption also underlies much of the work of international justice institutions that are spearheading the dramatic rise in transitional justice initiatives around the world. In contrast, the empirical cases presented in the book show the extent to which societies may be uninterested, unready, or even hostile to transitional justice. This political environment then creates favorable conditions for domestic elites to hijack the international transitional justice process for local political ends.

In addition, while domestic constituencies may at first strongly support transitional justice, this support is much more likely to hold if there is a domestic reversal of power—that is, if former victims are now in positions of authority and can put on trial their former victimizers. However, even in these circumstances, domestic commitment to transitional justice projects is likely to quickly dwindle if the trials or truth commissions expand their mandates to prosecute alleged perpetrators from the victim group currently in power. Put differently, this domestic commitment to justice that is the basis of much of transitional justice literature is very fickle and narrow; it does not extend to a full commitment to universal criminal accountability that pays no attention to identity politics (issues of ethnicity, religion, or race) and the victim/aggressor matrix. In plain words, the domestic public is much more likely to support transitional justice if its political opponents (the other guys) are put on trial. It will very rarely offer the same commitment if the perpetrators come from its own ranks.[1]

The empirical evidence for this skeptical view is abundant. Chapters 3 and 4 documented in detail the way in which Croatia and Bosnia, two states that were among the earliest supporters of the Hague tribunal, were enthusiastic champions of transitional justice as long as the international tribunal was putting Serbs on trial against Croats and Bosniacs. When the tribunal began indicting Croat and Bosnian nationals for crimes against the Serbs or against each other, the domestic commitment to international justice significantly dropped. A similar pattern has occurred in Rwanda, where the current government supports the trials of Hutu perpetrators but refuses to cooperate in sending the accused Tutsi to the ICTR.[2]

It is important to point out the problems with this basic assumption in transitional justice literature—that states adopt justice mechanisms because societies demand it—to show how identity politics can trump, or significantly alter, the social demand for justice, opening political space for elites to hijack the process, which in turn leads the justice project into a paradoxical outcome. The theoretical and empirical inadequacy of the ideal-type "demand from below" hypothesis is why this book has explored alternative mechanisms for domestic compliance with international norms and institutions.

---

1. A rare exception seems to be the "other" South African truth commission set up by the African National Congress to look into abuses of its own paramilitary forces. See Priscilla B. Hayner, *Unspeakable Truths: Confronting State Terror and Atrocity* (New York: Routledge, 2001).

2. For the problem of putting "winners" on trial in international courts, see Victor Peskin, "Beyond Victor's Justice? The Challenge of Prosecuting the Winners at the International Criminal Tribunals for the Former Yugoslavia and Rwanda," *Journal of Human Rights* 4 (2005): 213–31.

International Norms and Domestic Veto Players

The findings of this book also offer insights into the particular dynamic that is created when international normative interventions are pitted against powerful domestic veto players. Empirical cases indicate that domestic veto players or spoilers do not simply pose obstacles to international normative and institutional interventions. Rather, they manipulate or hijack the international norm by fulfilling its institutional requirements while ignoring the norm's substance. This process of norm hijacking then calls into question the very notion that international normative diffusion actually brings about social change. In the case of transitional justice, norm hijacking questions the fundamental premise of the literature that the transitional justice norm and its justice cascade actually produce justice. What in fact the norm produces under these circumstances is only an appearance that something is being done. This is an important insight into the relationship between domestic politics and international norms as well as the transitional justice policies themselves.

Norm hijacking, however, is contingent on a particular set of domestic political conditions and the strength and institutionalization of the norm itself. The findings of this book therefore offer another set of implications for a variety of domestic responses to international norms.

Under the domestic conditions described in this book, hijacking occurs when the international norm is strong (sanctions are clear and profound), but so are the domestic veto players. In such cases, domestic elites will attempt to subvert the substance, meaning, and purpose of the norm by fulfilling its institutional requirements. They will use international institutions to resolve domestic political fights. This is the dynamic that the cases of the former Yugoslavia illustrated.

But there are other possibilities as well. If the norm is strong and the veto players weak, the domestic response will be one of stalling. In such cases, international pressures are sustained, but domestic actors do not have the incentive to use international institutions to win over domestic political opponents. Instead, what they hope for is to gain some time by obstructing the process in anticipation that international attention will be diverted elsewhere. The third possibility arises when the international norm is weak or not fully institutionalized and veto players are strong; then we should expect outright rejection of the norm. Further testing of these hypotheses in a variety of international settings is a task awaiting future research.

Comparative Implications

This book has analyzed and explained the process of hijacked justice—a domestic elite strategy of using the international norm of transitional justice for local political purposes—in the context of the former Yugoslavia. The next step is broadening the argument and generalizing the findings beyond the empirical cases described in the book. A good start is to expand empirical research into cases that have very different histories of conflict, types of transition, and domestic constellations of power in the state. This will help nuance the argument to determine to what extent the general political setting and nature of conflict mattered for political consequences of international policy interventions in the field of transitional justice.

Hijacked Justice in Indonesia and East Timor

Indonesia is a good comparative case for exploring the causes and consequences of hijacked justice. The dispute in East Timor (Timor-Leste) was over very different sets of grievances from those in the former Yugoslavia.[3] The conflict not only resulted in partition but was part of a much larger project of decolonization. The international environment was also very different, with the United Nations playing a pronounced role in postconflict rebuilding. And yet with all these different domestic and international environmental components, the transitional justice process in Indonesia and East Timor suffered from many familiar characteristics of hijacked justice.

As a consequence of the international outrage over the atrocities the Indonesian army and militias had committed in East Timor in 1999, the United Nations Transitional Administration in East Timor (UNTAET) in 2000 established the Serious Crimes Investigation Unit (SCIU) located in Dili, East Timor, with the mandate to investigate and prosecute cases in the locales where atrocities had occurred. The SCIU closed down in May 2005, the result of a lack of political interest of both the Timorese government and the UN.[4] In its five years of operation, the SCIU indicted 391 individuals; 84 were convicted and 3 acquitted. The integrity of the trials, however, was deeply flawed. The trials lacked a consistent prosecutorial strategy, panels lacked basic facilities, defense quality was inadequate, and outreach to the victims' community and broader civil society was missing. Most damning, however, was the fact that the overwhelming majority of those indicted were living in Indonesia, beyond the reach of the SCIU, and the trials could effectively deal with only a limited number of very low-level perpetrators.[5]

---

3. For background on the violence in East Timor, see Joseph Nevins, *A Not-So-Distant Horror: Mass Violence in East Timor* (Ithaca: Cornell University Press, 2005).

4. Megan Hirst and Howard Varney, "Justice Abandoned?: An Assessment of the Serious Crimes Process in East Timor," International Center for Transitional Justice, New York, June 15, 2005.

5. Megan Hirst, "Too Much Friendship, Too Little Truth: Monitoring Report on the Commission of Truth and Friendship in Indonesia and Timor-Leste," International Center for Transitional Justice, New York, January 2008.

On the domestic side of the transitional justice ledger, the Indonesian government initially opposed any form of transitional justice for East Timor. Under growing international pressure, however, the government decided to establish the Ad Hoc Human Rights Court in Jakarta in 2001 to prosecute perpetrators of crimes in East Timor. The government offered the court as a countersolution to ever-louder international calls for an international tribunal for Indonesia, modeled after the already existing courts for Rwanda and Yugoslavia.[6] Appealing to its rights of sovereignty and its status as a transitional democracy that could deal with its own problems in a responsible manner, the Indonesian government promised to "take responsibility for providing justice for atrocities committed by its nationals in East Timor, and that it would do so in a credible manner."[7]

However, the Indonesian commitment to justice has been anything but credible. The trials in front of the ad hoc court have been widely judged as "intended to fail."[8] All eighteen of the Indonesians indicted for crimes against humanity in East Timor were acquitted or had their convictions overturned by higher courts.[9] The decision by the Indonesian appeals court in late 2004 to acquit or overturn the convictions of all Indonesians indicted for crimes against humanity in East Timor made it virtually impossible for any senior Indonesian military officer to be prosecuted for crimes in East Timor.[10] The main reason for continued impunity seems to be the lack of political will by the government to alienate the military by prosecuting senior civilian and military personnel.[11] Indonesia has also undermined the SCIU in East Timor by refusing to cooperate in sharing evidence, information, and other documentation, all of which has put the future of the local Timorese transitional justice project in serious peril.[12]

---

6. Indonesia was especially sensitive to the recommendations of the International Commission of Inquiry mandated by the UN Commission on Human Rights, which advocated an international tribunal for Indonesia. "Situation of Human Rights in East Timor," UN Doc. A/54/660, December 10, 1999; "Report of the International Commission of Inquiry on East Timor to the Secretary-General," UN Doc. A/54/726, S/2000/59, January 31, 2000.

7. Human Rights Watch, "Justice Denied for East Timor: Indonesia's Sham Prosecutions, the Need to Strengthen the Trial Process in East Timor, and the Imperative of U.N. Action," Background Briefing, Washington, DC, December 20, 2002.

8. David Cohen, "Intended to Fail: The Trials before the Ad Hoc Human Rights Court in Jakarta," International Center for Transitional Justice, New York, August 19, 2003.

9. International Center for Transitional Justice, "Indonesia: A Case of Impunity," June 30, 2008, http://www.ictj.org/en/news/features/1792.html.

10. Human Rights Watch, "Indonesia: Courts Sanction Impunity for East Timor Abuses," Washington, DC, August 7, 2004.

11. Open Society Justice Initiative and Coalition for International Justice, "Unfulfilled Promises: Achieving Justice for Crimes Against Humanity in East Timor," New York, November 2004.

12. Human Rights Watch, "Justice Denied."

In another preemptive strategy of preventing serious international involvement in Indonesian trials for East Timor, the Indonesian and Timorese governments established in 2005 a Commission of Truth and Friendship (CTF) to address the issues of the past. The Indonesian government made it clear that this new commission was set up as an alternative to the UN expert commission that would investigate the progress Indonesia and East Timor had made in fighting impunity for past crimes and that was supported by major international justice groups.[13] The new government of East Timor supported the CTF because it saw good neighborly relations with Indonesia as a priority over transitional justice, which it considered a fleeting concept and one that might damage Timorese diplomatic relations with its most powerful neighbor, Indonesia.[14] International justice activists strongly opposed this body on the grounds that it would offer amnesty provisions even for perpetrators of the most brutal atrocities, a stipulation that violated international norms on denial of impunity for serious crimes.[15] In addition, international justice organizations warned that the CTF lacked any credibility in either Indonesian or East Timorese civil societies, showed no concern for victims, and provided no mechanisms for obtaining evidence.[16] International human rights groups also heavily criticized the CTF for its treatment of victims and its preferential treatment of testimonies from military officers, militiamen, and bureaucrats without regard to the statements of victims.[17]

Because the CTF was so deeply flawed, the international justice groups also advised the international community not to cooperate with the commission until its mandate was changed to bring it in line with international human rights norms and standards.[18] The CTF issued a final report in July 2008. To the surprise of some skeptical international justice groups, the report did acknowledge Indonesian responsibility for atrocities committed in 1999 and did not ask for amnesty. The commission's findings, however, were very vague and did not identify a single individual perpetrator.[19] In response, Timorese and international transitional

---

13. John Aglionby, "Indonesia and East Timor to Investigate Murders," *Guardian*, December 23, 2004.

14. International Center for Transitional Justice, "Indonesia: A Case of Impunity."

15. International Center for Transitional Justice, "Timor Leste: ICTJ Activity," May 2008, http://www.ictj.org/en/where/region3/628.html.

16. International Center for Transitional Justice, "Joint NGO Statement on the Handover of the Report of the Commission of Truth and Friendship," July 15, 2008, http://ictj.org/en/news/features/1856.html.

17. Amnesty International, "Human Rights in East Timor 2008," London, May 2008.

18. International Center for Transitional Justice, "ICTJ Urges UN to Challenge Indonesia's Legacy of Impunity," May 4, 2007, http://www.ictj.org/en/news/press/release/1204.html.

19. Olivia Rondonuwu, "Indonesia, East Timor Leaders Regret Vote Bloodshed," Reuters, July 15, 2008.

justice groups renewed their request for an international tribunal to follow up on the heels of the CTF report by prosecuting individual perpetrators.[20]

The international alternative to the flawed domestic trials and the CTF was the Commission for Reception, Truth and Reconciliation (CAVR), a domestic truth commission strongly supported and heavily advised by international justice institutions, most actively the ICTJ. The CAVR worked from 2002 to 2005, when it submitted its final report, which contained over two hundred recommendations for the Timorese government, the United Nations, and the international community on justice, accountability, reparations and reconciliation. Indonesia in particular was requested to accept international support to strengthen its prosecutorial capacity. The report also recommended that the Security Council extend and strengthen the domestic transitional justice processes in East Timor, including restarting the failed SCIU trials. The Indonesian government was given six months to show progress on the commission's recommendations. If Indonesia failed to improve its record on transitional justice, the commission recommended that the UN Security Council, under Chapter VII, establish an international criminal tribunal.[21]

A particularly interesting aspect of the report is the statement that "the international community has an *obligation* to ensure justice for the crimes against humanity committed in East Timor in 1999."[22] International justice promoters therefore identified international actors in general and the UN in particular as the main agents of transitional justice processes in Indonesia and East Timor. In fact, Timorese president Xanana Gusmao has publicly appealed to the international community to take on the issue of justice and not let East Timor do it on its own: "The international community must take responsibility. Please don't give us this burden. We have enough to carry on our shoulders."[23]

To the great disappointment of international justice promoters, however, none of the CAVR recommendations have been acted upon.[24] In fact, President Gusmao initially refused to publicly release the report and submitted it only to the Timorese parliament.[25] Under international pressure, he later issued the report to the UN secretary general, but he has made no efforts to publicize its

---

20. International Center for Transitional Justice, "Joint NGO Statement."

21. Hirst, "Too Much Friendship."

22. Human Rights Watch, "East Timor: U.N. Security Council Must Ensure Justice," June 29, 2005, http://hrw.org/english/docs/2005/06/28/eastti11231.htm (emphasis added).

23. Shawn Donnan, "Justice Fails to Net Big Fish for Crimes in East Timor," *Financial Times*, December 10, 2003.

24. Human Rights Watch, "Timor-Leste: Candidates Should Prioritize Human Rights," April 4, 2007, http://hrw.org/english/docs/2007/04/04/eastti15639.htm.

25. International Center for Transitional Justice, "Timorese Parliament Should Release Truth Commission Report Immediately," November 28, 2005, http://ictj.org/en/news/press/release/250.html.

findings in East Timor.[26] While the clear power imbalance between Indonesia and East Timor helps illuminate somewhat the Timorese government's failure to actively support domestic justice efforts, it is still baffling why the government actively endorsed Indonesia's position on transitional justice. For example, President Gusmao used his Independence Day national address to praise the objectionable trials conducted in Indonesia.[27] This praise is even more curious since most transitional justice experts agree that Indonesia has been conducting trials as a way to sabotage, not advance, transitional justice for East Timor. In fact, local transitional justice activists argued that "it was sufficient simply to go through the motions of holding trials and that their content was of little consequence."[28]

As a consequence of the Indonesian lack of cooperation and the failure of the local Dili SCIU court, the consensus is growing in the international justice community that justice for victims of East Timor massacres will be denied.[29] While the international justice organizations and East Timor's civil society are continuing to appeal to the UN and other international agencies for a fresh approach to transitional justice—they favor an international tribunal—these efforts may be seriously undermined by international justice fatigue.[30] The United Nations and its agencies are unlikely to support the same process twice when new crises that need to be dealt with are emerging with unsettling regularity. But most significant, the Timorese government is opposed to setting up a new tribunal because improving relations with Indonesia is higher on the government's political agenda than commitment to a concept as fleeting as transitional justice. In many ways, it seems that the Indonesian hijacked justice strategy has been successful. By signaling to the international community that it is capable of dealing

---

26. Human Rights Watch, "World Report 2007: Timor Leste," New York, January 10, 2007.

27. "It is undeniable that the fact that Indonesia created an ad hoc court and tried military men, even generals, shows courage and determination to change the previous system. To the present, no country in Asia, not even the always lauded reconciliation process of South Africa, has shown such attitude of political courage." Gusmao's national address on May 20, 2004. Quoted in Hirst and Varney, "Justice Abandoned?"

28. Judicial System Monitoring Program (JSMP), "Justice for Timor Leste: Civil Society Strategic Planning for the Future of Serious Crimes," press release, September 27, 2004.

29. Human Rights Watch, "Justice Denied"; Cohen, "Intended to Fail"; Piers Pigou, "Crying without Tears: In Pursuit of Justice and Reconciliation in Timor-Leste: Community Perspectives and Expectations," International Center for Transitional Justice, New York, August 19, 2003; Human Rights Watch, "Indonesia: Courts Sanction Impunity for East Timor Abuses," August 7, 2004, http://www.hrw.org/english/docs/2004/08/06/indone9205.htm.

30. For example, in 2005 the UN established a Commission of Experts (COE) to evaluate transitional justice processes in Indonesia and East Timor. The commission issued its findings and recommendations in May 2005, but the UN Security Council has not discussed them in the more than three years since the report was completed. International Center for Transitional Justice, "Timor Leste."

with justice at home, Indonesia has in fact paved the way for justice to be at best delayed and at worst denied.

Hijacked Justice in Burundi

The pursuit of transitional justice in Burundi is another interesting illustrative case of the hijacked justice phenomenon. Violent conflict in Burundi has been raging for more than a decade between the rebel, majority Hutu, National Liberation Forces (FNL) and the combined forces of the Burundian military, traditionally dominated by the Tutsi minority, and a former rebel Hutu group, the Forces for the Defense of Democracy (FDD).[31] Widespread violence broke out in 1993, and after reports began coming in of deaths in the range of fifty thousand, the government of Burundi asked the United Nations to establish an international commission of inquiry to investigate the crimes. This request for a preliminary justice initiative was submitted without any domestic debate and without any serious input from civil society, but it was done in the wider context of regional developments at the time. In submitting a request for an international war-crimes commission, the Burundian government hoped that establishing a justice institution would prevent violence from escalating into mass genocide, like the one going on in similarly ethnically stratified neighboring Rwanda.[32]

The government officially submitted its request to the UN in September 1994. The following excerpt from the request is illustrative in its direct appeal to the expertise of international institutions as the best arbiters in helping Burundi deal with justice for mass atrocities: "What we tried to have is help from the international community; we were looking for *a kind* of international commission to help a judicial inquiry into the assassination of the President, into the massacres and into the impunity now going on."[33]

However, with the atrocities in Rwanda taking an unimaginable toll, UN Security Council was hesitant to establish a war-crimes commission, fearing this could spark further violence in Burundi and open the door to another Rwanda-like mass slaughter. Other international organizations expressed similar concerns

---

31. For background on the civil war in Burundi, see Timothy Longman, *Proxy Targets: Civilians in the War in Burundi* (New York: HRW, 1998); Human Rights Watch, "Emptying the Hills: Regroupment in Burundi," vol. 12, no. 4(A), New York, July 1, 2000; Human Rights Watch, "Burundi: Neglecting Justice in Making Peace," vol. 12, no. 2(A), New York, April, 2000; Caroline Sculier and Alison Liebhafsky Des Forges, "Everyday Victims: Civilians in the Burundian War," HRW, New York, December 1, 2003.

32. Hayner, *Unspeakable Truths.*

33. Amnesty International, "Rwanda and Burundi: A Call for Action by the International Community," AFR 02/24/95, London, September 1995, 22 (emphasis added).

but still advocated a commission for Burundi as an important step toward ending impunity. In fact, precisely because they argued that Burundi itself was incredibly polarized, international justice organizations came out strong in support of an internationally led transitional justice project, which would include identification of perpetrators as well as a wider reform of the Burundian judiciary, led by a task force of international justice advisers.[34]

While the impetus for creating a commission was a direct result of the unfolding events in neighboring Rwanda, the actual design of the commission was also the result of international transitional justice "contagion." The commission was designed in large part by the UN special envoy to Burundi, a Venezuelan lawyer who had played an integral part in the design of the truth commission in El Salvador.[35] The commission worked for ten months and was prepared to release its report on the massacres of 1993–94 and recommend measures to bring justice. However, on July 25, 1996, a coup overthrew the government of Burundi, and the report was withheld by the UN Security Council, which feared it could further exacerbate the conflict. After this initial delay, the report was finally released, indicating that "acts of genocide" had been committed in Burundi and recommending international jurisdiction over prosecution of war crimes.

After a new outbreak of fighting and a new ceasefire, there have been renewed efforts to establish a transitional justice mechanism in Burundi. The 2000 Arusha peace accords called for the establishment of a truth and reconciliation commission, as well as an international commission of inquiry. In 2004, the UN launched a mission to assess the feasibility and suitability of establishing these transitional justice institutions.[36] The UN, however, abandoned the plan for an international commission of inquiry and in 2005 issued a final report on transitional justice in Burundi. The so-called Kalomoh Report called for a truth commission and a special chamber for war crimes, crimes against humanity, and genocide to be located within the Burundian justice system.[37] The report unequivocally stated the necessity of establishing a commission but one "not necessarily in the shape and form requested by the Government of Burundi."[38] The UN Security Council endorsed the report in Resolution 1606 and advised the UN Secretary General

---

34. Ibid.

35. Hayner, *Unspeakable Truths*, 68. This was not the first time the El Salvadoran commission had been imitated. The design of the commission in El Salvador also served as Guatemala's main model when a truth commission was set up there.

36. For an overview of ICTJ activities in Burundi, see International Center for Transitional Justice, "Burundi: ICTJ Activity," March 2008, http://www.ictj.org/en/where/region1/512.html.

37. Ibid.

38. Letter from the UN Secretary General Kofi Annan to the UN Security Council, S/2005/258, March 11, 2005.

to initiate negotiations with the Burundian government on implementing the Kalomoh Report's recommendations.[39]

The government of Burundi, however, had its own plans for transitional justice, which sharply differed from the UN proposals. Unsatisfied with the broad scope of the Kalomoh Report, the government set up an ad hoc commission that would "negotiate" the Kalomoh Report with the UN.[40] When the negotiations began in 2006, the UN representatives failed to agree with the government of Burundi on the proposed transitional justice mechanisms. The holdout was on the part of the Burundian government, which refused to grant the prosecutor of the special court authority to decide which cases to bring to trial. The government's position was that only cases in which reconciliation had failed or participants had refused to cooperate would be sent to court. The Burundian and UN negotiators could also not negotiate the exact relationship between the two transitional justice mechanisms—truth commission and special court. Another point of contention was on proposed amnesty for war crimes. The ruling Defense of Democracy–Forces for the Defense of Democracy (CNDD–FDD) Party, a powerful veto player, favored reconciliation over prosecution for all crimes, a stance that made implementation of transitional justice mechanisms much more difficult to accomplish.[41]

As a consequence, justice for mass atrocities in Burundi is still an unfulfilled promise.[42] No definitive transitional justice mechanism is currently at work in Burundi, even though the Burundian government announced a law establishing a new national truth and reconciliation commission in 2004, with a sweeping mandate that would establish the truth about past crimes, identify the perpetrators, propose measures to promote reconciliation, and educate the population about the past.[43] This effort, however, appears to have been abandoned.[44]

In addition, the transitional justice process in Burundi operates within the larger context of the cycles of renewed warfare and postconflict peacebuilding. Because the emphasis of the peacebuilding process is on bringing former adversaries into the peace fold, it is sometimes at odds with the transitional justice agenda. For example, in order to accommodate the last rebel holdout group, the Palipehutu-FNL, any transitional justice process would probably have to offer immunity from prosecution, therefore directly contradicting the purpose of

---

39. UN Security Council Resolution 1606, S/RES/1606/2005, June 20, 2005.
40. International Center for Transitional Justice, "Burundi: ICTJ Activity."
41. Human Rights Watch, "Burundi: Donors Should Press for End to Impunity," May 22, 2007, http://hrw.org/english/docs/2007/05/21/burund15976.htm.
42. Amnesty International, "2008 Annual Report for Burundi," London, May 2008.
43. "Burundi Establishes NTRC," *News 24* (South Africa), January 5, 2005, http://www.news24.com.
44. International Center for Transitional Justice, "Burundi: ICTJ Activity."

the future special court.[45] Considering that Burundi has entered a new phase of political instability since the 2005 elections that put CNDD–FDD in power, hopes for a comprehensive transitional justice process are low.[46] Burundian human rights organizations have warned that the continuing silence about past abuses "contributes to the climate of impunity and growing insecurity."[47] International justice organizations have accused the government of showing "official indifference" to the issue of dealing with past violence.[48] After initial moves to adopt transitional justice models by imitating neighboring countries and fearing negative spillover effects from regional conflicts, Burundi has failed to sustain a long-term commitment to transitional justice.

With tactics of stalling and obfuscation, the Burundian government succeeded in deceiving the international community in the field of transitional justice. Justice for Burundian victims was denied, as Burundian elites felt squeezed between domestic political pressures to ignore past crimes and incentives to demonstrate their commitment to the rule of law to the international community, a dynamic very similar to the experience of the former Yugoslav cases explored earlier in this book.

Hijacked Justice in Cambodia

Thirty years since the fall of the genocidal Khmer Rouge regime, no systematic attempt has been made to hold surviving Khmer Rouge officials accountable for the estimated 1.5 million people killed under their rule between 1975 and 1979. The only trial of the Khmer Rouge was held by the Vietnamese after their invasion of Cambodia in 1979. This trial, however, was widely regarded as a sham and was not taken seriously either by the Cambodians or the international justice community.

The lack of accountability for the genocide in Cambodia has been tremendously troubling for promoters of transitional justice. The killing fields of Cambodia remain as haunting examples of some of the vilest crimes against humanity, and the continuing impunity of perpetrators has been a thorn in the side of the

---

45. International Center for Transitional Justice, "Burundi: Submission to the Universal Periodic Review of the UN Human Rights Council," July 14, 2008.

46. In 2007, the ruling coalition underwent a major crisis, which led to a coalition reshuffle. The CNDD–FDD vice president was recalled, which produced new tensions. Opposition leaders were also physically attacked. Human Rights Watch, "Burundi: Events of 2007," New York, January 31, 2008.

47. Human Rights Watch, "Letter to the United Nations Human Rights Council from Human Rights Organizations in Burundi," September 12, 2008, http://hrw.org/english/docs/2008/09/12/burund19797.htm.

48. International Center for Transitional Justice, "Burundi: Submission."

international justice community. Most notably, Khmer Rouge leader Pol Pot died in 1998 without ever having to answer for his crimes. In 2006, after years of international pressure, Cambodia finally established the hybrid international-domestic Extraordinary Chambers in the Courts of Cambodia (ECCC) to prosecute the former leaders of Democratic Kampuchea. The ECCC is housed within the Cambodian judiciary but is composed of both Cambodian and international judges, prosecutors, and defense teams.[49]

However, this long-awaited institution has been unusually controversial both within Cambodia and in the international justice community. The ECCC has been plagued with serious problems: the lack of impartiality and independence of the Cambodian judiciary, profound corruption, and inadequate legal capacity and training.[50] While the composition of the judiciary is mixed, and the court itself is supposed to be an example of a hybrid international/domestic court, in practice the court often operates as two separate units—Cambodian and international.[51]

There have been reports of corruption among Cambodian court administrators, including allegations of kickbacks to Cambodian government officials.[52] Human rights groups warned that housing the ECCC within the Cambodian judicial system would be risky, since corruption, incompetence, and payoffs are rampant. For example, Cambodian judges have been known to arbitrarily refuse to admit defense evidence or write up decisions before the trial has run its course. In trials deemed politically sensitive, judges often receive "guidance" from political officials.[53]

From the perspective of international justice standards, the ECCC also falls flat. International justice organizations have identified three key legal areas of concern: trials in absentia, lack of independence of the defense office and victims office, and insufficient access to public hearings.[54] Even though the ECCC's international composition is supposed to overcome these structural obstacles, international human rights activists have pointed to poor witness and victim

---

49. The Agreement between the United Nations and the Royal Government of Cambodia concerning the Prosecution under Cambodian Law of Crimes Committed during the Period of Democratic Kampuchea, July 2003, http://www.eccc.gov.kh/english/agreement.list.aspx.

50. Human Rights Watch, "Cambodia: Events of 2007," New York, January 31, 2008.

51. Open Society Justice Initiative, "Recent Developments at the Extraordinary Chambers in the Courts of Cambodia: October 2008 Update," New York, October 8, 2008.

52. Sara Colm, "Japan Can Help Cambodia's Quest for Justice," *International Herald Tribune*, May 29, 2008.

53. Sara Colm, "Killing Field Trials," *Bangkok Post*, March 3, 2008.

54. Human Rights Watch, "Extraordinary Chambers of the Courts of Cambodia: Letter to the Secretariat of the Rules and Procedure Committee," November 17, 2006, http://www.hrw.org/backgrounder/ij/cambodia1106.

protection programs and low transparency of the tribunal's operations and judicial proceedings.[55] Most significantly, the ECCC's narrow mandate focuses on a small group of alleged genocide masterminds—many of whom have long since died—and not on a more comprehensive investigation of direct perpetrators or even of broader social complicity in the genocide.[56] By the fall of 2008, the ECCC had in custody five suspected perpetrators. At a January 2008 international conference of potential donors to the court, ECCC officials indicated that they would pursue indictments against another three suspects.[57] If the numbers remain as low as this, it will represent a significant setback both for international promoters of transitional justice and for victims in Cambodia, who argue that large numbers of perpetrators live freely, including current members of the government, the military, and local administration.[58]

But more significant for the purposes of this analysis is that the Cambodian government has persistently interfered in the working of the hybrid court, hoping to push back the start of operations. The biggest practical obstacle was the government's refusal to agree on internal rules for the tribunal. Throughout the multiyear process of setting up the tribunal, the government engaged in various techniques of delay and obstruction, including endless negotiations, which tested the patience and endurance of UN experts but produced no concrete results.[59] The government also interfered more directly, as in February 2007, when it threatened to expel representatives of the Open Society Justice Initiative from the country in retaliation for their report on the rampant corruption among Cambodian staff of the ECCC.[60] The levels of corruption and lack of adequate response, including intimidation and retaliation against those who report it, have led international justice institutions to propose that donor countries who finance the court condition their future support on improvements in this area.[61]

The political dynamic that led to this stalling of transitional justice is rooted in the particular set of domestic political conditions in Cambodia. The Cambodian judiciary and legal system remain under the tight control of the government.

55. Amnesty International, "Extraordinary Chambers in the Courts of Cambodia: Recommendations to Address Victims and Witnesses Issues in the Internal Rules Effectively," London, January 1, 2007.

56. International Center for Transitional Justice, "Cambodia: ICTJ Activity," March 2008, http://www.ictj.org/en/where/region3/642.html.

57. Colm, "Japan Can Help."

58. Colm, "Killing Field Trials."

59. United Nations, "Report of the Secretary-General on Khmer Rouge Trials," A/57/769, New York, March 31, 2003.

60. Human Rights Watch, "Cambodia: Events of 2007."

61. The UNDP has already temporarily frozen its financial support of the court until the corruption allegations are cleared. Open Society Justice Initiative, "Recent Developments."

Judges, prosecutors, and security personnel appointed to the hybrid court are deeply loyal to the ruling elites and are unable to conduct free trials away from political interference. And, as in the cases in the former Yugoslavia, after much stalling, domestic elites finally allowed international transitional justice institutions to take place but then hijacked them for local political purposes. The Cambodian government indicated it would accommodate the UN and other international actors but only to maintain control over the judiciary and the entire domestic political process.[62] It is also in the government's direct interest to hold as few trials as possible so that it can claim to the international community that it has complied with pressures to hold trials while at the same time curtailing future prosecutions that might implicate current members of the Cambodian government, some of whom were Khmer Rouge soldiers themselves.[63]

More blatantly, the timing of the start of the trials was coordinated to overlap with the 2008 elections and give an added boost to the long-serving prime minister, Hun Sen. The Khmer Rouge trials were to serve a twofold purpose for Sen: to whitewash his personal complicity in the genocide (he was a Khmer Rouge soldier) but also to build his appeal—both domestically and internationally—as the leader who finally brought the Khmer Rouge to justice.[64] Instead of delivering justice to the Cambodian victims of genocide, this political exploitation of Cambodia's past in fact may produce exactly the opposite result.

Hijacked Justice and the International Criminal Court

The main argument of this book also has significant implications for newer international justice models such as the ICC.[65] The experience of the permanent international court has already provided plenty of examples of how domestic politics interferes with international justice processes and how international justice institutions can be used to pursue domestic political goals. The ICC was set up to avoid problems of hijacked justice, to provide an international legal environment that would prevent impunity, and to be a final step in the institutionalization of the

---

62. Human Rights Watch, "Cambodia: Government Interferes in Khmer Rouge Tribunal," December 5, 2006, http://hrw.org/english/docs/2006/12/05/cambod14752.htm.

63. Colm, "Killing Field Trials."

64. Christina Larson, "Festival of the Dead," *New Republic*, May 7, 2008.

65. As of October 2008, the ICC prosecutor has opened investigations in the Democratic Republic of Congo, Uganda, Sudan, and the Central African Republic. Four defendants are in ICC custody in The Hague. The ICC suffered a huge setback when its first trial, that of the Congolese suspect Thomas Lubanga, which was scheduled to begin in June 2008, was suspended indefinitely because of the prosecution's refusal to disclose exculpatory information to the court, jeopardizing Lubanga's chances of receiving a fair trial. Human Rights Watch, "Courting History: The Landmark International Criminal Court's First Years," New York, July 10, 2008.

international justice norm. This grand legal experiment, however, cannot avoid domestic politics in states where it operates but also in states on whose political will and support the ICC depends.[66] Three brief examples—from Uganda, the Democratic Republic of Congo (DRC), and Sudan—give evidence for the argument that the ICC is just as likely to produce the paradoxes of hijacked justice as were other transitional justice institutions described earlier in the book.

In January 2004, the government of Uganda invited the ICC to investigate crimes committed by the Lord's Resistance Army (LRA), a rebel force engaged in a protracted fight with the government in northern Uganda. By being the first state to refer an investigation on its territory to the ICC, the government hoped that the ICC indictments would discredit its domestic enemies (primarily the LRA) while painting Uganda as a regional leader who respected international law and institutions of justice. However, while the crimes the members of the LRA are accused of committing are by any measure hideous and the ICC indictments provide plenty of evidence to show the extent of the LRA brutality, it is also quite clear that the Ugandan government has used the international court as a tool in a domestic political fight. The ICC has investigated only atrocities committed by the LRA, even in the face of strong evidence that government forces have committed plenty of atrocities on their own. In fact, victims of the Ugandan civil war have said that they see both parties as equally guilty for their suffering.[67] The ICC, however, is reluctant to alienate the Ugandan government, on which it depends for its continuing investigations in the country. Many Ugandan community leaders and members of the political opposition are highly critical of the role the ICC has played in Ugandan domestic politics; in the words of a local politician, "The ICC has become [President] Museveni's political tool."[68] More generally, the ICC's involvement in the conflict, especially after it issued an indictment in

---

66. The continuing obstruction of the ICC by the United States is beyond the scope of this brief analysis. See Jamie Meyerfeld, "Who Shall Be Judge? The United States, the International Criminal Court, and the Global Enforcement of Human Rights," *Human Rights Quarterly* 25 (2003): 93–129; Jason Ralph, "International Society, the International Criminal Court and American Foreign Policy," *Review of International Studies* 31 (2005): 27–44; Robert C. Johansen, "The Impact of US Policy toward the International Criminal Court on the Prevention of Genocide, War Crimes, and Crimes Against Humanity," *Human Rights Quarterly* 28, no. 2 (2006): 301–31. For more on the U.S. efforts to weaken the court by forcing individual states to sign "nonsurrender agreements," see Judith Kelley, "Who Keeps International Commitments and Why? The International Criminal Court and Bilateral Nonsurrender Agreements," *American Political Science Review* 101, no. 3 (2007): 573–89.

67. United Nations Office of the High Commissioner for Human Rights, "Making Peace Our Own: Victims' Perceptions of Accountability, Transitional Justice and Reconciliation in Northern Uganda," Geneva, August 2007.

68. Quoted in Phil Clark, "Law, Politics and Pragmatism: The ICC and Case Selection in the Democratic Republic of Congo and Uganda," in *Courting Conflict? Justice, Peace, and the ICC in Africa,* ed. Nicholas Waddel and Phil Clark (London: Royal African Society, 2008), 42.

2005 of Joseph Kony, the LRA commander, was heavily criticized by diplomats, mediators, and humanitarian organizations, who all worried that the indictment would jeopardize delicate peace talks, prolong the conflict, and further threaten the displaced population of northern Uganda.[69] The ICC indictment, however, neither created domestic political chaos nor provided justice for the victims. Kony was not arrested, and the peace agreement was never implemented.[70]

In the DRC, President Joseph Kabila referred the investigation of war crimes in the DRC to the ICC in March 2004. The ICC opened investigations in June 2004, in the midst of fierce fighting between the Congolese government and rebels. The Congolese government and judicial authorities were in charge of arresting war-crimes suspects and transferring them to the ICC. While the government here clearly acted in accordance with its international obligations to cooperate with the ICC, it did so out of its narrow political interest in further weakening and demoralizing the rebel forces. In addition, the choice of indictments against specific individuals who fought in a relatively small, isolated area of the country indicated that the ICC was guided by politically strategic considerations in its case selection, by choosing to focus on conflict areas with the fewest implications for the government and President Kabila. In other words, had the ICC chosen cases in other regions, it would most likely have had to indict government forces, perhaps even implicate the president himself.[71] In this case, the Congolese government preempted potential political instability by inviting the ICC to prosecute rebel crimes and positioning itself as a guarantor of peace, while at the same time politically inoculating itself from further serious prosecutions.

However, the ICC encounters paradoxes of domestic politics even beyond the cases of government use of the court, as in Uganda and the DRC. Domestic politics encroaches on the mandate, conduct, and legitimacy of the ICC even in cases where the national government was not behind the decision to engage the ICC.

In July 2008, acting on a referral by the UN Security Council, Luis Moreno Ocampo, the ICC prosecutor, indicted Sudanese president Omar al-Bashir for genocide, war crimes, and crimes against humanity in Darfur. Since Bashir was the sitting head of state, the indictment was very politically sensitive and elicited many negative responses from international diplomats who worried that it would further complicate the delicate search for peace in Darfur. Some international humanitarian groups were also worried that they might be expelled from Darfur as the Sudanese government lashed out in revenge. International justice activists,

69. Nick Grono and Adam O'Brien, "Justice in Conflict? The ICC and Peace Processes," in Waddel and Clark, *Courting Conflict?*.
70. Paul Reynolds, "Bashir Move Bold but Problematic," BBC News, July 14, 2008.
71. Clark, "Law, Politics and Pragmatism."

however, argued that the indictment might in fact put added pressure on the Sudanese government to change its behavior in Darfur.[72] More pertinently, they argued, the indictment could not hamper the peace process because the peace process simply did not exist in any meaningful way.[73]

The Sudanese government, not surprisingly, used the ICC indictment to further rally domestic support, a tactic the governments of Serbia, Croatia, and Bosnia used extensively, as documented in earlier chapters of this book. The Sudanese government organized carefully orchestrated support rallies and announced it would ignore the arrest warrant for President Bashir because Sudan was not a signatory of the ICC and hence was not bound by its decisions.[74] Somewhat surprisingly, the government then arrested one of the two senior officials indicted by the ICC and announced it would hold domestic war-crimes trials. This move, however, was widely seen by human rights groups as a political stunt, a way for the government to improve its international image while controlling the process domestically to ensure no justice ever got done.[75] More important, perhaps, the government of Sudan attempted to circumvent the ICC's prosecution of President Bashir by setting in motion some kind of domestic justice process in exchange for the ICC's dropping Bashir's indictment. In fact, the Sudanese government officials disclosed that France had offered them a deal in which they would arrest and transfer another ICC indictee, a government minister accused of war crimes, in exchange for the ICC's suspending the indictment of President Bashir. The Sudanese government then calculated that offering a lower-ranked perpetrator, a *janjaweed* militiaman instead of a government official, would further shield the government from being implicated in the ICC's genocide indictment. This kind of domestic strategy can also further rally African allies, as Sudan makes a case that it is cooperating with international justice requests by conducting domestic trials while in fact using them as a smoke screen to deflect ICC pressures.[76] This strategy is also designed to showcase the apparent capacity of Sudan's legal system to handle complex war-crimes investigations, which in turn is an attempt to prevent the ICC from acting on Bashir's indictment.[77]

---

72. Lydia Polgreen and Marlise Simons, "The Pursuit of Justice vs. the Pursuit of Peace," *New York Times,* July 11, 2008.

73. Marlise Simons, Lydia Polgreen, and Jeffrey Gettleman, "Arrest Is Sought of Sudan Leader in Genocide Case," *New York Times,* July 15, 2008.

74. Lydia Polgreen, "Sudanese Protest War Crimes Case Against President at Scripted Rally in Capital," *New York Times,* July 14, 2008.

75. Associated Press, "Sudan to Conduct Its Own Darfur Trials," October 13, 2008.

76. Jeffrey Gettleman, "Sudan Arrests Militia Chief Facing Trial," *New York Times,* October 13, 2008.

77. "Sudan Completes Probe into Darfur Militia Leader," Reuters, October 14, 2008.

The domestic pushback against the international court in a political environment where accused war criminals still hold power is nothing to be surprised by. If anything, it would be surprising if the Sudanese government accepted the ICC indictments and arrested its own president. The broader implications of the ICC action in the region, however, are more interesting and worthy of mention.

The African Union's (AU) reaction to the ICC indictment of Bashir has been particularly strong. The AU Peace and Security Council stated that "the search for justice in Darfur should be pursued in a way that does not impede or jeopardize efforts aimed at promoting lasting peace."[78] A report from the AU's 142nd meeting further expressed concern that the principle of universal jurisdiction was being abused to target specifically Africans.[79] The overwhelming focus on Africa is in large part a practical reflection of the prevalence of ongoing or recently suspended human rights violations on that continent. The African focus, however, has awakened African sensitivities regarding issues of sovereignty and self-determination but also legacies of colonialism and Western imperialism.[80] African lawyers accused the ICC of pursuing "international justice fundamentalism."[81] Leading African academics warned that the ICC indictments were "assertions of neocolonial domination."[82] Many human rights activists interpreted this strong African pushback to mean that Africa had "lost confidence in the ICC" and was on its way to making Africa a zone free from the principle of universal jurisdiction.[83]

Other international justice experts, however, interpreted the ICC indictment of Bashir not necessarily as evidence of its anti-African agenda but as part of a broader prosecutorial strategy aimed at improving the ICC's international legitimacy and relations with the UN Security Council.[84] The indictment was issued in an international political environment where it is difficult to see which national or international actor would be either willing or able to arrest Bashir. Two peacekeeping missions operating in Sudan—the joint UN-African Union mission in Darfur (UNAMID) and the UN mission in Sudan (UNMIS) do not have the

---

78. Human Rights Watch, "African Union: Don't Trade Away Justice in Darfur," September 22, 2008, http://hrw.org/english/docs/2008/09/22/sudan19866.htm.

79. Human Rights Watch, "AU: Do Not Call for Suspending ICC's Investigation of President al-Bashir," September 19, 2008, http://hrw.org/english/docs/2008/09/18/sudan19848.htm.

80. Nicholas Waddel and Phil Clark, "Introduction," in Waddel and Clark, *Courting Conflict?*.

81. Chidi Odinkalu, "What If Ocampo Indicts Bashir? 2," June 16, 2008, http://www.ssrc.org/blogs/darfur/2008/06/16/what-if-ocampo-indicts-bashir-2.

82. Mahmood Mamdani, "The New Humanitarian Order," *Nation*, 287, September 29, 2008.

83. Alex de Waal, "Africa's Position on the ICC," September 23, 2008, http://www.ssrc.org/blogs/darfur/2008/09/23/africas-position-on-the-icc.

84. Phil Clark, "Ocampo's Darfur Strategy Depends on Congo," in *Oxford Transitional Justice Research Working Paper Series*, Oxford, August 20, 2008, http://www.csls.ox.ac.uk/otjr.php.

mandate to enforce ICC warrants, and both suffer from serious personnel and logistical problems and constant obstruction by the Sudanese government. In such a hostile international context, the ICC prosecutor may be using the Bashir case to further pressure the UN Security Council into approving greater peacekeeping operations in Sudan and in other countries where the ICC is conducting investigations, even if no actual trial is to take place.[85]

The strategies pursued by the ICC indicate that domestic politics remains intricately linked to the operations of this pillar institution of international justice. Domestic politics manifests itself in the ways in which national governments are able to manipulate the ICC prosecutorial strategy to fit with their local political needs. It is also manifest in continuing human rights abuses, where the governments use domestically unpopular ICC indictments to delegitimize the entire international community and with it international calls for broad normative and behavioral change. Finally, the ICC makes decisions that are in its own bureaucratic interest, which may or may not be in line with either the preferences of human rights groups or the victims themselves.

The fundamental problem facing ICC investigations is the paradox of pursuing justice in the midst of violent conflict or simultaneously with ongoing peace processes.[86] One of the most prescient criticisms leveled against the investigations, even from noted human rights activists, is the potential of making things worse, of "international justice fundamentalism"—pursuing individual accountability that may trump broader efforts to bring peace. If the ICC is to continue to promote the goals of international justice, it should take domestic politics seriously—but not by pursuing a prosecutorial strategy that looks to victims like cozying up to one side in the conflict. Instead, the ICC needs to make a better case for why the goals of justice, universal, uncompromised, not regional-specific justice, are in the interest of all of society, not just of its leaders.

Hijacked justice, therefore, is not unique to the Balkans, nor is it unique to specific institutional models of justice. Domestic elites are able to use quite different international mechanisms of transitional justice in widely varied political environments and for a multitude of different local reasons: to get rid of domestic political opponents, to cozy up to the international community, to preempt serious international justice processes by holding sham domestic trials, or— simply and most damagingly—to obtain an international shield of legitimacy for continuing justice impunity at home.

---

85. Ibid.

86. The ICC can investigate only those crimes committed after the Rome Statute took effect in 2002, U.N. Doc. A/CONF.183/9.

Theoretical Implications

This book contributes to broader theoretical debates in political science, particularly to the scholarship in international relations and transitional justice as well as regional area studies of the Balkans. It builds on existing explanations of international normative diffusion and compliance by offering a theoretical twist: under specific domestic conditions, domestic actors will use international norms for local political purposes, producing outcomes very different from the goals and objectives of the international norm. The theoretical approach presented in the book specifies the different kinds of international pressures that states are subjected to and then explains what kinds of political strategies domestic elites develop to react to such pressures. This model contributes to the ongoing debates about the mechanisms of normative diffusion and adoption by providing a domestic politics approach to normative compliance. The book therefore further unpacks the concept of compliance to explore not only *whether* states comply with international norms and institutions but also *how* they go about complying and *why.*

Finally, this book opens up space for more general questions about the interplay between domestic politics and the international sphere and the domestic political impact of international norms and institutions. It invites more discussion about the role of norms and ideas in world politics. As we have seen, international norms often have effects that were unintended by their creators but very much intended by the domestic actors that use them. I suggest we use these theoretical findings to develop a broader research program that fundamentally rethinks the relationship between international norms and transnational activism by identifying domestic conditions that provide limits and opportunities for international policy interventions.

The book also contributes to the growing literature on transitional justice, memory politics, and, more broadly, the politics of human rights. It broadens the scope of inquiry in transitional justice scholarship to explain the process of transitional justice adoption and compliance, the actors involved, and the role international norms have in producing particular domestic political outcomes. It questions some of the foundational assumptions of transitional justice literature to offer a new theoretical explanation for why transitional justice mechanisms often disappoint and under what domestic conditions political entrepreneurs use them for political countermobilization.

However, the theoretical implications of this book extend well beyond international norms of transitional justice into other areas of international politics. I expect similar relationships to develop when other international policies are adopted under conditions similar to the ones I identify in areas such as, for example, antidrug policies, terrorism, or human trafficking—empirical areas well worthy of further ethnographic research.

Last, the book contributes to the rich body of literature on the former Yugoslavia and the Balkans. It shows how the politics surrounding the breakup of the former Yugoslavia are far from resolved and offers some lessons for policymakers and international activists dealing with similar situations worldwide. The book provides further evidence of the effects international actors, who have played a major role in the region, have had on domestic political outcomes. It also accounts for the significant political variation among the three states. Even with the shared legacy of war and membership in the former federal state, the three countries followed dramatically different transitional paths, which were dependent on highly localized domestic political conditions. The book also shows how the Balkan states continue to be inextricably politically linked to one another and how international action in one of the states affects—positively but also adversely—politics in all of them. Many years after the war, the countries of the former Yugoslavia continue to mirror one another; they base their policies in reaction to their neighbors, and they appeal to international legitimacy by comparing one another's accomplishments. The social interpretations of the violent past that broke them apart, however, continue to further drift away. The truths about the war and the crimes that were committed are incommensurable and still deeply entrenched in ethnic and national mythologies.

Avoiding Hijacked Justice

The findings of this book provide plenty of support for the skeptical view of transitional justice and its domestic and international institutions. If transitional justice is structurally prone to producing the paradoxes documented here, then why not jettison the idea altogether and support amnesties for human rights abuses for the benefit of political stability?[87] This is an important policy question with a complex answer.

First, let us attempt a counterfactual. What would politics look like in postconflict states in the absence of international pressure to carry out some model of transitional justice? What would Serbia look like if the international community had not coerced the government to arrest and transfer Milošević to The Hague? Judging from the continuing political instability in Serbia following Milošević's ousting from power in 2000 and the waves of resurging nationalism that kept

---

87. Jack L. Snyder and Leslie Vinjamuri, "Trials and Errors: Principle and Pragmatism in Strategies of International Justice," *International Security* 28, no. 3 (2003): 5–44.

right-wing governments in power, it is certainly plausible to argue that Milošević would have found a way to reassert himself as a political powerbroker in Serbia. In fact, it is quite likely that he would have fought his way back into power.[88] The international court here served as a big vacuum, sucking out the worst perpetrators from the streets and corridors of power and contributing to political stability.

Second, the international trials have created a deep reservoir of evidence from documents and witness testimonies about the atrocities that occurred. This evidence can then be tapped into sometime in the future, when there is more domestic political will to tackle the issue of past violence and when new generations may show renewed interest in the legacies of human rights abuse. The experience of transitional justice in Argentina can be a good example of this. Younger generations, sons and daughters of the "disappeared" in the state terror of 1976–83, have used the evidence collected during the early trials in the 1980s to press the government for new trials and more public discussion about the victims of state terror decades after the atrocities happened.[89] Transitional justice institutions, therefore, can help preserve a historical memory of the past that can be fully explored in a more favorable political environment.

Finally, transitional justice is important for the society that produced the perpetrators. It is important for the health of the nation to distinguish right from wrong. It is important for the society to know that human rights abuses, war crimes, and genocide are wrong. This acknowledgment of the difference between appropriate and inappropriate ways to conduct politics and resolve conflict is necessary for the recapturing of a lost sense of justice in the society that was complicit in massive human rights abuses.[90]

This book, then, does not argue against the idea of transitional justice. In fact, it argues that transitional justice is essential if states and societies where crimes were carried out are to develop a political culture of human rights. The paradox of hijacked justice, however, presents a serious challenge for transitional justice efforts, as the window of opportunity for acknowledging abuses and prosecuting the perpetrators is often very restricted. This is not a process that can drag on forever. The patience of the population facing other pressing needs during the transition is limited, and the attention span of international organizations and individual states will also be narrow as urgent new crises arise around the globe. The most serious outcome of this strategy—and one that domestic elites

---

88. Dejan Anastasijević, "Perfect Villains, Flawed Tribunal," *Washington Post*, July 20, 2008.

89. Kathryn Sikkink, "From Pariah State to Global Protagonist: Argentina and the Struggle for International Human Rights," *Latin American Politics and Society* 50, no. 1 (2008): 1–29.

90. Nenad Dimitrijević, "Justice beyond Blame: Moral Justification of (the Idea of) a Truth Commission," *Journal of Conflict Resolution* 50, no. 3 (2006): 368–82.

purposefully undertake—is to use transitional justice as a legitimating tool for inaction at home.

This book has argued for a maximalist interpretation of transitional justice. It does not call for an end to transitional justice projects but for more comprehensive international policies that take into account the inevitable domestic contestation they will set in motion. International pressures on states to begin a serious reassessment of their past should not end. Instead, international involvement should increase, but it should take a different form. International actors should engage in more substantive, sustained, and broad transitional justice projects beyond just counting the number of indictments and length of convictions and sentences. We should promote comprehensive education reform, which includes textbook and curriculum reform, that clearly presents evidence of crimes committed, the nature of the conflict, and the political environment that made the atrocities possible and even popular among wide segments of society. International organizations should promote media professionalization, specialization, and education in the field of transitional justice—how to investigate war crimes, how to write about them, how to present evidence, how to protect the victims. Domestic political elites can be socialized, persuaded, and rewarded for opening the black box of the past in a politically responsible manner. New generations of political leaders can be educated to understand and appreciate the importance of separating right from wrong for the future of their country.

Finally, international actors should do all they can to strengthen the political culture of transitional justice. Whether or not a country cooperates with an international tribunal and holds domestic trials or commissions of inquiry is not the only, or even the best, indicator of a state's commitment to dealing with the past. Only when stories about the past are wide open—when societies can talk about what happened, how, and why, who was to blame, and who stood idly by—will the path to achieving justice truly begin.

Index

Ademi, Rahmi, 93, 96
Ad Hoc Human Rights Court (Jakarta), 173
African Union (AU), 187
African Union Peace and Security Council, 187
al-Bashir, Omar, 185
Albright, Madeleine, 88
amnesty, 25, 42, 45, 70, 147–48, 174, 179
Amnesty International, 142
Anastasijević, Dejan, 61n100, 76n154
"anti-Hague patriots," 11, 38. *See also* "Stop the Hague"
apology, 18, 65, 118, 152, *See also specific countries*
Argentina, 16, 19, 68, 191
army. *See* military
Arusha peace accords, 178
Ashdown, Lord Paddy, 151, 157–58, 162
Association for Citizens of Truth and Reconciliation, 146

Balkans, 8, 38, 56, 116. *See also* Yugoslavia (former)
conflict/war in the, 38, 60, 95, 127, 138, 166, 188–90. *See also* Yugoslav conflict/wars
Banac, Ivo, 109n119
Bass, Gary, 27
Belgium, 17, 80
Belgrade, 1, 40, 42, 46, 48, 53–54, 59, 64, 73, 77, 80, 84, 128
Bijeljina, 153
Biserko, Sonja, 44n21, 55n71, 60n94, 74n147
Blaškić, Tihomir, 90, 119, 129
Blind Justice, 133
boomerang model, 7, 34–35
Boraine, Alex, 53–54
Bošić, Mladen, 161
Bosnia. *See* Bosnia-Herzegovina
Bosnia-Herzegovina (BH), 61
advocates of transitional justice in, 143, 145, 159, 162. *See also* human rights activists, in Bosnia
conservatives/hard-liners in, 151
and compliance, 168
courts in, 128, 132, 134–35, 141, 143–45, 160

demand for justice in, 122–23, 153–54, 156
domestic use of transitional justice in, 123, 131, 135, 140, 146, 149, 159–65
ethnic cleansing in, 124
ethnic politics in, 159
and the EU. *See* EU, and Bosnia
and the ICTY. *See* ICTY, and Bosnia
instrumental adopters in, 160–61
intelligence services in, 157–58, 161
international demands on, 126, 146. *See also* international pressure, in Bosnia
international organizations in, 126, 159, 162
judiciary in, 125, 140, 157
military in, 124, 127, 129, 156–57, 158n167, 161
number of war dead in, 154–56
old-regime loyalists, 123, 128, 132, 156, 158
Parliament in, 125, 127, 148–49, 158
police in, 124–25, 135, 139, 141, 145, 156–58, 161
public opinion in, 154n150
refugees in, 130, 153, 157
resisters in, 159–61
and transitional justice, 122–23, 139–40, 142, 144–45, 153–54, 156, 158, 161, 163
trials in. *See* war-crimes trials, in Bosnia
true believers in, 159, 162
truth commission. *See* truth and reconciliation commission, in Bosnia
truth-telling in, 123
victimization in, 156–57
war in, brief history, 123–25
See also civil society, in Bosnia; truth, perception of in Bosnia
Bosnian Commission for Missing Persons, 149
Bosnian Council of Ministers, 149
Bosnian Human Rights Chamber, 151
Boyle, Francis, 138
Bratunac, 63, 66
Brussels, 2, 98, 115
Budiša, Dražen, 87, 92, 94
bureaucratic pressure. *See* international pressure, bureaucratic
Burundi, 16, 177–80

193

CPSIA information can be obtained at www.ICGtesting.com
Printed in the USA
LVOW11s0244020916

502860LV00009B/35/P